Rabbi Marcus Jastrow and His Vision for the Reform of Judaism

A Study in the History of Judaism in the Nineteenth Century

Jews of Poland

Series Editor—Antony Polonsky (Brandeis University)

Rabbi Marcus Jastrow and His Vision for the Reform of Judaism

A Study in the History of Judaism
in the Nineteenth Century

MICHAŁ GALAS

Translated by Anna Tilles

Boston
2013

Subsidized by the National Program for Development of Humanities
in Warsaw, grant no. 0213/FNiTP/H31/80/2011

NARODOWY PROGRAM ROZWOJU HUMANISTYKI

Library of Congress Cataloging-in-Publication Data:
A catalog record for this book is available from the Library of Congress.

© 2013 Academic Studies Press
All rights reserved

ISBN 978-1-64469-033-8
ISBN 978-1-61811-356-6 (electronic)

Book design by Ivan Grave
Published by Academic Studies Press in 2013
28 Montfern Avenue
Brighton, MA 02135, USA
press@academicstudiespress.com
www. academicstudiespress.com

Contents

Foreword to the English Edition ... vii
Foreword ... ix
Introduction: Judaism in the Nineteenth Century: A General Overview ... xvii
    The Haskalah and the Reform of Judaism in Germany ... xvii
    The Influence of Reform in Judaism in the Polish Lands ... xxvi
    Judaism in the United States ... xxxi

PART I: EUROPE ... 1

Chapter 1: The Early Years ... 2
    Rogoźno: Jastrow's birthplace ... 2
    Jews in Rogoźno ... 4
    Marcus Jastrow in Rogoźno and Poznań ... 12
    Studying in Berlin and Halle ... 16
Chapter 2: Jastrow in Warsaw, 1858–1862 ... 21
    The Synagogue on at Daniłowiczowska Street ... 25
    Jastrow the Preacher ... 33
    Changes in the Liturgy ... 39
    Education and Culture ... 46
    The Lomdei Torah Society ... 50
    The Salon: Among Young People ... 53
    Educational Reform ... 56
    Polish-Jewish Relations and Reform Ideas in Polish Sermons ... 59
    Jastrow the Revolutionary ... 73
Chapter 3: Mannheim ... 89
Chapter 4: Return to Warsaw, 1862–1863 ... 96
Chapter 5: Worms ... 104

Part II: The United States of America 109

Chapter 6: Congregation Rodeph Shalom 110
    Jastrow as the Rabbi and Preacher of the Congregation
    Rodeph Shalom 112
Chapter 7: Controversies 130
    The Conflict between Jastrow and Wise 130
    Defending American Jews 130
    The Controversy with Samuel Hirsch 143
Chapter 8: Liturgy: The *Minhag Jastrow* 152
Chapter 9: Jastrow and the "Historical School" 160
    Maimonides College 161
    Toward a New Seminary 167
Chapter 10: *Wissenschaft des Judentums* 173
    "Jastrow's Dictionary" 173
    The Jewish Encyclopedia 179
    The Jewish Publication Society 182

Conclusion 187
Appendix I: Jastrow's Leter to Rabbi Jacob S. Raisin 192
Appendix II: Aleksander Kraushar, "Kartka z niedawnej
    przeszłości" 194
Appendix III: Selections from Jastrow's March 1, 1861, Sermon 198
Appendix IV: Jastrow's Letter to the Synagogue Council of
    Mannheim 200
Appendix V: Jastrow's Farewell Sermon 205
List of Abbreviations 209
List of Illustrations 210
Bibliography 212
Index 241

Foreword to the English Edition

My adventure with Marcus Jastrow started at the University College London Library, when by chance I came across an article published in the United States (probably an article by Henrietta Szold), which discussed his biography, focused on his life in America. At the time, I associated Marcus Jastrow with his patriotic activities in Warsaw in the years 1861–1863, and had no idea that Jastrow had had a second life, so to speak, in the USA. Drawn into the story, I decided to find out more about this fascinating character and, consequently, to write a book about him, which was published in Polish in 2007.[1] Encouraged by the positive reviews the book received in Poland,[2] Germany,[3] and the UK,[4] and motivated by Professors Antony Polonsky, Jonathan Sarna, Marc Saperstein, and Stefan Schreiner, as well as Rabbi Dov Marmur, I decided to prepare an English edition. I am deeply grateful to Professors Antony Polonsky and Jonathan Sarna for their support at all stages of this work, from research to publishing. Their valuable comments and corrections improved both the translation and the content of my work. I hope that this volume book can offer new information, and that it will be an inspiration for undertaking further studies on this important figure.

I would like to thank Igor Nemirovsky and Sharona Vedol of Academic Studies Press for their assistance in preparing this publication, and especially for their patience. I am also grateful for the financial assistance of the National Program for Development of Humanities in Warsaw. Valuable contributions to this book were made by its translator, Anna Tilles, and by Jessica Taylor-Kucia, who agreed to do a proofreading. I would like to thank them both for their

---

[1] Michał Galas, *Rabin Markus Jastrow i jego wizja reformy judaizmu. Studium z dziejów judaizmu w XIX wieku*, Krakow: Wydawnictwo Austeria, 2007.

[2] Jan Doktór, in *Kwartalnik Historii Żydów/Jewish History Quartely*, no. 1 (2008): 100–101.

[3] Elvira Grözinger, in *PaRDeS: Zeitschrift der Vereinigung für Jüdische Studien e.V* 15 (2009): 182–184.

[4] Ludwik Finkelstein, in *European Judaism* 44, no. 2 (Autumn 2011): 141–143.

valuable comments and for catching mistakes that were missed in the first version of the text.

I would also like to thank all of the institutions, particularly the American Jewish Archives in Cincinnati, who have graciously granted permission for the reproduction in these pages of photographs and documents in their collections.

Krakow, Poland, 29 April 2013.

Foreword

Rabbi Dr Marcus Jastrow (1829–1903) took part in numerous major events in the history of nineteenth-century Judaism. He was, for example, not only a witness to but also an active participant in the events that led to the emergence and formation of the major denominations in modern Judaism. At several points in his life he found himself at the center of the most important occasions and ideological disputes among the followers of Judaism in nineteenth-century Germany, in the Kingdom of Poland, and in the United States. His active involvement in building a Jewish community that would be open to the world and at the same time faithful to the basic values of tradition offers a unique opportunity to investigate his interesting and turbulent life, so full of unexpected turns. It also enables us to learn about and better understand the events and processes that took place in the main Jewish centers of the nineteenth century.

Jastrow lived and worked in many towns, but the most important were Rogoźno (Rogasen) and Poznań (Posen), where he was born and received his early education; Berlin and Breslau, where he studied and where his views were shaped; and Warsaw, Mannheim, and Worms, where he worked as a preacher and a rabbi. In Warsaw he became famous not only as a preacher at the German Progressive Synagogue on Daniłowiczowska Street, but also, and primarily, as a symbol of Polish-Jewish fraternization. Another place that featured in Jastrow's life was Philadelphia, in the USA, where he developed his preaching work and, above all, where he got involved in the battle for the shape of American Judaism.

Unfortunately, Marcus Jastrow is almost absent from modern historiography, and if not for two events in his life he would have been completely forgotten. In Poland and in Polish-Jewish historiography, he is remembered as a participant in the Polish-Jewish fraternization of 1861, which he, along with Rabbi Baer Meisels, came to symbolize, as they were immortalized in a number of paintings.[1] In Jewish

---

[1] See Henryk Pillati, *Pogrzeb pięciu ofiar manifestacji w Warszawie roku 1861* (1865), National Museum in Krakow, and Aleksander Lesser, *Pogrzeb pięciu*

historiography, he is known as the author of the first dictionary of Talmudic language in English, *A Dictionary of the Targumim, the Talmud Babli and Yerushalmi, and the Midrashic Literature*,[2] which is still used today, and which is known to all students and teachers of Jewish studies as "Jastrow's Dictionary."

The research which led to the writing of this book was not easy for many reasons, but one of the most significant reasons was that Jastrow lived, studied, and worked as a rabbi and preacher in many countries. His career, full of unexpected turns, was divided into two important stages: a European stage and an American one. For various reasons, considerable parts of his printed and archived legacy, as well as documents and publications relating to his life, were destroyed or lost during certain events in his life. This book does not claim to offer a presentation of Jastrow's full biography; its primary objective is to delineate his views on the reform of Judaism. Out of necessity, it also contains a number of biographical elements, some of which are published here for the first time, in order to aid in developing a better understanding of the vicissitudes of Jastrow's life, actions, and the context in which he operated.

No critical biography of Jastrow exists in Polish historiography apart from an entry in *Polski Słownik Bibliograficzny* ("Polish Bibliographical Dictionary").[3] Although he is mentioned in works by Artur Eisenbach,[4] Zofia Borzymińska,[5] Alina Cała,[6] Krzysztof

---

ofiar manifestacji w Warszawie roku 1861 (1867), National Museum in Krakow. Reproductions of both pictures are included in this book.

[2] Marcus Jastrow, Ph.D. Litt.D., *A Dictionary of the Targumim, the Talmud Babli and Yerushalmi, and the Midrashic Literature: with an Index of Scriptural Quotations* (London: Luzac & Co.; New York: G.P. Putnam's Sons, 1903), vol. I–II.

[3] Artur Eisenbach, Eligiusz Kozłowski, "Markus Jastrow," in *Polski Słownik Biograficzny*, vol. XI (Wrocław-Warsaw-Kraow: 5) 70–71.

[4] Artur Eisenbach, *Emancypacja Żydów na ziemiach polskich 1785–1870 na tle europejskim* (Warsaw: PIW, 1988), passim; idem, *Kwestia równouprawnienia Żydow w Królestwie Polskim* (Warsaw: Książka i Wiedza, 1972), passim.

[5] Zofia Borzymińska, *Szkolnictwo żydowskie w Warszawie 1831–1870* (Warsaw: ŻIH, 1994), see index.

[6] Alina Cała, *Asymilacja Żydow w Królestwie Polskim (1864–1897)* (Warsaw: PIW, 1989), 78, 373. Cała was one of the first authors to note the importance

Makowski,[7] and more recently, from a new perspective, by Marcin Wodziński,[8] he is mainly depicted as an advocate of the assimilation or emancipation of the Jews, a maskil, or an integrationist. Thus these books touch upon only certain aspects of his activity in Poznań and Warsaw, almost completely omitting his achievements as a religious reformer and preacher.[9]

In Jewish historiography, on the other hand, interesting publications were written by Natan M. Gelber[10] and Jakub Szacki[11] before the Second World War. They mainly concern Jastrow's involvement in the Polish-Jewish fraternization between 1861 and 1863, his preparations

---

of the issue of religion in discussing the problem of assimilation, but she was referring to a period after Jastrow's departure from Warsaw.

[7] Krzysztof Makowski, *Siła Mitu. Żydzi w Poznańskiem w dobie zaborów w piśmiennictwie historycznym* (Poznań: Wydawnictwo Poznańskie, 2004), see index.

[8] Marcin Wodziński, *Oświecenie żydowskie w Królestwie Polskim wobec chasydyzmu. Dzieje pewnej idei* (Warsaw: Cyklady, 2003), 161–165, 190–191, 201–203 and passim. See also the English edition of that book, *Haskalah and Hasidism in the Kingdom of Poland: A History of Conflict* (Oxford: The Littman Library of Jewish Civilization, 2005), see index.

[9] See also Michał Galas, "Rabbi Marcus Jastrow: A Symbol of Polish-Jewish Relations in the 19th Century," *Newsletter of the Skalny Center for Polish and Central European Studies, University of Rochester* (2006): 5; Michał Galas, "Rabbi Marcus Jastrow (1829–1903)," in *YIVO Encyclopedia of Jews in Eastern Europe*, ed. Gershon Hundert (New Haven, CT: Yale University Press, 2008), 819; Michał Galas, "Jewish-Polish Relations in the writings of Rabbi Marcus Jastrow," in *Jewish Studies at the Central European University* 6 (2011): 39–53; Michał Galas, "Rabin Markus Jastrow (1829–1903) i jego droga z Rogoźna do Warszawy," *Studia Historica Slavo-Germanica* 28 (2008–11): 155–174.

[10] Natan M. Gelber, "Dr Mordechai (Markus) Jastrow" (in Hebrew), *He-Avar* 11 (1964): 7–26; Natan M. Gelber, "Akt zbratania polsko-żydowskiego przed powstaniem styczniowym 1863–1864," *Almanach żydowski na rok 5678* (1918); Natan M. Gelber, "Zur Geschichte der Judenfrage," *Zeitschrift für Osteuropäische Geschichte* (1914): 491, 507; Natan M. Gelber, *Die Juden und der polnische Aufstand 1863* (Vienna: R. Löwit, 1923), 71–84, 193–195, passim.

[11] Jakub Szacki, "Yidn un der Poylisher oyfshtand fun 1863," *Historishe shriftn. YIVO* 1 (1929): 423–468; Jakub Szacki, *Geschichte fun Yidn in Warshe*, vol. II (New York: YIVO, 1948), 209–214, 234–236, passim; Jakub Szacki, *Yidishe bildungs-politik in Poyln fun 1806 biz 1866* (New York: YIVO, 1943), 138–149, passim.

for the January uprising, and his work on the development of Jewish education in the Kingdom of Poland.

Jastrow is almost completely absent from German historiography, except for Samson Rothschild's book on the rabbis of Worms[12] and some general entries in encyclopedias and dictionaries.[13]

In English-language publications, Jastrow appears in a few biographies written in the period after his arrival in Philadelphia in 1866,[14] as well as after his death in 1903. The latter publications were prepared by his friends and students Henrietta Szold[15] and David Amram.[16] In the 1960s Moshe Davis mentioned Jastrow in the context of the "historical school" and the history of Conservative Judaism in America.[17] Other important publications are Eric Friedland's studies on changes in the liturgy and on the *Avodat Israel* prayer book compiled by Marcus Jastrow and Benjamin Szold.[18] Jastrow has fallen into obscurity in the

---

[12] Samson Rothschild, *Beamte der Wormser jüdischen Gemeinde (Mitte des 18. Jahrhunderts bis zur Gegenwart)* (Frankfurt a. M: J. Kaufmann Verlag, 1920), 32–37.

[13] The most comprehensive details may be found in *Die Rabbiner der Emanzipationszeit in den deutschen, böhmischen und großpolnishen Ländern 1781–1871*, ed. Carsten Wilke, vol. 1 of *Biographisches Handbuch der Rabbiner*, Part 1, (Munich: Saur, 2004), 479–480.

[14] Benjamin Szold, *Auch ein Wort über Jastrow und Hirsch, von…, Rabbiner der Oheb-Shalom-Gemeinde zu Baltimore* (Baltimore, 1868).

[15] Henrietta Szold, "Marcus Jastrow," *PAJHS* 12 (1904): 181–183; Henrietta Szold, "Marcus Jastrow," in *The American Jewish Year Book 5665. September 10, 1904, to September 29, 1905*, vol. 6, ed. Cyrus Adler and Henrietta Szold (Philadelphia: Jewish Publication Society, 1905), 401–408.

[16] David W. Amram, *Memorial address on the tenth anniversary of the Reverend Doctor Marcus Jastrow Rabbi emeritus of the Congregation Rodef Shalom by…, (delivered at the Synagogue of the Congregation Rodef Shalom, Shemini Atsereth 5674-October 23, 1913)*, [Philadelphia] 1913.

[17] Moshe Davis, *Emergence of Conservative Judaism: The Historical School in 19th Century America* (Philadelphia: Jewish Publication Society of America, 1963), see index; Moshe Davis, *Yahadut Amerikah be-hitpathutah* (New York: Bet ha-Midrash le-Rabanim be-Ameriḳah 1961), 54–60.

[18] Eric L. Friedland, "Marcus Jastrow and Abodath Israel," in *Texts and Responses: Studies Presented to Nahum N. Glazer on the Occasion of his Seventieth Birthday by his Students*, ed. Michael A. Fishbane and Paul R. Flohr (Leiden: Brill, 1975), 186–200; Eric L. Friedland, "'Were Our Mouths Filled with Song': Studies in Liberal Jewish Liturgy* (Cincinnati, OH: HUC Press, 1997), 55–70;

last ten years, and his name does not even appear in the bibliographical dictionaries of individual denominations.[19]

Studies on the history of Congregation Rodeph Shalom in Philadelphia, where Jastrow spent almost half of his life as a rabbi and rabbi emeritus, are also important sources, and do discuss Jastrow's activities to a certain degree.[20]

The lack of serious biographical and bibliographical essays meant that research had to be done practically from scratch, beginning with preparing a bibliography of Jastrow's works. This was not at all easy, as he was involved in the preparation of many drafts of acts and regulations and wrote a number of texts which he did not sign, mainly for political reasons and to avoid criminal liability. Many of his publications were confiscated by censors. Finding his works in American libraries also posed difficulties, even in the case of those works that were published in the United States. Jastrow had many of his sermons and occasional lectures published as brochures, but I have not been able to find all of them. In some instances, a few copies of a lecture remained, but in others—as in the case of the open letter to the Mannheim Synagogue Council[21]—only one copy remains (in the case of the aforementioned letter, the copy is currently at the Jewish National and University Library in Jerusalem). Finally, due to the poor condition of nineteenth-century American newspapers and the fact that collections were missing some items, I was not able to access all of Jastrow's articles, though the crucial ones are included in my bibliography.

Eric L. Friedland, "The Historical and Theological Development of the Non-Orthodox Prayerbooks in the United States' (Ph.D. diss., Brandeis University, 1967), 94–114, 285–288.

[19] See and cf. the following: K.M. Olitzky, L. Sussman, M. Stern, eds., *Reform Judaism in America: A Bibliographical Dictionary and Sourcebook* (Westport-London: Greenwood Press, 1993); P.S. Nadell, ed., *Conservative Judaism in America: A Bibliographical Dictionary and Sourcebook* (Westport-London: Greenwood Press, 1988). Neither of the books contains a biography of Jastrow, though there are entries for his lesser-known colleagues.

[20] E.g., Edward Davis, *The History of Rodeph Shalom Congregation Philadelphia: 1802–1926* (Philadelphia, 1927).

[21] Marcus Jastrow, *Offenes Schreiben an den Grossh. Synagogenrath in Mannheim* (Mannheim, 1862).

Following the trail laid by Jastrow's life, I conducted archival research in Poland, Germany, and the United States. In Poland, research was mostly done in Archiwum Państwowe, Poznań (the State Archive in Poznań, APP), Muzeum Regionalne im. Wojciechy Dutkiewicz, Rogoźno (Wojciecha Dutkiewicz Regional Museum), Archiwum Główne Akt Dawnych, Warsaw (Central Archive of Historical Records, AGAD), Żydowski Instytut Historyczny, Warsaw (Jewish Historical Institute, ŻIH), Biblioteka Jagiellońska, Kraków (Jagiellonian Library), and Zakład Narodowy im. Ossolińskich, Wrocław (Ossolineum Library). In Germany, research was done in Centrum Judaicum Archiv, Berlin (New Synagogue Berlin Centrum Judaicum Archives, CJA), the university archives in Berlin and Halle, and the city archives of Mannheim and Worms. The most useful archives in the United States were the American Jewish Archives in Cincinnati (AJA), where the largest number of documents was found. One of the very interesting sources found there was a manuscript (and partial typescript) of a draft biography of Jastrow compiled on the basis of his letters,[22] which have unfortunately been lost. That biographical compilation, most likely written by Henrietta Szold and David Amram, has often been the only source of information about an aspect of Jastrow's life. It nevertheless contains numerous mistakes, especially regarding his European period. Other important archives in which research was done include the archives of the Jewish Theological Seminary and the Center for Jewish History in New York, the Philadelphia Jewish Archives Center at the Balch Institute, the Rodeph Shalom Congregation Archives, the Institute of Advanced Judaic Studies, the University of Pennsylvania Archives in Philadelphia, and the Jewish Museum of Maryland in Baltimore.

The subject of this book—Rabbi Marcus Jastrow and his vision of the reform of Judaism—determines both the book's layout and the use of the materials collected. From the beginning, Jastrow had fairly clearly developed views on the need for religious reform in Judaism, and the shape that those reforms should take, and these remained stable, despite all the changes of environment and the locations he studied and worked in as a rabbi and preacher (Poznań, Berlin, Warsaw, Mannheim, Worms, and Philadelphia). His views on this particular

---

[22] American Jewish Archives (AJA), Small Collection (SC) no. 5686, also known as the *Marcus Jastrow Near Print File = NPF*.

topic were influenced mainly by his teachers and mentors, but also by people he came into contact with, the era in which he lived, and the needs that arose and the experience he gained in the course of pursuing his preaching work in different communities. He himself wrote that when he took up the post of rabbi in Warsaw he understood progress as spreading education and culture, while in Mannheim and Worms he concentrated on moral advancement in the spiritual development of the followers of Judaism and people in general—and he subsequently attempted to combine the two in Philadelphia.[23]

The primary sources for this monograph, through which Jastrow's life story and his views in particular are perceived and analyzed, are his own works—archival and published—some of which were previously unknown. Thus, in this volume there are numerous quotes and annexes containing selected source texts that illustrate Jastrow's work and explain the contents of this monograph. There are also other important papers and pamphlets, often polemicizing with Jastrow's ideas, which were printed in the period in question. Individual chapters are supplemented by significant biographical details to facilitate a better understanding of the actions and beliefs of our "main protagonist."

The type, number, and accessibility of sources for specific periods dictate the approach to the subject and the size of individual chapters. In order to better understand Jastrow's views and the background of the events and changes in nineteenth-century Judaism, major events in the history of Judaism are outlined in the introduction, with a focus on the issue of the Reform movement in Judaism and new movements and denominations in European and American Judaism. The book is complemented by additional materials, such as pictures, copies of documents, and photographs of Jastrow and his family from various places and times of his life.

My research project benefitted from the interest and support of many institutions, without which my archival and library research would not have been possible. I am grateful for the support I received from the Fulbright Foundation, whose scholarship enabled me to conduct research at Brandeis University during the 2002–2003 academic year. I would also like to express my gratitude to the American Jewish

---

[23] Marcus Jastrow, "Antwort an Herrn I.M. Wise in Cincinnati, auf dessen Aufsatz betitelt "Das Pamphlet"," *Deborah*, September 20, 1867, 10.

Archives for the Loewenstein-Wiener Fellowship that enabled me to conduct research there, as well as to the Deutscher Akademischer Austauschdienst (German Academic Exchange Service, DAAD), for supporting my research in German archives. This book could not have been published without the support of many people who helped me and offered advice at various stages of the project. Among those I would especially like to thank are Antony Polonsky and Jonathan Sarna of Brandeis University, Stefan Schreiner of the University of Tübingen, Garry Zola and Kevin Proffitt of the American Jewish Archives, David B. Ruderman, Arthur Kiron, Seth Jerchower, and Judith Leifer of the University of Pennsylvania, Eleonora Bergman of the Jewish Historical Institute in Warsaw, Gershon Hundert of McGill University, Krzysztof Makowski of Adam Mickiewicz University, Poznań, and Lidia Kubit of Tuchów.

Introduction

Judaism in the Nineteenth Century: A General Overview

During his lifetime, Rabbi Marcus Jastrow experienced firsthand all of the major problems and phenomena of nineteenth-century Judaism in Germany, Poland, and the United States. Before I embark on the story of his life, and above all his views on the reform or reforms of Judaism, therefore, I shall attempt to outline the main trends and characters that may have had an influence on Jastrow's views, and the major events that occurred during his lifetime in the places in which he lived.

The nineteenth century brought many changes to the history of Jews and Judaism, turning an almost homogenous society based on religious customs and laws into a socially, culturally, and religiously pluralist society. These changes began in the seventeenth and eighteenth centuries with religious crises such as mystical and messianic movements, as well as the influence of the Enlightenment and the quest for equality by sections of the Jewish community. The Haskalah, the Jewish enlightenment, had a remarkable impact on the form of nineteenth-century Judaism, and its problems. It caused a real revolution which, to varying degrees, affected the lives of Jews in all the countries of the Diaspora in Europe and the United States. The organizations, ideologies, denominations, and divisions that emerged as a result of these processes form the basis for the present state of the Jewish world. But Orthodox, Reform, and Conservative Judaism were not solely the results of processes of internal change in the Jewish community: they were also, to a large extent, results of reactions to and relations with the external world.

The Haskalah and the Reform of Judaism in Germany

At the end of the eighteenth century, arguments rooted in the ideology of the Enlightenment were voiced in France and some German states in support of the granting of equality and full emancipation to Jews.[1]

---

[1] Eisenbach, *Emancypacja Żydów*, 126–135.

Those opinions also began to gain popularity among the Jews themselves, who needed to find an appropriate reaction to the new situation and the opportunities it presented. Moses Mendelssohn, known as the "father of the Haskalah," defined the ideological framework of the Jewish response to the new era in his works and speeches. This framework constituted a compromise, including the modernization of Jewish life but not at the expense of loyalty to religious tradition, to which he was faithful until his death. However, his desire for Jewish emancipation and participation in political, social, cultural, and economic life required certain changes and compromises from the Jews.[2] The attitude that Mendelssohn and the maskilim called for involved, above all, the adoption of the language of the country of residence, and the renunciation in intellectual life of Yiddish, the "shameful jargon," in favor of Hebrew, the "real" Jewish language. Jews were also to become more similar to their Christian neighbors through changes to their dress and lifestyle, and this could not be achieved without a reform of traditional Jewish education. For Mendelssohn, who considered himself a spiritual heir of Maimonides, there was no dissonance in accepting secular education and teaching—not only was this not a transgression of the law, but it was a necessity of the new era. Therefore, the advocates of the Haskalah attached great importance to Jewish schooling and education at all levels, which would include the teaching of vernacular languages and secular subjects, as well as vocational training for professions previously inaccessible to or forbidden for Jews. Another fundamental postulate advocated by the supporters of the Haskalah was loyalty toward the state and its authorities. The ideas and principles of the Haskalah movement first gained expression in the German-speaking countries and soon spread throughout Western and Central Europe and Russia.[3]

---

[2] For more about Mendelssohn, see Salomon Łastik, *Z dziejów oświecenia żydowskiego. Ludzie i fakty* (Warsaw: PIW, 1961), 24–30; Michael A. Meyer, *The Origins of the Modern Jew: Jewish Identity and European Culture in Germany, 1749–1824* (Detroit: Wayne State University Press, 1967), 11–28; and Aleksander Altman, *Moses Mendelssohn: A Biographical Study* (Tuscaloosa: University of Alabama Press, 1973), which also contains an extensive bibliography.

[3] Cf. Shmuel Feiner, *Haskalah and History: The Emergence of a Modern Jewish Historical Consciousness*, trans. Chaya Naor and Sondra Silverston (London: The Littman Library of Jewish Civilization, 2002); Shmuel Feiner and

Mendelssohn saw no discrepancy between the ideology of the Haskalah and the values of traditional Judaism. He was a true follower of Judaism for the rest of his life, though he was treated by many not as a reformer but as a heretic who did more harm than good for the Jews and Judaism.[4] His students and future maskilim interpreted the emancipation and participation of Jews in social life in a number of ways. By the end of the eighteenth century, there were four movements based on different interpretations and understanding of the Haskalah.

The first consisted of emancipation being seen as merely a stage in the process of full assimilation and, consequently, departure from Judaism or even conversion to Christianity. The second movement completely rejected the Haskalah as a heresy and a road to secularization. The third was initiated by those maskilim who, like Mendelssohn, sought to reconcile the values of Haskalah with traditional Judaism. The fourth, which is the one of greatest interest to us here, was led by those followers of the Haskalah who wanted to neither abandon Judaism nor reject emancipation. They tried to find a compromise with a modernizing reform of Judaism. This reform was to consist of removing those elements of Judaism which, according to the advocates of this trend, were an obstacle to full emancipation and contact with and acceptance by their Christian neighbors.[5]

David Sorkin, eds., *New Perspectives on the Haskalah* (London: The Littman Library of Jewish Civilization, 2001); Jacob S. Raisin, *The Haskalah Movement in Russia* (Philadelphia: Jewish Publication Society of America, 1913); and Łastik, *Z dziejów oświecenia*.

[4] His translation of the Bible into German became the symbol of the Haskalah, but at the same time, to opponents of the movement it was an example of a departure from tradition. Thus there were cases of public burnings of "Mendelssohn's Bible"; see, e. g., Majer Bałaban, *Historja Żydów w Krakowie i na Kazimierzu* (Krakow: "Nadzieja," 1936), vol. II, 540–541. For other religious conflicts, see also Shmuel Feiner, "Między Lesznem a Berlinem. Pierwszy spór ortodoksji z haskalą i jego religijne oraz społeczne implikacje," in *Duchowość żydowska w Polsce. Materiały z międzynarodowej konferencji dedykowanej pamięci profesora Chone Shmeruka Krakow 26–28 kwietnia 1999*, ed. Michał Galas (Krakow: Księgarnia Akademicka, 2000), 279–286.

[5] Meyer, *The Origins*, 85–114; Michael Meyer, "Jewish Communities in Transition," in *German-Jewish History in Modern Times*, vol. II of *Emancipation*

The movement for reform in Judaism was therefore deeply rooted in the Haskalah, though the two movements were not the same. We need to remember that in the German-speaking countries, the ideas of the Haskalah and, later, Reform Judaism reached above all communities and individuals in larger cities—Berlin, Königsberg, Hamburg, Frankfurt—where they found fertile ground. The movement's impact also depended on political and religious factors. As noted by Michael Meyer, the movement for reform in Judaism had more followers and greater influence where the Protestant Church was stronger.[6] It should not come as a surprise, then, that the first attempts to introduce reforms took place in the Kingdom of Westphalia, where the law was similar to French law at the time.[7] They were initiated by the consistorial president of the Jewish community in Kassel, Israel Jacobson, and were mainly aimed at adapting Judaism to the modern world through copying Protestant forms of worship. Thus the initial reforms sought to make synagogue services more attractive through the adoption of socially appropriate behavior and appearances, and the introduction of sermons, in the vernacular, which focused mostly on issues of morality and spiritual development. The first such sermon was delivered by Joseph Wolf of Dessau in 1808. In time, choral singing and organ music were introduced, and prayers recited in Hebrew were replaced by prayers in German. The role of the rabbi changed as well—he was no longer an authority and "oracle" in matters of religious law, but rather a priest and teacher of religion whose role and function was comparable to that of a pastor.[8] Jacobson started delivering services in the new form in Seesen in 1810, and in Berlin when he moved there in 1815. He established a synagogue in his home in Berlin,

---

    and Acculturation: 1780–1871, ed. Michael A. Meyer and Michael Brenner (New York: Columbia University Press, 1997), 90–105.

[6] Ibid., 90–127. Some scholars see a parallel between the Reformation and the Reform movement in Judaism, though it seems that such influences were quite limited. The Protestant Reformation was undoubtedly held up as an example of religious revival by Jews, cf. Michael A. Meyer, *Response to Modernity: A History of the Reform Movement in Judaism* (Detroit: Wayne State University Press, 1995), 17–18; Michael A. Meyer, "Judaism and Christianity," in *German-Jewish History in Modern Times*, vol. II, 168–198.

[7] Eisenbach, *Emancypacja Żydów*, 126–128.

[8] Meyer, *Jewish Communities*, 106–108.

holding Reform services there regularly. In 1818, about 25 percent of the Jewish residents of Berlin participated in such Reform services.[9] New synagogues, such the Hamburg Temple founded in 1818, resembled churches rather than old Jewish prayer houses in their décor. Although the reformers tried to make sure that the changes did not transgress traditional religious laws, the innovations threatened centuries-old customs, so naturally they were attacked by opponents of the Haskalah and the Reform movement.[10] The only non-Orthodox community at the time was the community of Hamburg, which brought out a new, bilingual, Hebrew-German prayer book[11] and new synagogue by-laws. The most important modification they made to the prayer service was the elimination of those sections which mentioned the return of the Jews to the Land of Israel under the leadership of the Messiah. This change suggested that Germany, or any other country inhabited by Jews, could replace Erets Yisra'el, because the religious goal and ideals of the Jewish faith could be achieved anywhere. The word used for the synagogue—temple—was based on similar ideological attitudes, which held that the Holy Temple would not be rebuilt, but every house of prayer could be considered a temple. Early reform-minded Jews were advocates of secular education, too, and their children often attended Christian schools.

At the beginning of the nineteenth century, voices were raised in favor of further changes in doctrine and worship in order to achieve the goal of emancipation and "coming out of the ghetto." David Friedländer, a student of Mendelssohn's, was the first to signal further changes in the liturgy and faith.[12] However, the program of reform

---

[9] Ibid., 125.

[10] For more about the first attempts to introduce reforms, and their consequences, see ibid., 119–123.

[11] *Seder ha-Awodah. Ordnung der öffentlichen Andacht für die Sabbath- und Festtage des ganzen Jahres. Nach dem Gebrauche des Neuen-Tempel-Vereins in Hamburg* (Hamburg [1819]). It is considered one of the first Reform prayer books. See Jakob J. Petuchowski, *Prayerbook Reform in Europe: The Liturgy of European Liberal and Reform Judaism* (New York: World Union for Progressive Judaism, 1968), 2.

[12] For more about this important figure, see Meyer, *The Origins*, 57–84. Friedländer is also known for writing a book on Jewish reform in the Kingdom of Poland, commissioned by Archbishop Franciszek Malczewski Skarbek: David Friedländer, *Über die Verbesserung der Israeliten des Königreich*

would crystalize later, during the three rabbinical conferences of Brunswick (1844), Frankfurt (1845), and Breslau (1846).[13] Two trends dominated the Reform movement in Judaism during this period. One was identified with Abraham Geiger, who gained popularity and reputation first as a scholar of Jewish history affiliated with the Verein für Cultur und Wissenschaft der Juden in Berlin, and later as a leading figure of the Reform movement. He was a rabbi in Breslau for many years, and between 1872 and 1877 a lecturer at the Hochschule für die Wissenschaft des Judentums, the main rabbinical seminary and research center of Reform Judaism in Germany. Geiger's views originated in observations he made in the course of his academic research. He believed that in every era Judaism reflected the aspirations of the Jews at that time and was a reaction to existing conditions. Judaism was, therefore, an evolving religion, and changes in Judaism had always been evolutionary rather than revolutionary. The principles of his vision of Reform Judaism were included in a prayer book published in 1854 in which he omitted references to resurrection, angels, the rebuilding of the Temple, and the return to the Land of Israel. Geiger also reinterpreted the personal Messiah and messianic hope as universal, not specifically national. He rejected the idea of chosenness and many religious laws, among them the dietary laws.[14]

Another leading figure, this one associated with a more radical branch of the Reform movement, was Samuel Holdheim, who advocated changes in Judaism but supported a more revolutionary approach. His understanding of the Bible and the Talmud was also more radical: he held that they contained both the eternal and unchangeable values of monotheism and morality and laws and rulings that related to specific historical events and situations. Holdheim

---

Pohlen. Ein von der Regierung daselbst im Jahr 1816 abgefordertes Gutachten (Berlin, 1891). See Krzysztof Pilarczyk, *Literatura żydowska od epoki biblijnej do haskali* (Krakow: Wydawnictwo UJ, 2006), 307.

[13] For more about the conferences and their resolutions, see David Philipson, *The Reform Movement in Judaism* ([New York]: KTAV, 1967), 140–224.

[14] For more about Abraham Geiger and his doctrine, see Ken Koltun-Fromm, *Abraham Geiger's Liberal Judaism* (Bloomington: Indiana University Press, 2006); *Abraham Geiger and Liberal Judaism. The Challenge of the Nineteenth Century*, compiled with a biographical introduction by Max Wiener, trans. from German Ernst J. Schlochauer (Philadelphia: Jewish Publication Society of America, 1962).

proposed that the latter should be removed, as they had no normative value. He rejected the Oral Torah on the basis of a belief that "the Talmud speaks out of the consciousness of its age and for that time it was right; I speak out of the higher consciousness of my age and for this age I am right."[15] In addition, Holdheim did not believe in the Messiah or the return to the Land of Israel, and he abolished the observance of the second days of religious holidays in the Diaspora. He wanted Judaism to be a universalist religion devoid of nationalistic and particularistic elements; hence, he advocated a form of worship similar to that of Christianity. He not only supported the idea that the German language should replace Hebrew as the language of sermons and prayers, but he also moved the observance of the Sabbath from Saturday to Sunday. Holdheim's radical views found few followers in Germany, and most of those few were in Berlin, though his ideology found adherents among the radical reformers in America.[16]

Through their education and questions about true Judaism, the advocates of religious reform and the Haskalah contributed to the emergence of an interest in academic research into Jewish history and attempts to learn about the essence of Judaism, free from the accretions of centuries. One of the first initiatives they led was the founding of the already mentioned society, the Verein für Cultur und Wissenschaft der Juden, whose main aim was to lead Judaism to self-awareness and to make the Jewish world known to the Jews.[17] One of the best-known members of the society was Leopold Zunz, one of the founders of the Wissenschaft des Judentums movement, which gave rise to modern Jewish Studies.[18] To the proponents of Wissenschaft des Judentums and Zunz, the goals of the movement were on the one hand to initiate research into the Jewish religious, historical, cultural, and literary heritage using contemporary scholarly methods, and on the other hand to bring that tradition into the "bloodstream" of the

---

[15] Meyer, *Response to Modernity*, 83.

[16] For more about Samuel Holdheim, see ibid., 77–84.

[17] Meyer, *Jewish Communities*, 131.

[18] See Michael Brenner, Stefan Rohrbacher, eds., *Wissenschaft vom Judentum; Annäherungen nach dem Holocaust* (Göttingen: Vandenhoeck & Ruprecht, 2000); David Nathan Meyers, "The Ideology of Wissenschaft des Judentums," in *History of Jewish Philosophy*, ed. Daniel H. Frank and Oliver Leaman (London: Routledge, 1997), 706–720.

German and wider European awareness as an important element of universal human heritage.

One of the crucial figures in the Wissenschaft des Judentums movement was Zacharias Frankel, who initially joined the supporters of religious reform and even took part in the first and second conferences of Reform rabbis in Brunswick (1844) and Frankfurt (1845), though he withdrew from the second conference in protest at what he considered the too far-reaching reforms proposed by Geiger and others. He was particularly opposed to the ideas of removing the Hebrew language from the liturgy and replacing it with German, and eliminating all references to messianism. Frankel believed that the core values of Judaism were "unchangeable and imperative"[19] because they were derived from revelation. He held the view that it was permissible to reform customs based on the Oral Law, as the Oral Law did not come from revelation but from the sages, and was shaped over thousands of years of Jewish history and experience. As such, the Oral Law deserved respect, though changes to it were permissible. Such a stance required turning to the study of the history and collective experience of the Jews, which had had a greater formative influence on Judaism than theology had.[20] He described what he was trying to achieve as "Positive-Historical Judaism."

Frankel believed that Jews constitute only a "religious, spiritual community conditioned by faith—they have an identity only inasmuch as they keep their faith. Therefore, Jews form a religious community only, like any denomination present in a given country."[21]

He held that every religion evolves, but any changes in Jewish rituals should be introduced in a manner that does not violate the core values of Judaism. He supported reforms that would help Jews adapt to their new conditions—primarily educational reforms. Apart from Geiger, Frankel was the best educated advocate of religious reform, and they were both candidates for the post of director and lecturer at the newly established Jewish Theological Seminary of Breslau,

---

[19] Often referred to as "positive," cf. Meyer, *Jewish Communities*, 141.

[20] Cf. Arthur Hertzberg, Aron Hirt-Manheimer, *Żydzi. Istota i charakter narodu*, transl. B. Paluchowska (Warszawa: Mada, 2001), 172. (English: Arthur Hertzberg, Aron Hirt-Manheimer, Jews: the essence and character of a people, [San Francisco]: HarperSanFrancisco, 1998.)

[21] Quoted after Meyer, *Jewish Communities*, 145.

founded in 1854.[22] Eventually, it was Frankel who was elected head of the seminary, and he who shaped it and imposed on it a particular vision of teaching and academic research. Frankel also contributed to the seminary's evolution into the main center of moderate reform, which was referred to as "Positive-Historical" Judaism at the time. The lecturers at the seminary were eminent historians in various fields of study: Heinrich Graetz, Jacob Bernays, Manuel Joël, Benedict Zuckermann, David Rosin, Marcus Brann, and many others. Frankel had also been the founder in 1851 of the *Monatsschrift für die Geschichte und Wissenschaft des Judenthums*, the most important scholarly periodical of the "positive-historical school."[23]

In the mid-nineteenth century the structure of Reform or Positive-Historical Judaism had not yet been formed. Hence, the majority of followers gathered around the most prominent individuals. However, there were also a number of figures, both rabbis and laymen, who supported the reforms without engaging in the activity of such circles, for instance Isaac Noah Mannheimer and the well-known and respected rabbi Dr Michael Sachs, who were advocates of moderate reform.

The responses of Orthodox circles to the ideology of the Haskalah and the attempts at reform varied. The Gaon of Vilna (Rabbi Elijah ben Shlomo Zalman Kremer), the Hasidic leaders, and later the leader of modern Orthodoxy, Rabbi Moses Sofer of Bratislava, were profoundly opposed to any changes in the established Jewish tradition. Sofer even went so far as to declare that anything "new is forbidden by the Torah."[24] He was against secular education, changes in dress, and efforts toward emancipation. Sofer pronounced the followers of the Enlightenment and Reform heretics.

The prominent German Orthodox rabbi Samson Raphael Hirsch differed from Sofer in his views, as he sought a compromise between Judaism and the modern world. He considered Moses Mendelssohn

---

[22] The full name of the seminary was *Das Jüdisch-Theologische Seminar— Fränckelscher Stiftung*.

[23] *Die Monatsschrift für Geschichte und Wissenschaft des Judentums*, published between 1851 and 1939, was the leading academic journal, and was copied by other propagators of Jewish studies around the world (e. g. *Miesięcznik Żydowski* [Jewish Monthly] published in the 1930s).

[24] Hertzberg, Hirt-Manheimer, *Żydzi*, 167.

to be an example attesting to the fact that such a compromise was possible. Hirsch held that it was the Jews, not Judaism, that were in need of reform. He thus accepted acculturation to a certain extent, particularly in terms of dress, use of the local language, and access to secular education. Hirsch's philosophy, "*Torah im derekh eretz*—Torah in association with "the way of the land"," involved loyalty to the values of Judaism combined with participation in the social life of the country of residence. He initially joined forces with Frankel against the radical reformers, and even expressed his willingness to become a lecturer at the seminary in Breslau. When Frankel turned him down, Hirsch distanced himself from him and started his own movement, commonly known as "Neo-Orthodoxy."[25]

These are four reactions to the challenges of the Haskalah in the field of religion that were characteristic of the experiences of German Jews in the nineteenth century. Jastrow came into contact with each of these ideologies and most of their leaders, and the impacts of those contacts would echo in his future work.

The Influence of Reform in Judaism in the Polish Lands

The subject of religious reform in Judaism is often overlooked in the historiography of the nineteenth-century history of Jews and Judaism in the Polish lands, or it is discussed in a few sentences, usually accompanied by the statement that progressive ideas and the Reform movement in Judaism did not have any significant impact in this part of Europe due to the strength of Jewish Orthodoxy and Hasidism.

Michael Meyer, the most distinguished modern historian of Reform Judaism, disagrees with this view, arguing that contemporary

---

[25] Jacob Breuer, ed., *Fundamentals of Judaism: Selections from the Works of Rabbi Samson Raphael Hirsch and Outstanding Torah-true Thinkers*, ed. Jacob Breuer (New York: Published for the Rabbi Samson Raphael Hirsch Society by P. Feldheim, 1969); Samson Raphael Hirsch, *The Nineteen Letters*, trans. Karin Paritzky, revised and with a comprehensive commentary by Joseph Elias (New York: Feldheim Publishers, 1995); Noah H. Rosenbloom, *Tradition in an Age of Reform: The Religious Philosophy of Samson Raphael Hirsch* (Philadelphia: Jewish Publication Society of America, 1976); and Mordechai Breuer, *The "Torah-im-derekh-eretz" of Samson Raphael Hirsch* (Jerusalem: Feldheim Publishers, 1970).

historians of Judaism and Jewry have been neglectful of the history of the movement for Jewish religious reform in Central and Eastern Europe (mainly with the Polish lands in mind). He designates certain research areas which should be explored first, in order to be able to state with certainty the extent of the influence of Jewish religious reform in that part of Europe. The most crucial of these are: to locate the phenomenon of religious reform in Eastern Europe; to determine the origins of reform in the context of both the political and the intellectual milieux of Eastern European Jewry, and particularly in relation to the model of the religious reform originated by German Jews; and to assess the scope and depth of the movement's influence and the character and consequences of reform ideology in religious and secular contexts.[26] Meyer's only article on Eastern Europe is limited mainly to Russia, though he does also mention the phenomenon of religious reform in the Polish lands.[27] He maintains that only one small group of Jews, those in the German synagogue in Warsaw, introduced radical Reform services and sermons delivered in Polish. However, he notes, the Polish progressives, who tended to be wealthy and assimilated, were not aware of their affiliation with a worldwide movement.[28] While Meyer is clearly correct about the need for more research, this judgment is flawed.

Warsaw was indeed the first Polish city to boast a "German" synagogue, which was established in 1802.[29] The main centers of

---

[26] Michael A. Meyer, "The German Model of Religious Reform and Russian Jewry," in his, *Judaism within Modernity: Essays on Jewish History and Religion* (Detroit: Wayne State University Press, 2001), 279.

[27] It is significant that Meyer does not differentiate between Warsaw and Odessa in this respect, and he writes: "Toward the middle of the nineteenth century, "German" prayer services were established in a number of Russian cities: in Odessa, Warsaw, Riga, and Vilna." Meyer, "The German Model of Religious Reform and Russian Jewry," 281. Cf. idem, *Response to Modernity*, 197–198.

[28] Ibid., 339.

[29] The term "progressive synagogue" in the Polish lands corresponds with "reform" or "liberal" synagogue in Germany at that time. In Austria-Hungary, reformers were also known as Neologs. See Michael A. Meyer, "Religious Reform," in *YIVO Encyclopedia of Jews in Eastern Europe*, www.yivoinstitute.org/pdf/reform.pdf, 2–3. See also Michał Galas, "The Influence

reform in Judaism in the Polish lands were synagogues or houses of prayer referred to as "progressive," "reform," "German," "Polish," or as "temples." Unfortunately, in the historiography of nineteenth-century Jewish history in the Polish lands, much more attention has been devoted to the processes accompanying the Haskalah and religious reform in Judaism, i. e., to acculturation, assimilation, secularization, and integrationism,[30] than to strictly religious aspects of this development.[31] The few works on the impact of the religious reform movement deal mainly with the histories of individual communities or synagogues, and rarely touch upon specifically religious issues such as liturgical changes, rabbis and preachers, the contents of sermons, and modifications to services—themes that could be summarized as "what Polish progressives in the nineteenth century believed and how they expressed their religiosity." No comprehensive biographies or critical studies have been written about the great preachers and advocates of Polish-Jewish fraternization, such as Abraham Goldschmidt, Marcus Jastrow, Izaak Cylkow,[32] Izaak Kramsztyk, Samuel A. Poznański, and

---

of Progressive Judaism in Poland: An Outline," *Shofar. An Interdisciplinary Journal of Jewish Studies* 29, no. 3 (2011): 55–67.

[30] The most important publications on this subject include Tomasz Gąsowski, *Między gettem a światem. Dylematy ideowe Żydow galicyjskich na przełomie XIX i XX wieku* (Krakow: Księgarnia Akademicka, 1996); Scott Ury, "Pod szubienicami...". Polityka asymilacji w Warszawie przełomu wieków," in *Duchowość żydowska w Polsce*, ed. Michal Galas, 309–326; Stefan Kieniewicz, "Assimilated Jews in Nineteenth-Century Warsaw," in *The Jews in Warsaw: A History*, ed. Władysław T. Bartoszewski and Antony Polonsky (Oxford: Basil Blackwell, 1991), 151–170; Antony Polonsky, *The Failure of Jewish Assimilation in Polish Lands and Its Consequences* (Oxford: Oxford Centre for Hebrew and Jewish Studies, 2000).

[31] Stephen D. Corrsin also points this out in his very valuable article, which is at the same time a sort of review of Meyer's works on Eastern Europe. See Stephen D. Corrsin, "Progressive Judaism in Poland: Dilemmas of Modernity and Identity," in *Cultures and Nations on Central and Eastern Europe: Essays in Honor of Roman Szporluk*, ed. Zvi Gitelman et al. (Cambridge, MA: Harvard University Press, 2000), 89–99.

[32] On Cylkow see Michał Galas, ed., *Izaak Cylkow. Życie i dzieło* (Krakow-Budapest: Wydawnictwo Austeria, 2010).

Moses Schorr of Warsaw, or Szymon Dankowicz[33] and Ojzasz Thon[34] of Krakow, as well as many others. Let us hope that this book prompts the filling of this gap.

The truth is that there were not many such progressive communities, and their existence was limited to larger towns, particularly those in the Prussian partition. Nevertheless, the Warsaw "German" synagogue, with which Jastrow was affiliated from 1858, existed as early as the beginning of the nineteenth century. In 1852, a "Polish" synagogue affiliated with the rabbinical school was also established there.[35] In addition, Progressive communities with their own synagogues existed in Łódź, Vilna, and Zhytomyr, and in Galicia in Lviv, Tarnopol, Brody,

---

[33] On Dankowicz see Michał Galas, ed., *Synagoga Tempel i środowisko krakowskich Żydów postępowych* (Krakow—Budapeszt: Wydawnictwo Austeria, 2012) and Alicja Maślak Maciejewska, *Życie i działalność Szymona Dankowicza (1834–1910)* (Krakow—Budapeszt: Wydawnictwo Austeria, 2013).

[34] See, e. g., Michał Galas, "Ojzasz (Jehoshua) Thon (1870–1936)—Prediger und Rabbiner in Krakau (Eine Erinnerung anlässlich seines 75. Todestages)," *Judaica. Beiträge zum Verstehen des Judentums*, no. 3 (2011): 311–321; Michał Galas, "Three Views of Jewish Acculturation to Polish Culture in the 19th and Early 20th Twentieth Century Krakow," in *Jewish Lifeworlds and Jewish Thought: Festschrift presented to Karl E. Grözinger on the Occasion of his 70th Birthday* (Wiesbaden: Harrassowitz Verlag, 2011), 245–251.

[35] See the following to learn about progressive institutions in nineteenth-century Warsaw: *Z dziejów Gminy Starozakonnych w Warszawie w XIX stuleciu*, vol. I, *Szkolnictwo*, Warsaw 1907, 41–140; Zofia Borzymińska, *Szkolnictwo żydowskie w Warszawie*, 78–93, passim; Zofia Borzymińska, "Przyczynek do dziejów szkolnictwa żydowskiego w Warszawie w XIX wieku, czyli jeszcze o Szkole Rabinów," *Biuletyn ŻIH* 3–4 (1984): 183–196; Antony Polonsky, "Warszawska Szkoła Rabinów: orędowniczka narodowej integracji w Królestwie Polskim," in Galas, ed., *Duchowość żydowska w Polsce*, 287–308; Aron Sawicki, "Szkoła Rabinów w Warszawie (1826–1863)," *Miesięcznik Żydowski* 1–2 (1933): 244–274; Sara Zilbersztejn, "Postępowa Synagoga na Daniłowiczowskiej," *Biuletyn ŻIH* 74 (1970): 31–57; Alexander Guterman, "The Origin of the Great Synagogue in Warsaw on Tłomackie Street," in *The Jews in Warsaw: A History*, ed. Władysław T. Bartoszewski and Antony Polonsky, 182–211; Alexander Guterman, *Me-hitbolelut la-leumiyut: perakim be-toldot bet ha-keneset ha-gadol ha-sinagogah be-varshah 1806–1943* (Jerusalem: Karmel 1993); Jürgen Hensel, "Wie "deutsch" war die "fortschrittliche" jüdische Bourgeoisie im Königreich Polen? Antworten anhand einiger Beispiele aus Warschau und Lodz," in *Symbiose und Traditionsbruch. Deutsch-jüdische Wechselbeziehungen in Ostmittel- und Sudosteuropa (19. Und 20. Jahrhundert)*, ed. Hans Hecker and Walter Engel (Essen: Klartext, 2003), 135–172.

Kraków, and Stanisławów.³⁶ In the inter-war period, there was one in almost every big town in the Republic of Poland. Reforms were introduced by means of the German language almost everywhere, and with time German was superseded by Polish. The model for nineteenth-century Polish progressives was the Viennese reform known as the Viennese rite, implemented by the local rabbi Isaac Noah Mannheimer and cantor Solomon Sulzer. The Viennese reform introduced moderate changes which did not violate Jewish law and were characterized mostly by decorum and esthetics in services, sermons delivered in German, and an abbreviated liturgy.³⁷

---

36   For more about progressive synagogues and institutions in the Polish lands in the nineteenth century, see Majer Bałaban, *Historia lwowskiej Synagogi Postępowej* (Lviv: Nakł. Zarządu Synagogi Postępowej, 1937); Majer Bałaban, *Historia projektu szkoły rabinów i nauki religii mojż. na ziemiach polskich* (Lviv: Nakładem Przełożeństwa Zboru Izraelickiego, 1907); Hanna Kozińska-Witt, *Die Krakauer Jüdische Reformgemeinde 1864–1874* (Frankfurt a.M.: Peter Lang Verlag, 1999); Hanna Kozińska-Witt, "Stowarzyszenie Izraelitów Postępowych w Krakowie 1864–74," in *Duchowość żydowska w Polsce*, ed. Michael Galas, 309–326; Julian Bussgang, "The Progressive Synagogue in Lwow," *Polin: Studies in Polish Jewry* 11 (1998): 127–153; Verena Dohrn, "The Rabbinical Schools as Institutions of Socialization in Tsarist Russia, 1847–1873," *Polin: Studies in Polish Jewry* 14 (2001): 83–105; Efim Malamed, "The Zhitomir Rabbinical School: New Materials and Perspectives," *Polin: Studies in Polish Jewry* 14, 105–116; L. Streit, *Dzieje synagogi postępowej w Stanisławowie* (Stanisławów: Nakładem Zarządu Synagogi Postępowej w Stanisławowie, 1939); Leszek Hońdo, "Das Verhältnis der Juden in Westgalizien zur polnischen und deutschen Kultur an der Wende vom 19. zum 20. Jahrhundert," in *Symbiose und Traditionsbruch*, ed. Hans Hecker and Walter Engel, 81–94.

37   Mannheimer's activity was an exemplar for many progressive rabbis in the Polish lands. One example may be his participation, along with Catholic and Protestant clergymen, in the funeral of the soldiers who died during the Hungarian Revolution of 1848. The picture which documents that event resembles A. Lesser's painting of the funeral of 5 victims of the demonstration of 1861. Cf. Meyer, *Jewish Communities*, 198, illustration 23. For more about Mannheimer, see Marsha L. Rozenblit, "Jewish Identity and the Modern Rabbi: The Cases of Isak Noa Mannheimer, Adolf Jellinek, and Moritz Guedemann in Nineteeth-Century Vienna," *Leo Beck Institute Year Book* (1990): 103–131; David Ellenson, "The Mannheimer Prayerbooks and Modern Central European Communal Liturgies: A Representative Comparison of Mid-Nineteenth-Century Works," in his *Between Tradition and Culture: The Dialectics of Modern Jewish Religion and Identity* (Atlanta, GA: Scholars Press, 1994) 59–78; Robert S. Wistrich, *The Jews of Vienna in the*

Judaism in the United States

Reform ideas came to America, as they had to the Polish lands, from Germany, with Jewish immigrants. In the history of the Jews in America, the period between 1820 and 1880 is referred to as "the German period," as people from German-speaking countries constituted the core of Jewish immigration to America at the time. During those years, the number of Jews increased from 6,000 in 1830 to about 300,000 in 1880.[38]

The influx of Jewish immigrants from Germany had an impact on changing the face of Judaism in the United States, which had hitherto been dominated by Sephardic Jewry. From then on, Ashkenazi Jews, or "German Jews," as they were called there, began to dominate and influence the customs of both old and newly established congregations. However, in the initial period, the Jews who arrived in the New World were predominantly economic immigrants striving to improve their material and social situation. They perceived America as the "promised land," where everybody was equal and free to do as they pleased. Jewish congregations were organized by communities on the basis of voluntary membership and were independent of one another. Each was governed by a board elected from among its members, and religious matters were attended to by *hazanim* (cantors), who also led worship.

The first rabbi in America arrived in 1840. Abraham Joseph Rice (Reiss), who came from an Orthodox community in Bavaria, became the rabbi of the Baltimore Hebrew Congregation. What was characteristic not only of Rice but of every subsequent rabbi who came to America in his era was his aspiration to lead all American Jews and to impose his own standards and practices on them. Leaders of Orthodox communities wanted to declare Rise "the chief rabbi of the United States."[39]

Age of Franz Joseph (Oxford: Published for the Littman Library by Oxford University Press, 1989), 98–115; Meyer, *Response to Modernity*, 144–151.

[38] See Jonathan D. Sarna, *American Judaism: A History* (New Haven-London: Yale University Press, 2004), 375. A good general description of this period is provided in Hasia R. Diner, *A Time for Gathering: The Second Migration 1820–1880* (Baltimore-London: Johns Hopkins University Press, 1992).

[39] Harold I. Sharfman, *The First Rabbi: Origins of Conflict between Orthodox and Reform: Jewish Polemic Warfare in pre-Civil War America* (Malibu, CA: Pangloss Press, 1988).

Despite these hopes, the structures of the Jewish communities and their mutual independence made it impossible to establish structures similar to those in Europe. The rabbis' striving for domination caused theological conflicts and discussions on the form of Judaism in the United States and the limits of acculturation in the New World, since the mostly German Orthodox Jews acculturated relatively quickly and needed to adapt their traditional Judaism to the new conditions. Therefore, many initially Orthodox "German" communities reformed quickly. The acculturation, or rather Americanization, of Judaism[40] was advocated early on by Isaac Leeser of Westphalia, the *hazan* of the Sephardi Congregation Mikveh Israel in Philadelphia, who introduced sermons and education in English. Leeser was also the founder and editor of the first English-language Jewish monthly magazine, *The Occident and American Jewish Advocate*, and founded the first rabbinical school in America. Nevertheless, he opposed radical reforms of Judaism that would violate Jewish law.[41] His views were shared and his work was continued by Sabato Morais, Henry Pereira Mendes, Benjamin Szold, Alexander Kohut, Marcus Jastrow, and many other rabbis in Philadelphia, New York, and Baltimore who, in opposition to radical reforms, contributed to the establishment of the Jewish Theological Seminary in New York and the development of Conservative Judaism.[42]

---

[40] See Leon A. Jick, *The Americanization of the Synagogue, 1820–1870* (Hanover and London: Published for Brandeis University Press by the University Press of New England, 1992).

[41] For more about Leeser, see Lance J. Sussman, *Isaac Leeser and the Making of American Judaism* (Detroit: Wayne University Press, 1995); Davis, *Emergence of Conservative Judaism*, 347–69; and Sarna, *American Judaism*, 77–111.

[42] Davis, *Emergence of Conservative Judaism*; Herbert Parzen, *Architects of Conservative Judaism* (New York: J. David, 1964); Sidney H. Schwarz, *Law and Legitimacy: An Intellectual History of Conservative Judaism, 1902–1973* (Ph.D. diss., Temple University, 1981); Daniel J. Elazar and Geffen Rela Mintz, *The Conservative Movement in Judaism: Dilemmas and Opportunity* (Albany: State University of New York Press, 2000); Robert Gordis, *Understanding Conservative Judaism* (New York: The Rabbinical Assembly, 1978); Abraham J. Karp, "A Century of Conservative Judaism in the United States," in *The History of Judaism in America: Transplantations, Transformations, and Reconciliations*, part I, ed. J.S. Gurock (New York–London: Routledge, 1998), 213–272; Abraham J. Karp, "The Origins of Conservative Judaism,"

On the other hand, there were signs of reforms to American Judaism as early as in the first decades of the nineteenth century. The first signals came from Charleston, Baltimore, New York, and Richmond, where congregations of Sephardi origin sought change. Then, with the influx of German Jewish immigrants the first Reform Societies were established as seedbeds of Reform congregations. The first Reform congregations to be founded were the Har Sinai Congregation in Baltimore in 1842, the Emanuel Congregation in New York in 1845, and the Chicago Sinai Congregation in 1857. The first Reform rabbis and advocates of reform were active in the United States from the 1840s.[43]

In 1846 Isaac Mayer Wise came to America, and he quickly became one of the most important figures in the Reform movement. In 1848, he wrote:

> The majority of our congregations in this country have been established but a few years back; they are generally composed of the most negative elements of all the different parts of Europe and elsewhere; they have been founded and are now governed for the most part by men of no considerable knowledge of our religion…[44]

Isaac Mayer Wise was an Orthodox Jew, educated in Bohemia, who only embarked upon his career as a Reform rabbi once he was in the United States. Before his arrival in America he lived in Prague and Vienna for some time, and it was in those two cities that he came into contact with the ideas of Reform Judaism. Upon his arrival in the United States in 1846, he was appointed rabbi of the Beth El congregation of Albany, NY. Wise immediately introduced certain innovations, such as family pews, a mixed choir, and confirmations for both boys and girls. In 1848 he made a proposal to establish an organization uniting all the congregations in America, which would follow a rite adjusted to the conditions of American Judaism. He was

---

Conservative Judaism 14, no. 4 (1965): 33–48; Marshal Sklare, *Conservative Judaism: An American Religious Movement* (New York: Shocken Books, 1972).

[43] Meyer, *Response to Modernity*, 225–325.

[44] Nathan Glazer, *American Judaism* (Chicago: University of Chicago Press, 1972), 32.

removed from his office as rabbi of the Beth El congregation when he publicly announced that he did not believe in the coming of a personal Messiah or in bodily resurrection. However, together with his supporters, he soon formed a new Reform congregation, the Anshe Emeth. In 1854 Wise went to Cincinnati, Ohio, where he became rabbi of the Bnai Jeshurun congregation. He remained in that post until his death in 1900. It was during his time there that Cincinnati became the center of Reform Judaism in the United States, with Wise as its "founding father." Opinion-forming magazines and periodicals such as *The Israelite*[45] (in English) and *Die Deborah* (in German) were published there. In 1855, the first rabbinical conference in the country was held in Cleveland, on Wise's initiative. His intention was for the conference to introduce "peace and unity" into American Judaism. However, it was criticized both by Conservative Jews, among them Leeser, and radical reformers, such as David Einhorn of the Har Sinai congregation in Baltimore, who had previously been Samuel Holdheim's successor as chief rabbi of Mecklenburg-Schwerin. Two strong branches of Reform Judaism, differing in their approach to the issue of traditional Jewish law and the revelation at Sinai, existed in America from that time on.

Wise sought to establish an organization that would gather all of the American congregations. He also planned to found a rabbinical school and compile a common prayer book to be used by the whole of American Jewry. In 1856, he published *Minhag Amerika*, a prayer book that he intended for that purpose. Even though it did not gain much support, the prayer book became an inspiration for other rabbis preparing new versions of prayer books for their congregations.[46] In his papers, Wise criticized anyone who opposed his projects, such as the founding of the first national Jewish organization, and came out against any initiatives which did not further his purpose.

Wise achieved his goals, not as the leader of American Judaism but as the leader of the followers of Reform, when he founded the Union of American Hebrew Congregations in Cincinnati in 1873, and

---

[45] The weekly was later published under the title *The American Israelite*.

[46] The following study is evidence of how many such prayer books were compiled at this time: Sharona R. Wachs, *American Jewish Liturgies: A Bibliography of American Jewish Liturgy from the Establishment of the Press in the Colonies through 1925*. Historical Introduction by Karla Goldman, Liturgical Introduction by Eric L. Friedland (Cincinnati: HUC Press, 1997).

a seminary for training rabbis—the Hebrew Union College—in 1875. He was the first president of the college, and in 1889 became president of the Central Conference of American Rabbis, the principal organization of Reform rabbis.[47] These institutions did not embrace the whole of American Jewry, as was Wise's dream, but they did give rise to the formation of Reform Judaism in the United States.

A consequence of this was the emergence of certain ideas in opposition to Reform Judaism, which developed into separate institutions marking the beginning of Conservative and Orthodox Judaism in America.[48]

This short overview aims to show how the face of Judaism changed within a short period of time in the nineteenth century, influenced by the advocates of religious reform in the countries in which Jastrow was active. Naturally, the Reform movement took varying forms and had differing impacts in different countries, due not only to internal opposition but mainly to diverse laws which either permitted the founding of independent Reform communities or congregations or forbade it. The movements and characters delineated above will accompany us in subsequent parts of this book.

---

[47] James G. Heller, *Isaac M. Wise: His Life, Work and Thought* (New York: Union of American Hebrew Congregations, 1965); Sefton D. Temkin, *Creating American Reform Judaism: The Life and Times of Isaac Mayer Wise* (London-Portland, OR: The Littman Libarary of Jewish Civilization, 1998).

[48] Marc Lee Raphael, *Profiles in American Judaism: The Reform, Conservative, Orthodox, and Reconstructionist Traditions in Historical Perspective* (San Francisco: Harper & Row, 1988).

Part I

Europe

Chapter 1
The Early Years

Rogoźno: Jastrow's Birthplace

Like many other towns in Greater Poland (Wielkopolska), Rogasen, the place of Jastrow's birth and youth, has a long and turbulent history. Now called by its Polish name, Rogoźno, it is located about 50 kilometers north of Poznań (German Posen), on the road to Piła[1] (German Schneidemühl).

Rogoźno was granted town privileges in 1280 by Duke Przemysław II. The municipal charter authorized Jan and Piotr Dedz to found a town under Magdeburg Law.[2] In the thirteenth and fourteenth centuries, Rogoźno and the surrounding villages were royal estates managed by the starost general of Greater Poland.[3] In the sixteenth century, the town and its environs were bestowed on Queen Bona by King Sigismund I the Old. It became an important center of crafts in northern Greater Poland, as well as the administrative center of the royal estate,[4] and it was famous for smelting iron from local bog ores until the beginning of the sixteenth century. With time, numerous craft guilds were established, including tailors'', brewers'', butchers'', shoemakers'', and drapers' guilds.[5] Rogoźno flourished until the

---

[1] Its population is currently approximately 12,000.

[2] See Mieczysław Brust, "Rogoźno w czasach najdawniejszych i w średniowieczu," in *Dzieje Rogoźna*, ed. Zygmunt Boras (Poznań: Wydawnictwo Lega, 1993), 29–31; Jan Hinczewski, "Kalendarium dziejów Rogoźna," *Rogozińskie Zeszyty Historyczne* 1 (1989): 3. However, the town was not a lucky one for Przemysław II: he was murdered there on February 8, 1296.

[3] Brust, "Rogoźno w czasach najdawniejszych," 48.

[4] Jerzy Łojko, "Od początku XVI wieku do końca Rzeczypospolitej szlacheckiej," in *Dzieje Rogoźna*, 64–65.

[5] For more on the development of crafts, see Mieczysław Brust, *Zarys dziejów rzemiosła rogozińskiego 1248–1998* (Rogoźno: Cech Rzemiosł Różnych w Rogoźnie, 1998), 3–38, for the period in question.

war with Sweden in 1655–1660, during which Swedish troops passed through it twice, causing extensive devastation to the area. The situation improved in the mid-eighteenth century, when Rogoźno New Town was granted municipal rights[6] and cloth-making and tailoring industries developed in New and Old Rogoźno.[7]

After the Second Partition of Poland, Rogoźno came under Prussian rule. Greater Poland was part of the region known as Southern Prussia, and Rogoźno fell within Poznań Department, Oborniki (Obornik) County. In 1794 the Prussian authorities decided to merge the two towns, New and Old Rogoźno, into one, though the integration was not completed until 1798. During the partitions, until 1820, the textile industry was particularly prosperous. In the nineteenth century, Rogoźno was also famous for its copperware and its trade in cloth, grain, and livestock. The merging of New and Old Rogoźno and the influx of settlers from Prussia triggered numerous ethnic and economic conflicts. According to the *Indaganda* (Urban Survey), in 1794 there were 1,996 people in Old Rogoźno: 959 Catholics, 936 Jews, and 101 Lutherans; while New Rogoźno had a population of 954, comprising 729 Lutherans, 113 Catholics, 108 Jews, 3 Reformers, and 1 Greek.[8] Later the proportions of Catholics (mostly Poles), Lutherans (mostly Germans), and Jews balanced out at about a third for each nationality and denomination.

Manufacturers in Rogoźno had a guaranteed right to trade directly with Russia, the main recipient of cloth from local shops until the 1820s. Nonetheless, economic growth was restricted by frequent fires, the most tragic of which occurred in 1794 (when the synagogue and the Jewish hospital, among other buildings, burned down), 1803, 1806, 1823, 1841, and 1847.[9]

---

[6] Rogoźno New Town was granted its municipal charter in 1750 on the initiative of Władysław Szołdrski, the Rogoźno starost. See Łojko, "Od początku XVI wieku," 72–73.

[7] Rogoźno was the sixth-biggest cloth manufacturer in Greater Poland. See Brust, *Zarys dziejów rzemiosła rogozińskiego*, 24.

[8] The Indaganda of Rogoźno was translated and published in Janusz Esman, *Opis Rogoźna z 1794 roku* (Rogoźno, 1989), see in particular 6, 16.

[9] Idem, "Rogoźno pod zaborem pruskim," in *Dzieje Rogoźna*, 104–105; see also Brust, *Zarys dziejów rzemiosła rogozińskiego*, 29–30.

Jews in Rogoźno

Unfortunately, there has thus far been no comprehensive study on the history of Jews in Rogoźno.[10] Thus, information about Rogoźno's Jews primarily comes from a variety of general works about Greater Poland and Jews in the region. It may be assumed that Jews inhabited Rogoźno soon after it was granted town rights: Żydowska (Jewish) Street, previously called Plebańska (Rectory) Street, already existed by the end of the fifteenth century.[11] One of the first mentions of Jews in Rogoźno was made in the June 23, 1565, survey of Rogoźno county. It lists shoemaking workshops, of which sixteen were owned by Christian townsmen and five were owned by Jewish craftsmen.[12]

---

[10] The few available sources on the history of Jews in Rogoźno are scattered, and their largest number may be found in Centrum Judaicum Archiv in Berlin (CJA), see *Ortsregister* in *Quellen zur Geschichte der Juden in den Archiven der neuen Bundesländer*, ed. Stefi Jersch-Wenzel and Reinhard Rurup, vol. 6: *Stiftung "Neue Synagoge Berlin—Centrum Judaicum,"* part I–II (Munich: Saur, 2001); Michael M. Zarchin, *Jews in the Province of Posen: Studies in the Communal Records of the Eighteenth and Nineteenth Centuries* (Philadelphia: The Dropsie College for Hebrew and Cognate Learning, 1939), mentions municipal documents from Rogoźno in the Jewish Theological Seminary Archives, see 3–5, but unfortunately my efforts to find them were in vain. The best study is Jacob Jacobson's *Zur Geschichte der Juden in Rogasen* (Berlin 1935) (typescript); I accessed the copy in the Leo Baeck Institute Archives in New York, Jacob Jacobson Collection; it is 27 pages long including quoted sources. Other books worth mentioning are A. Heppner and J. Herzberg, *Aus Vergangenheit und Gegenwart der Juden und der jüdischen Gemeinden in den Posener Landen nach gedruckten und ungedruckten Quellen*, part II (Koschmin–Bromberg, 1909), 897–901; and Ehud M.Z. (Chaikin) Cain, *From Prussia with Love* (Jerusalem, 2002), 85–91 and passim, though it would be unwise to overestimate the credibility of the information included there. For more on individual people with ties to Rogoźno, see also Michael Brocke and Juliusz Carlebach, eds., *Biographisches Handbuch der Rabbiner*, part 1, *Die Rabbiner der Emanzipationszeit in den deutschen, böhmischen und grosspolnischen Ländern 1781–1871*, ed. Carsten Wilke, vol. 1–2 (Munich: Saur, 2004), index; and *Pinkas ha-Kehilot: Encyclopedia of Jewish Communities*, vol. VI, *District Poznań and Pomerania* (Jerusalem: Yad Vashem, 1999), 117–120.

[11] Brust, "Rogoźno w czasach najdawniejszych," 35, 39.

[12] Brust, *Zarys dziejów rzemiosła rogozińskiego*, 13. See also Andrzej Tomczak, et. al., eds., *Lustracja województw wielkopolskich i kujawskich 1564–1565* (Bydgoszcz: Bydgoskie Towarzystwo Naukowe, 1961), part I, see especially 47–50, 245–259.

Surveys from later periods also mention Jewish craftsmen in Rogoźno who at the end of the seventeenth century were engaged in many other professions previously the exclusive domain of Christian craftsmen.[13] There were Jewish bakers, glaziers, goldsmiths, and tailors.[14] The growing Jewish population and influence contributed to the establishment of a separate Jewish district, where all the necessary institutions, such as a synagogue, a *mikveh*, and a cemetery, were located. Despite growing competition from Jewish tradesmen and craftsmen, serious conflicts were never reported, and the town was always open to Jews. An episode relating to a person named Rabbi Isaac, who was executed in 1656 for collaboration with the Swedish army, is interesting but does not affect the general opinion of the mutual relations and will not be discussed in detail here.[15]

Rogoźno developed further in the eighteenth century and became famous for cloth manufacturing. Its prosperity triggered an influx of new settlers, especially Jews and Germans. Between 1768 and 1794, the population of Old Rogoźno increased by 1,261, and that of New Rogoźno by 370 people.[16] As mentioned previously, in 1794 there were 936 Jews in Old Rogoźno and 108 Jews in New Rogoźno.[17]

The *Indaganda* lists Jewish craftsmen who were members of the local guilds in Old Rogoźno. It includes 4 bakers, 20 butchers, 2 glaziers, 2 goldsmiths, 56 tailors, 55 merchants, 5 haberdashers, and 12 cloth-makers.[18] There were also Jewish craftspeople who did not

---

[13] Brust, *Zarys dziejów rzemiosła rogozińskiego*, 16.

[14] For more on the Jewish contribution to the development of trade in Rogoźno see ibid., 12–27, especially 25–26. The register of professions and numbers of Jewish tradesmen is also to be found in the *Indaganda*, see Esman, *Opis Rogoźna*, 8–9, 16–17.

[15] Brust, "Rogoźno w czasach najdawniejszych," 66–69; Cain, *From Prussia with Love*, 85–86. Jacobson writes that the whole Jewish community of 40 families was annihilated on that occasion. Jacobson, *Zur Geschichte der Juden in Rogasen*, 2.

[16] I am quoting data from Brust, "Rogoźno w czasach najdawniejszych," 79.

[17] Esman, *Opis Rogoźna*, 6, 16. Jacobson, *Zur Geschichte der Juden in Rogasen*, 5, gives the total number of Jews as 1,004.

[18] Esman, *Opis Rogoźna...*, 8–9.

belong to any of the guilds: 3 barber surgeons, 3 midwives, 3 musicians, and 9 cap-makers.[19]

The only Jew on the list for New Rogoźno is an innkeeper.[20] Rogoźno had all the institutions of Jewish religious life: - a synagogue, prayer houses, and a cemetery. A *Chevra Kadisha* and separate Jewish legal and school systems existed from the seventeenth century.[21]

In the Prussian partition, the Rogoźno Jews were mainly engaged in cloth-making, tailoring, and trade, with cloth-making becoming their specialty in the first decades of the nineteenth century. The Jews also became influential in the municipal government, though their presence in the town council was reduced to a quarter of the total number of councilors in 1841.[22] However, many of Rogoźno's Jews lived in modest conditions or even poverty. According to Zarchin, in 1833 there were at least 300 beggars among the 1,300 Jews.[23]

In 1836 a three-year school for Jewish children was established in Rogoźno, but 10 illegal cheders banned by the authorities continued to operate.[24] Other organizations which existed at the beginning of the nineteenth century included a *Gemilut Chasadim*,[25] a *Chevra Kadisha*, a Talmud Torah Association, a society of women and unmarried girls, and an association for Jewish history and literature.[26]

In 1835 there were 349 Jewish households in Rogoźno. The register of Jewish professions included two assistant rabbis, a cantor, a teacher, a *shochet*, and two *soferim* (scribes).[27]

---

[19] Ibid., 9.

[20] Ibid., 19–20.

[21] Idem, "Rogoźno pod zaborem pruskim," 137.

[22] Ibid., 111.

[23] Zarchin, *Jews in the Province of Posen*, 85.

[24] Heppner, Herzberg, *Aus Vergangenheit und Gegenwart der Juden*, 900; Cain, *From Prussia with Love*, 90.

[25] The statute of this organization may be found in CJA, 1, 75 A Ro 2, No. 2, ID no. 6639.

[26] Heppner, Herzberg, *Aus Vergangenheit und Gegenwart der Juden*, 900–901; Cain, *From Prussia with Love*, 90.

[27] For the full list of professions see Jacobson, *Zur Geschichte der Juden in Rogasen*, 13.

Among the well-known members of the nineteenth-century Jewish community in Rogoźno were the *dayanim* Moses ben Mendel Mendelshon (d. 1839) and Chaim ben Yakov Weil (d. 1847). We also know that Simon Halevi Feibelmann, the former rabbi of Kalisz, was the rabbi of the Rogoźno community between 1819 and 1834. He was succeeded in 1840 by Moses ben Josef Feilchenfeld, who served the community until his death in 1872.[28] Feilchenfeld was also Jastrow's first instructor in religion and the one who prepared him for his service as a rabbi. He maintained contact with Rabbi Michael Sachs from Berlin, who later had a significant influence on Jastrow's views. The subsequent rabbis in Rogoźno were Dr. Elias Plessner (from 1873 until 1885), Dr. Ludwik A. Rosenthal (from 1886 until 1895), and Dr. Isaac Auerbach (from 1895 until 1901).[29]

What distinguished Rogoźno was that it had one of the highest proportions of Jewish residents of any town in Greater Poland.[30] Jews comprised approximately 30–35% of the town's population, and this proportion remained stable throughout the first half of the nineteenth century.[31]

---

[28] He signed his contract with the community of Rogoźno on December 28, 1839, and one of the representatives of the community was Abraham Jastrow, CJA, 75 A Ro 2, No. 5, ID no. 6642, 8–9. Rabbi Feilchenfeld's surname was sometimes spelled Veilchenfeld; see Brocke and Carlebach, eds., *Biographisches Handbuch der Rabbiner*, part 1: *Die Rabbiner der Emanzipationszeit*, 871–872. This entry includes short biographies of other rabbis and *dayanim* connected with Rogoźno. See also Cain, *From Prussia with Love*, 87.

[29] Heppner, Herzberg, *Aus Vergangenheit und Gegenwart der Juden*, 899.

[30] See *Liczba głów żydowskich w Koronie z taryf roku 1765*, eds. F. i J. Kleczyńscy, Archiwum Komisji Historii Akademii Umiejętności, vol. VIII (Krakow: Akademia Umiejętności, 1898), 391–392.

[31] In 1848 Rogoźno was inhabited by 1,836 Jews, 1,660 Catholics, and 1,373 Protestants. In 1859 there were 1,381 Jews, 1,571 Catholics, and 1,556 Protestants. These data come from Brust, "Rogoźno w czasach najdawniejszych," 110. Cf. Hinczewski, *Kalendarium dziejów Rogoźna*, 19–21, and Sophia Kemlein, *Żydzi w Wielkim Księstwie Poznańskim 1815–1848. Przeobrażenia w łonie żydostwa polskiego pod panowaniem pruskim*, afterword by Krzysztof Makowski, trans. Zenon Choderna-Loew (Series: Wielkopolska: historia, społeczeństwo, kultura, vol. 12) (Poznań: Wydawnictwo Poznańskie, 2001), 417.

Ethnic relations in Rogoźno and the whole of Greater Poland, particularly at the time of the Spring of Nations witnessed by Jastrow, are probably crucial to understanding his story and attitude. Rogoźno was atypical in Greater Poland, especially its eastern part, as Poles were in a minority there from the beginning of the nineteenth century. This was due to the settlement of German and Jewish craftsmen and merchants there at the time of the Polish Commonwealth in an attempt to rebuild the towns of Greater Poland following wartime destruction.

It is a widely held view in both Polish and foreign historiography that the Jews in Greater Poland were decidedly in favor of affiliating with German culture and strongly supported Prussian rule, which is said to have led to many conflicts with Poles. However, contemporary research on this topic, especially by historians of the younger generation, such as Sophia Kemlein[32] and Krzysztof A. Makowski[33] in particular, shows a different picture of the Jews and their attitude toward ethnic issues in the Poznań province in the nineteenth century.

---

[32] See especially Kemlein, *Żydzi w Wielkim Księstwie Poznańskim*. Other publications by this author are "Żydzi wśród Niemców i Polaków (wzajemne stosunki, uprzedzenia i konflikty w Wielkim Księstwie Poznańskim w pierwszej połowie XIX wieku)" in *Żydzi w Wielkopolsce na przestrzeni dziejów*, ed. Jerzy Topolski and Krzysztof Modelski (Poznań: Wydawnictwo Poznańskie, 1999), 128–148; "The Jewish Community in the Grand Duchy of Poznań under Prussian Rule, 1815–1848", *Polin. Studies in Polish Jewry* 14 (2001): 49–67; "Między tradycją a nowoczesnością—intelektualiści żydowscy w Poznaniu w pierwszej połowie XIX wieku," *Kronika Miasta Poznania* 2 (1998): 77–90.

[33] Special attention should be given to the ground-breaking work by Krzysztof A. Makowski, *Siła mitu. Żydzi w Poznańskiem w dobie zaborów w piśmiennictwie historycznym* (Poznań: Wydawnictwo Poznańskie, 2004). Please refer to its extensive bibliography on the subject. Other publications by Makowski include "Gdy na ulicach Poznania, obok polskiego, powszechnie rozbrzmiewał język niemiecki i żydowski. Niemcy i Żydzi w Poznaniu w latach 1815–1848," *Kronika Miasta Poznania* 3 (1996): 48–65; "Ludność żydowska wobec wydarzeń Wiosny Ludów na ziemiach polskich," in *Żydzi w obronie Rzeczypospolitej, materiały konferencji w Warszawie 17 i 18 października 1993 r.*, ed. Jerzy Tomaszewski (Warsaw: Cyklady, 1996), 43–63; "Żydzi wobec Wiosny Ludów w Wielkim Księstwie Poznańskim," in *Żydzi w Wielkopolsce na przestrzeni dziejów*, 149–167; and "Verzeichnis der israelitischen Absolventen von Gymnasien im Grossherzogtum Posen in den Jahren 1815–1848," *Nordost-Archiv*, NF vol. 1, 1992, H. 2, 457–460.

In the period after the Second Partition of Poland, Jews in Greater Poland were anxious to maintain their autonomy, particularly in the sphere of religion and culture, as they had under the First Republic of Poland. Attempts to introduce religious reforms, and strivings for Berlin-style assimilation, had few supporters and even those were only in bigger urban centers. Rogoźno is an example of such a town, and no institutions foreign to traditional Judaism existed until the mid-nineteenth century.[34] Moreover, Jews from Greater Poland were called "Polish Jews' or "Ostjuden" by their co-religionists from Prussia, with all the implications that entailed. Jastrow himself, when he was in America, was contemptuously called a "Polish Jew" by Jewish immigrants from Prussia, though Yiddish, not Polish or German, was the language of everyday life for most Jews in the area, who were culturally and religiously more similar to Jews from Congress Poland or Galicia.[35] Therefore, it should not be surprising that any attempts to restrict Polish Jews' autonomy and scope of religious influence were met with resistance and opposition. There were protests when the education reform of 1824 abolished traditional cheders,[36] and elementary schools — "Freischulen" — were established for Jewish children, with the help of the British Society for the Promotion of Christianity Among the Israelites in the province of Poznań.[37] One such school was even established in Rogoźno.[38] After that period illegal cheders[39] were still run, and there was probably one in Rogoźno in the 1830s, in which Jastrow's first teacher, Rabbi Moses Feilchenfeld, taught. There is much evidence that Jews from the Poznań province supported Polishness, especially at decisive points during the Napoleonic Wars and during

---

[34] See, e. g., the table of religious reforms illustrating the implementation of religious reforms and the employment of rabbis with religious education in Jewish corporations of the Grand Duchy of Poznań between 1834 and 1848, in Kemlein, *Żydzi w Wielkim Księstwie Poznańskim*, 259.

[35] Artur Kiron writes that Jastrow spoke Yiddish at home too. See http://www.library.upenn.edu/exhibits/cajs/jastrow/01.html (28.04.2013)

[36] Makowski, *Siła mitu*, 410.

[37] Kemlein, *Żydzi w Wielkim Księstwie Poznańskim*, 97–98.

[38] Christopher M. Clark, *The Politics of Conversion: Missionary Protestantism and the Jews in Prussia 1728–1941* (Oxford — New York: Clarendon Press, Oxford University Press, 1995), 205.

[39] Kemlein, *Żydzi w Wielkim Księstwie Poznańskim*, 152.

the existence of the Duchy of Warsaw and the January and November uprisings.[40] Krzysztof Makowski writes:

> ...Poznań Jews were continuously in touch with the Polish culture. Their relations with Poles in the first half of the nineteenth century should also be considered appropriate. Most, not to say virtually all, Israelites had some command of Polish. ...Jews learned Polish in schools at the time—not only in gymnasiums but also in elementary schools.[41]

Indeed, the author gives more examples of such Polish-Jewish coexistence and cooperation, from Jewish booksellers and publishers publishing Polish newspapers and books to Jewish members of Polish patriotic organizations.[42]

Polish upsurges and hopes for political independence were also reflected in Rogoźno, both during the time of the Duchy of Warsaw and later, under the Grand Duchy of Poznań. It is known that 24 residents of Rogoźno took part in the November Uprising of 1830–1831.[43]

On the eve of the Spring of Nations, insurrectionary hopes were raised by the distribution of leaflets by emissaries of the Plebeians' Union informing the reader of an imminent uprising.[44] As early as in January 1846, many of the guilds convened secret meetings. The Prussian authorities, alarmed by the situation, appointed a new municipal guard. In 1846, a conflict broke out between Poles and Jews in Rogoźno; in March and April, a few stores were devastated and a few people injured as a result of riots, fights, and anti-Jewish outbursts by

---

[40] For more on this topic, see, e. g., Makowski, *Siła mitu*, 174, 408–409, 412, and *Żydzi w obronie Rzeczypospolitej*, 31–71, and the list there of older publications on the topic.

[41] Makowski, *Siła mitu*, 411.

[42] E.g. Ludwik Merzbach was a co-founder and for some time also the publisher of *Kurier Poznański*, and Maksymilian Peiper was a member of the clandestine Tomasz Zan Society in Ostrów Wielkopolski. He was also the publisher of the only Polish collection of Jastrow's sermons in 1862. For more examples, see Makowski, *Siła mitu*, 418–422. Also see Kemlein, *Żydzi w Wielkim Księstwie Poznańskim*, 312–390.

[43] Esman, "Rogoźno pod zaborem pruskim," in *Dzieje Rogoźna*, 115.

[44] Ibid., 116.

Polish Catholic residents. There is no basis, however, for thinking that most people supported such attitudes. The Polish National Committee sent delegates from Poznań to investigate and neutralize the situation on the spot.[45]

The cause of the conflict is not known. It has been established that one of its consequences was the suspension of the mayor, Zimmerek, a German Catholic who often took the side of the Polish residents of Rogoźno.[46] During the famine in Greater Poland a year later, in 1847, however, both Polish and Jewish inhabitants of Rogoźno participated in the lootings that took place.[47]

Catholic churches were also important places in which nationalist attitudes in Rogoźno were shaped. The rector of the parish of St Vitus, Fr. Feliks Laskowski, was a particularly significant figure. Through his activities, especially his passionate sermons, he encouraged Poles to mobilize and urged young people to join the insurrectionary forces. However, in May 1848, the entry of the Prussian forces into Rogoźno marked the beginning of a period of repressions of participants in the Polish patriotic campaigns. Soldiers severely beat up Zimmerek, the mayor, calling him "a Polish mayor and Polish spy."[48] Fr Laskowski was also a victim of these incidents, getting beaten by drunken soldiers. Esman writes that the wounded priest was rescued and hidden by the Jewish merchant Abraham Jastrow,[49] who was none other than Marcus Jastrow's father. Was Abraham Jastrow's demeanor a reflection of broader views among the Jews or an example of his individual humanitarian attitude? Did the events of those years and his father's conduct affected Marcus's future attitude toward Poles and Christians in general? It is difficult to answer these questions unequivocally, but it is certain that Jastrow's upbringing left its imprint and had

---

[45] For more on the incidents in Rogoźno in 1846–1848, see Esman, "Rogoźno pod zaborem pruskim," 16–123; Hinczewski, "Kalendarium dziejów Rogoźna," 18–19.

[46] Esman, "Rogoźno pod zaborem pruskim," 117.

[47] Kemlein, Żydzi w Wielkim Księstwie Poznańskim, 365. For more on Polish-Jewish relations between 1830 and 1847, see 357–365.

[48] Esman, Wiosna Ludów w Rogoźnie, 13.

[49] Esman, "Rogoźno pod zaborem pruskim," 122–123; Esman, Wiosna Ludów w Rogoźnie, 13. The incident is the only one in the Polish historiography of Rogoźno in which Jastrow's family is mentioned.

an effect on his actions in the future. Jastrow was most likely aware of the events taking place in Rogoźno and Poznań, and they probably shaped his future attitude toward nationalist movements and Polish independence aspirations.

Marcus Jastrow in Rogoźno and Poznań

The Jastrow family most likely settled in Rogoźno at the end of the eighteenth or the beginning of the nineteenth century. The family name attests to the fact that they were relative newcomers. In the civil status records of the Jewish community of Rogoźno, in the entry relating to Marcus Jastrow's birth, Abraham is listed as Jastrauer.[50] Therefore, it may be assumed that Abraham Jastrow was linked to the town of Jastrow (in Polish, Jastrowie), north of Piła, which was also inhabited by Jews.[51] It is not known when Abraham or his family arrived in Rogoźno, though it may be speculated on the basis of the form of the family name that it would have been during the Prussian partition or, conversely, that it was upon his arrival that the surname was given to Abraham.[52]

The details we have about Jastrow's family and youth are scarce. Abraham, the father, was a merchant[53] active in the Jewish community, which beginning in 1833 was called a corporation. From his signatures on documents of the Rogoźno corporation we know that he was

---

[50] National Archives in Poznań (APP), Akta stanu cywilnego gminy żydowskiej Rogoźno, ref. no. 3, 1829, item 22, and ref. no. 5, 1834 item 36—this entry relates to Marcus's brother Isaac.

[51] In 1765 there were 411 Jews in total in Jastrow and Piła. See *Liczba głów żydowskich w Koronie*, 391–392, and Brust, "Rogoźno w czasach najdawniejszych," 79.

[52] Cf. B. Brilling, "Adoption of Family Names by Jews in Prussia (1804)," *Avotaynu. The International Review of Jewish Genealogy* 1, no. 2 (1985): 23–25.

[53] A few sources refer to him as "Handelsmann" or "Kaufmann," cf. APP, *Księga metrykalna gminy żydowskiej Rogoźno*, APP ref. no. 3, item 22; APP, *Friedrich Wilhelms Gymnasium zu Posen—Gimnazjum im. Fryderyka Wilhelma w Poznaniu (1834–1920)*, ref. no. 41. "Verzeichnis der in das Königl. Friedrich Wilhelms Gymnasium in Posen: aufgenommenen Schüler. 1934–1851," 245–246.

a member of its Representative Council.[54] He died in 1869.[55] Marcus was the eldest son, and was born on June 5, 1829, in Rogoźno.[56] He had two brothers,[57] Chaim[58] and Isaac.[59] Isaac continued the family trading tradition and was also an alderman in the town council for 42 years. He performed various important functions in the Jewish community for over 20 years. On his 80th birthday, in 1914, he received a certificate of appreciation for his work for the town and the honorary title of *Stadtaeltester*.[60] In relation to this event, an article was published about Isaac in the local newspaper,[61] though it unfortunately does not mention anything about the early years of his life that could shed some light on the whole Jastrow family.

It seems that Marcus was destined to become a rabbi from the beginning. He received his first education in an elementary school in Rogoźno,[62] and at the same time studied the Bible and the Talmud under the supervision of Rabbi Moses Feilchenfeld as one of his *bachurim*. He was taught secular subjects and the Polish language by a teacher named Wolf from the Polish elementary school.[63]

---

[54] See, e. g., CJA, 75 A Ro 2, No. 5, Id. no. 6642, sheet 9b; Id. no. 6646; Id. no. 6638; Id. no. 6643.

[55] With his death, Marcus Jastrow inherited 1,600 Reichsthaler, AJA SC no. 5686, 1.11.1869, [114].

[56] APP, *Księga metrykalna*, ref. no. 3, item 22—Abraham Jastrauer is given as the father and Jette [Rolle] as the mother.

[57] Jastrow's biographies do not mention any other siblings, and there is only information about the two brothers.

[58] Chaim Levin, born on May 13, 1832, APP, *Księga metrykalna*, ref. no. 4, item 23. In the copies of Marcus Jastrow's correspondence, a Herman Jastrow appears as well. It is likely that Chaim and Herman are the same person. Cf. AJA, SC no. 5686, Letter from Herman Jastrow from Rio Janeiro of 6.11.1863.

[59] Isaac, born on August 25, 1834, APP, *Księga metrykalna*, ref. no. 5, item 6.

[60] The certificate is currently in the possession of the Wojciecha Dutkiewicz Regional Museum in Rogoźno.

[61] See *Rogasener Wochenblatt*, August 2, 1914.

[62] AJA SC no. 5686, 1. Contains a note that the school was a Polish elementary school.

[63] Ibid.

On April 1, 1845, Jastrow enrolled in the Friedrich Wilhelms Gymnasium zu Posen, and went into Class III.[64] The entry under "previous school" in the register reads: "Privatunterricht."[65] The gymnasium was established in 1834 as a result of the reorganization of an earlier one, which had been divided into two: the Saint Maria Magdalena Gymnasium with Polish as the language of instruction, and the Friedrich Wilhelms Gymnasium zu Posen for German youth, with classes taught in German. Before 1848, many Poles and Jews also attended that gymnasium, however, with Jews making up about 10%[66] of the student body before 1848 and later, in the 1870s, as much as 50%.[67]

Students of Polish origin were not a rarity prior to 1848, though. In the 1847/1848 school year, there were 366 students at the gymnasium, 187 Protestant, 42 Catholic, and 137 Jewish; while in the 1849/1850 school year, there were 432 students: 235 Protestant, 20 Catholic, and 177 Jewish.[68]

Kazimiera Chojnacka wrote:

> The curriculum in the gymnasium was the same as in other standard Prussian gymnasiums. It was intended for German Protestant youth; however, at the beginning [until 1848] this rule was not observed rigorously and quite a few Poles attended the school too. This brought about the introduction of the Polish language as an additional language of instruction alongside German. There were also Polish teachers, such as the Polonist Popliński, 1837–8, and Polish literature and language teacher Józef Łukasiewicz, 1838–1842. Mathematics, physics, and the history of Polish literature were taught by Dr Karol Libelt, 1841–1844, and Polonist and Romance philologist Dr Rymarkiewicz. This state of things lasted until the uprising broke out during

---

[64] Most biographies give 1846 as the year of his enrolment in that school.

[65] The full entry is as follows: "Markus Jastrow—nr 53 (554), 1 Apr. 1845, geb. in Rogasen, 13. Mai 1830 [sic!!!], Confession—mosaische, Vater:—Kaufmann in Rogasen, Privatunterricht, Klasse IIIb"—APP, *Friedrich Wilhelms Gymnasium,* ref. no. 41, "Verzeichnis," 245–246.

[66] According to K. Makowski, "*Verzeichnis der israelitischen Absolventen,*" 457.

[67] According to Kazimiera Chojnacka, the author of the introduction to an inventory of the school, APP, *Friedrich Wilhelms Gymnasium.*

[68] APP, *Friedrich Wilhelms Gymnasium,* ref. no. 46, "Verzeichnis."

the Spring of Nations, when the Polish students came to the gymnasium ostentatiously wearing red and white ribbons on their clothes. Most of them left the school after the failure of the uprising.[69]

Jastrow most likely observed this atmosphere, and he cannot have been indifferent to it. After 1848, when Polish became an additional subject, Jastrow learned it for at least five semesters.[70] At the gymnasium he met a number of his future friends. One of them, Manuel Joël, started his education in the same year as Jastrow and went on to become a rabbi and lecturer at the Jewish Theological Seminary in Breslau. He helped Jastrow a number of times, and they met again later, during their studies in Berlin and Halle. Both were friends with Rabbi Michael Sachs.[71] At the gymnasium he also met his first love, Paulina W.[72]

In the fall of 1850 Jastrow's health deteriorated: he suffered from a chronic cough and nervous instability,[73] and his health problems were to persist throughout his life.

There is some evidence that Jastrow must have been an outstanding student at the gymnasium, as during the graduation ceremony on March 3, 1852, he gave a speech on behalf of a group of students. This was recorded by *Allegemaine Zeitung des Judentums*, which reported that there were 478 students at the gymnasium in the 1851/1852 school year, including 227 Jews. It was also mentioned in the newspaper that 6 out of the 12 graduates were Jewish, and that Marcus Jastrow spoke on the class's behalf.[74]

---

[69] Ibid., p. 3, For more about the history of that gymnasium see Makowski, "Verzeichnis der israelitischen Absolventen"; Herman Starke, *Zur Geschichte des Königlichen Wilhelms Gymnasiums zu Posen* (Poznan 1884); *75 Jahre (1834–1909) Friedrich-Wilhelms Gymnasium in Posen* (Poznan 1908).

[70] As indicated by gymnasium documents; see APP, *Friedrich Wilhelms Gymnasium*, ref. no. 46 and 47.

[71] For more on Manuel Joël, see *Biographisches Handbuch der Rabbiner*, Teil 1, *Die Rabbiner der Emanzipationszeit*, 489–490.

[72] Vestiges of their correspondence may be found in AJA, SC no. 5686 [6, 7, 12].

[73] AJA, SC no. 5686, [5].

[74] *Allgemeine Zeitung des Judentums* (AZJ) 1852, 18 (26.04.1852), 209.

Studying in Berlin and Halle

After he graduated from the gymnasium in Poznań, Jastrow left for Berlin, where he embarked on a course of study on May 6, 1852. According to university records, he studied the history of philosophy, logic, Greek philology and literature, medieval history, and psychology.[75] He graduated and received his diploma on June 30, 1855.[76]

Jastrow maintained contact with his family in Rogoźno during his studies, and even filled in for his father as a representative in the Jewish community—his signature appears on financial documents of the Jewish corporation in Rogoźno from 1853 and 1856.[77]

He was also summoned to Poznań in order to be examined by the military committee. On August 13, 1852, he was assigned to the Ersatz-Reserv in Berlin, and on October 1, 1852, following a medical examination in Poznań, he was exempted from military service due to his chronic lung disease.[78]

During his time in Berlin, Jastrow also applied himself to rabbinical studies in order to receive *semicha*—rabbinic ordination. He had, as discussed, studied under Rabbi Moses Feilchenfeld in Rogoźno and Poznań, and in Berlin he was associated with Rabbi Michael Sachs (1808–1864), who became his teacher and mentor. It must have been Sachs who influenced many of Jastrow's views on the possibility of introducing reforms to Judaism. Sachs was the preacher and substitute rabbi (Prediger und Rabbinatassessor) of the Berlin Jewish community from 1844 until his death. He had a secular education as well: he had earned a philological degree in Berlin and received his PhD in Jena in 1835 for a thesis on Homer. Sachs was one of the pioneers of the Wissenschaft des Judentums movement, and his hobby was researching and translating medieval poetry of Spanish Jews.[79] He also translated the Bible into German with Leopold Zunz in 1835. As a rabbi and

---

[75] AJA, SC no. 5686, [8] (June 30, 1855); Universitatsarchiv Humboldt-Universitat zu Berlin, *Abgangszeugnis 16. Mai—3. August 1855*.

[76] Ibid.

[77] CJA, 1, 75 A Ro 2, no. 8, Id. no. 6645.

[78] AJA, SC no. 5686, 7.

[79] Michael Sachs's main work was *Religiöse Poesie der Juden in Spanien* (Berlin: Veit, 1845).

preacher he paid particular attention to prayer and rituals, and during his close relationship with Jastrow spent a lot of time publishing prayer books in bilingual Hebrew and German versions.[80] His conservative views are evident in his *siddur* and *mahzor*, which Jastrow later wanted to publish in Polish.[81] Sachs's moderately conservative views on reform were limited to plans of purging Judaism of the accretions of the Middle Ages and adjusting Jews to life in the modern world. Nonetheless, even those ideas met with criticism from the more traditional members of the community.

Some innovations in the ritual and order of services were introduced in the Berlin community on Sachs' initiative. Certain prayers were said in German, *piyutim* were removed from prayer books as a medieval influence, and choral singing was added. In addition, Sachs preached in German, and his sermons were very popular.[82] However, he opposed the introduction of organs and music into the synagogue as non-halakhic.[83] As the rabbi of the Berlin community, he could not afford any new conflicts, and instead he tried to maintain equilibrium between the supporters of reform and the supporters of Orthodoxy. His special field of interest was the literary and poetic heritage of Spanish Jews.[84]

Rabbi Michael Sachs was also politically active, as demonstrated by the fact that during the March Revolution of 1848 he took part in the funeral of the victims of street demonstrations alongside Christian ministers and gave a speech.[85]

---

[80] Sachs's publications include *Die Festgebete der Israeliten,* Neu übersetzt und erläutert, 9 Bde (Berlin, 1855–1856); *Das Gebetbuch der Israeliten mit vollständigem, sorgfältig durchgesehenem Texte*. Neu übersetzt und erläutert (Berlin, 1858).

[81] AJA, SC no. 5686, February 26, 1859, 28.

[82] M. Sachs, *Predigten,* ed. David Rosin, Bde. I–II (Berlin: Gerschel, 1866–1869). For more see M. Schad, "Rabbiner Dr. Michael Sachs als Prediger: "Ich mus einen neuen Menschen für die alte Lehre fordern"," in *Neuer Anbruch: Zur deutsch-jüdischen Geschichte und Kultur,* ed. M. Brocke, Aubrey Pomerance, and A. Schatz (Berlin: Metropol, 2001), 191–204.

[83] Meyer, *Response to Modernity,* 124.

[84] *German-Jewish History,* ed. Meyer and Brenner, 342.

[85] Ibid., 284. For more on Michael Sachs see, e. g., D. Lukas and Heike Frank, *Michael Sachs—Der konservative Mittelweg. Leben und Werk des Berliner Rabbiners zur Zeit der Emanzipation* (Tübingen: Mohr, 1992), and Margit

When in Berlin, Jastrow maintained close contact with Manuel Joël,[86] a friend from gymnasium with whom he studied, and Rabbi Sachs. In the 1850s Sachs became a tutor and mentor for many young Jews who, on the one hand, chose to study secular subjects at the University of Berlin and, on the other, wished to broaden their knowledge of Judaism and devote themselves to rabbinical careers in the future. Sachs tutored many students, and Jastrow and Joel in particular developed a true admiration for him. Sachs met with his students in his private apartment, facilitating closer and less formal relations. He had a great influence on Jastrow and his views on the form of potential reforms of Judaism.[87]

After Sachs's death, Jastrow wrote a letter of condolence to his widow. In return, he received a letter in which she called him "a true disciple" of her husband.[88]

Another important person who influenced the young Jastrow and became his friend was Rabbi David Rosin, an associate of Sachs's and the director of a Jewish school in Berlin, who later also a lecturer at the Jewish Theological Seminary of Breslau.[89]

Jastrow established a friendly relationship in Berlin with Heinrich Graetz, a distinguished historian who later supported him during various periods of his life.

While he was studying in Berlin, Jastrow received his rabbinic ordination (*semicha*) from Rabbi Moses Feilchenfeld from Rogoźno. The ordination was confirmed in 1857 by Rabbi Wolf Landau,[90] the

---

Schad, *Rabbiner Michael Sachs: Judentum als höhere Lebensanschauung*, (Hildesheim — New York: Olms, 2007).

[86] For more about him, see Isaak Heinemann, "Manuel Joëls wissenschaftliches Lebenswerk. Festvortrag anlässlich der Gedächtnisfeier des Jüdisch-Theologischen Seminars am 31. Oktober 1926" (Breslau: Jüdisch-Theologisches Seminar Fraenckel'scher Stiftung, 1927); Guido Kisch, ed., *Das Breslauer Seminar* (Tübingen: Mohr, 1963), 255 ff; and Marcus Brann, *Geschichte des jüdisch-theologischen Seminars in Breslau* (Breslau: T. Schatzky, 1904), 86–88, 126 ff.

[87] Lukas, Frank, *Michael Sachs*, 118.

[88] AJA, SC no. 5686, [94], 21.04.1865.

[89] M. Brann, *Geschichte des jüdisch-theologischen Seminars*, 97–99, 115, 128–129.

[90] He was probably related to the rabbi of Rogoźno, Moses Feilchenfeld, through his wife. For more about him, see *Biographisches Handbuch der*

rabbi of Gniezno, who gave Jastrow a certificate authorizing him to teach and pass judgments on religious matters, and by Rabbi Dr Michael Sachs from Berlin, who confirmed Jastrow's qualifications to serve as a rabbi on March 27, 1857.[91]

Upon the completion of his studies in Berlin, Jastrow continued his secular education at the university in Halle. At the time, Jews could not obtain doctorates from the University of Berlin; therefore, they most often continued their education and received doctorates at the universities in Halle or Jena. Jastrow obtained his doctorate in history, philosophy, and classical studies from the University of Halle on February 19, 1856.

His dissertation, *De Abraham ben Meir Aben Esrae principiis philosophiae*,[92] written in Latin, was 70 pages long and presented the views of ben Meir, one of the most notable representatives of Jewish Neo-Platonism, a poet, Bible commentator, grammarian, and astronomer, who lived in Spain in 1088–1176. Jastrow's doctoral thesis was never published. It seems that he drew the inspiration to write on that specific topic from his master and teacher Michael Sachs, who was interested in the world of Spanish Jews, as well as from David Rosin, who later devoted many of his monographs to Abraham ibn Ezra.[93]

After his promotion in October 1856, Jastrow received a job offer to teach in a religious Jewish school in Berlin. Its headmaster, David Rosin, commended Jastrow for his dedication and skills.[94] On January 1, Jastrow became a teacher at the school, and he officially worked there until August 2, 1858.[95]

In the meantime, he was looking for a better-paid job in view of his planned marriage to Bertha Wolfssohn from Poznań, seeking

---

Rabbiner, ed. Brocke, Carlebach, Teil 1, *Die Rabbiner der Emanzipationszeit*, 563–564; Adolf Diamant, *Chronik der Juden in Dresden* (Darmstadt: Agora, 1973), 98–99, 162–165, passim.

[91] AJA, SC no. 5686, [11].

[92] The manuscript of Jastrow's dissertation is in Universitätsarchiv Halle, Rep. 21 I no. 35; for other documents relating to his studies in Halle and doctorate, see Universitätsarchiv, Halle, Rep. 21 II no. 84.

[93] See for instance David Rosin, *Reime und Gedichte des Abraham ibn Esra*, vol. 1–2 (Breslau 1884–1888).

[94] AJA, SC no. 5686,[10], 10.1856.

[95] AJA, SC no. 5686, [10], 1.01.1857; [11], 9.11.1827; [24], 2.08.1858.

Bertha Wolfssohn-Jastrow (1834–1908).

a rabbinical position in a smaller town. Among the towns he applied to were Gorzów Wielkopolski and Stargard Szczeciński.[96] He also talked to Michael Sachs about a teaching vacancy in a community school for girls in Berlin. In a letter dated May 5, 1858, he wrote to his future wife:

> ...I went to Dr. Sachs to speak to him about the position at the girls' school. The majority of the directors favor me and I shall therefore at once apply to the directors of the congregation in writing. If I obtain a salary of 400 Reichsthaler per annum, I shall not readily accept a position in a small town, and with the help of God we shall acquire what is needful, and after I am here my earnings will increase easily through increase of salary or multiplication of my labors. And we shall have the enjoyment of living in Berlin, not to be despised...[97]

Marcus Jastrow's wedding to Bertha Wolfssohn[98] took place in Poznań on May 16, 1858. It seems that the marriage was their personal choice, to judge from their letters, which show great mutual devotion.[99]

---

[96] See *Biographisches Handbuch der Rabbiner*, ed. Brocke, Carlebach, Teil 1, *Die Rabbiner der Emanzipationszeit*, 479.

[97] AJA, SC no. 5686, [17], 5.05.1858.

[98] Bertha Wolfssohn was born on February 21, 1834, according to AJA, SC no. 5686 [18].

[99] AJA, SC no. 5686, passim.

CHAPTER 2

JASTROW IN WARSAW, 1858–1862

When planning his new life with a family in mind, Marcus Jastrow sought a position that would guarantee him not only financial security, but also professional satisfaction. As previously mentioned, he was interested in working as a teacher in Berlin or as a rabbi in a smaller town. Unexpectedly, though, the post of preacher in the progressive synagogue at Daniłowiczowska Street in Warsaw, also known as "the German synagogue," became vacant.

Encouraged by Heinrich Graetz, the most distinguished nineteenth-century historian of the Jews, who was very close to Jastrow and possibly related to him, and the outgoing preacher, Rabbi Dr. Abraham Meyer Goldschmidt, who had just received an offer of the post of rabbi in Leipzig, Jastrow decided to apply for the vacancy. Graetz and Goldschmidt both recommended him as a man well educated in both Jewish and secular studies who would serve the progressive Jewish community of Warsaw well. The Synagogue Committee's requirement was that the candidate should know Polish, or at least French, in addition to German, so the fact that Jastrow did not need to learn Polish from scratch was to his great advantage.[1]

Jastrow arrived in Warsaw on January 8, 1858, at the invitation of the synagogue authorities, in order to give a trial sermon, which was treated like an interview.[2] His rival was a Rabbi Feilchenfeld, who sometimes preached there, but unfortunately we do not know anything else about Feilchenfeld, though it is unlikely that he was

---

[1] Sara Zilbersztejn, *Postępowa synagoga na Daniłowiczowskiej w Warszawie (przyczynek do historii kultury Żydów polskich XIX stulecia)*, Master's thesis written at the University of Warsaw under the supervision of Professor Majer Bałaban, 1933/34, p. 28, ŻIH Archive, Master's theses no. 57 (manuscript). An abridged version of this thesis was published in *Biuletyn ŻIH* 74 (1970): 31–57.

[2] Gelber, "Dr. Mordechai (Markus) Jastrow," 8.

the Feilchenfeld who taught Jastrow and had been the rabbi of Rogoźno.[3]

Marcus Jastrow and his sermon must have made a good impression, as Dr. Adolf Bernhard wrote to him as early as May 3, saying that Rabbi Abraham M. Goldschmidt had recommended him to the committee and was inviting him to Warsaw for Shavuot.[4] A few days later, Goldschmidt sent another letter, in which he invited Jastrow to a conference in Leipzig.[5] Nevertheless, Jastrow remained unsure whether to accept the nomination, and his letters to his future wife reveal that he was considering various other possibilities of employment such as teaching at the girls' school in Berlin.[6] However, despite it being a busy period in Jastrow's family life (he married Bertha Wolfssohn on 16 May in Poznań),[7] he maintained the contact with the synagogue in Warsaw.

A month later, Jastrow traveled to Warsaw again in order to discuss the details of his contract and duties with representatives of the Committee of the Synagogue at Daniłowiczowska Street. In a letter to his wife, he writes that Warsaw seemed to be a slightly odd and foreign place:

> Last night at one o'clock I arrived: half sleeping I left the train, a Jewish boy took possession of me and dragged me to the examiner of passports. I looked around expecting to be looked for or called to, but heard and saw nothing. I approached the examiner. "Where are you going to lodge?" "I do not know". "Go back and find a place." (with a gentle push in the breast) I suggest Hotel de l'Europe and my passport is taken. The boy takes me to a cab; the cabman, a Jew, gives me his number hanging as a chain around his neck and I hasten to the baggage room. Trunk and satchel are examined, taken to the cab and off to the hotel. But "nie ma stancyi" is heard, "Germańce": get out. Forward to Hotel de Rome. After a long wait they take me to a room and just as I am about to make myself at home two men enter unannounced, Messrs. Centerschwer and Elsenberg

---

[3] Zilbersztejn, *Postępowa synagoga na Daniłowiczowskiej w Warszawie*, 29.
[4] AJA, SC no. 5686, 3.05.1858, [14].
[5] Ibid.
[6] Ibid., 5.04–05.1858, [15–17].
[7] Ibid., 5.16.1858, [17].

of the commitee, who announce that a sudden hoarseness of the Shammes prevented him from calling out loud and they were misled by my unrabbinical hat.[8]

The talks must have been a success, even though they probably did not end with the signing of a contract. However, on July 16, 1858, Rabbi Goldschmidt sent Jastrow, who was in Berlin, congratulations on having been chosen as his successor as preacher in the progressive synagogue in Warsaw. In his letter, Goldschmidt also laid out his expectations regarding Jastrow's service as rabbi, at the same time praising the environment in which he was to work:[9]

> Congratulating him on his election at Warsaw. "I did not want a bungler to succeed me to act as a foil, on the contrary I wanted to see the work created by me, and thank God, fairly well developed, to be well cared for and advanced... You have a congregation the like of which hardly can be found in Germany, friendly, receptive, not yet blasé, on the contrary, rather given to enthusiasm."[10]

Jastrow came to Warsaw again on July 21 in order to discuss the terms of his contract, which to his dismay was concluded only verbally. Nevertheless, he was reassured by Jakub Centnerszwer (1798–1880), the mathematician and teacher at the Rabbinical School in Warsaw, who told him that Rabbi Goldschmidt's contract had been the same, and that all of its terms had been fulfilled.[11] In addition, Centnerszwer mentioned that when Goldschmidt was leaving, he had received a gift of 388 rubles.[12] The main terms of the contract agreed to by Jastrow were as follows:[13]

---

[8] Ibid., Warsaw, 6.25.1858, [19].

[9] Aleksander Kraushar maintained friendly relations with Abraham Goldschmidt's son Julian after Goldschmidt had left. See Aleksander Kraushar, *Kartki z pamiętnika Alkara* (Krakow: G. Gebethner i Spółka, 1910), 112–115.

[10] Ibid., Leipzig, 7.16.1858, [21].

[11] Ibid., Warsaw, 7.22.1858, [23].

[12] See Zilbersztejn, *Postępowa synagoga na Daniłowiczowskiej w Warszawie*, 28, footnote 5.

[13] I list them after Zilbersztejn, *Postępowa synagoga na Daniłowiczowskiej w Warszawie*, 29.

he was contractually obliged to serve as preacher of the synagogue at Daniłowiczowska Street for five years, but the committee reserved the right to terminate the contract after each six-month period, in which case Jastrow would be paid a six-month salary. His annual salary was set at 900 rubles.[14] In addition to the salary, he would be given an allowance to purchase new furniture for the apartment he would live in (with a study, dining room, kitchen, and hall)[15] from the synagogue's funds, though this was to remain in the synagogue's possession. Jastrow was required to start preaching in Polish no later than a year after the start of his job. One of his duties as preacher was also to establish a religious school alongside the synagogue and teach in it, in a manner that matched the committee's guidelines, for it was the committee that elected the rabbi and was his superior. After concluding the contract, Jastrow vowed to the members of the committee that he would devote himself to his work "in order to fully satisfy his community's strivings."[16]

The person who helped Jastrow settle in was Jakub Centnerszwer, who sent a plan of the Warsaw apartment to Berlin so that Jastrow would be able to buy furniture. Centnerszwer also informed Jastrow that the books he had sent to Warsaw were soon to pass through censorship. He suggested that any books necessary for Jastrow's work in Warsaw, such as the Talmud, the *Arba'ah Turim*, the *Shulhan arukh*, or the works of Maimonides, should be bought in Berlin, as they were not as easily available in Warsaw and were more expensive there.[17]

---

[14] According to AJA, SC no. 5686, 7.21.1858, [22], the salary was initially supposed to be 700 rubles. It seems, based on the committee's report for 1860–61, that the committee was satisfied with Jastrow's work and that his salary was increased to 1,100 rubles per annum. This was justified as follows: "Our appreciation for our preacher's service to the community is so ubiquitous that the committee's expression of gratitude is merely a faint echo of the voice of the community." Quoted from Zilbersztejn, *Postępowa synagoga na Daniłowiczowskiej w Warszawie*, 29.

[15] Some sources mention furniture for three rooms, e. g., AJA, SC no. 5686, 7.21.1858, [22].

[16] Minutes from the meetings of the committee of the synagogue (2.09.1858), quoted after Zilbersztejn, *Postępowa synagoga na Daniłowiczowskiej w Warszawie*, 29.

[17] AJA, SC no. 5686, 7.22.1858 [23].

Prior to his departure for Warsaw, Jastrow bade an official farewell to the representatives of the Jewish community of Berlin, who thanked him for his work in the religious school.[18] Afterward, Jastrow stayed in Breslau between August 16 and 19, where he most likely met with his teachers and friends Heinrich Graetz, Manuel Joël, and David Rosin, whom he often turned to for help and advice.

The Jastrows arrived in Warsaw on Sunday, August 22, 1858. First to greet them, at the station in Skierniewice, were Mathias Rosen and his daughter, with flowers and a basket of fruit; the Committee of the Synagogue welcomed them with bread, salt, and a formal dinner in Warsaw.[19]

The Synagogue at Daniłowiczowska Street

The synagogue Marcus Jastrow was to work in was the oldest progressive synagogue in Warsaw, and possibly in the Polish lands.[20] The history of the synagogue at Daniłowiczowska Street goes back to the turn of the nineteenth century, when a group of Jews from Prussia

---

[18] The ceremony took place on August 2, 1858, AJA, SC no. 5686 [24].

[19] Ibid. [25].

[20] Unfortunately, no comprehensive monograph has been written about that synagogue, and most documents relating to its history were destroyed during the Second World War. Thus Zilbersztejn's Master's thesis has become a source. One of the surviving manuscripts is the so-called *Gold Book* discovered by Eleonora Bergman in the ŻIH Archive, Gmina Warszawska fo. 199/1, *Bericht über Entstehung, Entwicklung und Tendenz der Synagoge Daniłowiczowskastrasse 615 (die deutsche Synagoge genannt) verfasst und seiner teuren Gemeinde gewidmet von dem Prediger derselben Dr. Abraham Meyer Goldschmidt, Warschau am 24. Februar 1858*. The book contains a brief history of the synagogue up to 1858, 3–27, and reports on the activities of the Committee of the Synagogue, the history of its foundation, and the foundation act of the Great Synagogue on Tłomackie Street. See also Eleonora Bergman, "Złota Księga Wielkiej Synagogi w Warszawie," in *Izaak Cylkow*, 57–70; Eleonora Bergman, "Synagoga na ulicy Daniłowiczowskiej (1800–1878) —próba rekonstrukcji,", in *Rozdział wspólnej historii. Studia z dziejów Żydów w Polsce ofiarowane profesorowi Jerzemu Tomaszewskiemu w siedemdziesiątą rocznicę urodzin* (Warsaw: Cyklady, 2001), 113–128. Another important study on this topic is Jürgen Hensel's article "Wie "deutsch" war die "fortschrittliche" jüdische Bourgeoisie im Königreich Polen?," 135–172.

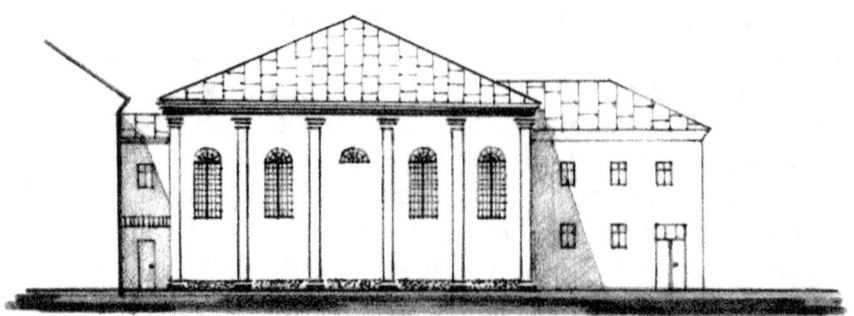

Reconstruction of the synagogue at Daniłowiczowska Street,
by Eleonora Bergman

settled in Warsaw. They were markedly different from other Warsaw Jews in their dress and in the fact that German was their everyday language. On the initiative of one of them, Isaak Flatau, a prayer house was set up, in his home at 616 Daniłowiczowska Street. From the very beginning it was referred to as *Die deutsche Schul*, *Deutsche Synagoge*, or just "the German synagogue." Those who attended the synagogue—initially Flatau's family and friends—were called "German Jews." Such terms were used for a long time, well into the second half of the nineteenth century.[21]

In the lifetime of the synagogue's founder, there was little that set the synagogue itself and its rituals apart from the other synagogues and prayer houses in Warsaw, aside from the "European" dress, the décor, and the order of service. We have no knowledge of any attempts to introduce reforms at that time. The synagogue itself consisted of two rooms, one for men and one for women.[22] After Flatau's death in

---

[21] For more about the early history of the synagogue, see also Hilary Nussbaum, *Szkice historyczne z życia Żydów w Warszawie od chwili pierwszych śladów pobytu ich w tem mieście do chwili obecnej* (Warsaw: K. Kowalewski, 1881), 91–95; and Bergman's detailed study "Synagoga na ulicy Daniłowiczowskiej," 113–129.

[22] This is confirmed by Nussbaum, *Szkice historyczne z życia Żydów w Warszawie*, 93–94. See also Bałaban, *Historia lwowskiej Synagogi Postępowej*, 7, and Zilbersztejn, *Postępowa synagoga na Daniłowiczowskiej w Warszawie*, 7.

1806,[23] the synagogue building was inherited by people who were not interested in the continuation of the synagogue's activities. Following numerous conflicts and supplications to the authorities, in 1815 the "German Jews' were finally able to congregate for services there again. Eleonora Bergman rightly points out that in one of the supplications from that period, a rift in the community of Warsaw Jews is clearly visible. On September 15, 1815, representatives of the synagogue—Samuel Kronenberg, Izaak Simon Rosen, Jakub Epstein, and a person referred to only as Landshutter—wrote the following letter to the superintendent of police:

> Advanced residents of the Mosaic Faith have no more than this one house, in which no one lives, for services and it is located on a street at a distance from others. There is no danger of fire, because the candles are put out right after the end of the service, and the door is closed. In addition the building is brick and does not adjoin other buildings. [...] We request it the more that there is disharmony between us and the rest of our brothers, who are different from us in their dress and looks, and it would disturb our service if we were forced to have it in the same place as them.[24]

From that time the synagogue ceased to be a private synagogue and became the synagogue of the "Congregation of German Israelites," operating continuously until 1843, when a new, temporary synagogue was built on the adjoining plot because there was not enough space for all the worshippers in the "old" synagogue. The temporary synagogue consisted of one large room and a gallery for women. It operated in this form until 1849, when a new synagogue was built at 615 Daniłowiczowska Street.[25] The synagogue existed in that building

---

[23] According to Kazimierz Reychman, *Szkice genealogiczne*. Serja I (Warsaw, 1936; reprinted: Warsaw: Wydawnictwo Artystartystyczne i Filmowe, 1985), 69, I. Flatau died on April 5, 1807. Cf. Bergman, "Synagoga na ulicy Daniłowiczowskiej," 115.

[24] AGAD, KRSW 5753, cat. 20v, quoted after Bergman, "Synagoga na ulicy Daniłowiczowskiej," 116–117.

[25] For more about the architecture and issues related to the construction of the synagogue, see ibid., 116–118.

until 1878, when the Great Synagogue on Tłomackie, which brought together all Warsaw's Progressives, was opened.[26]

Despite the fact that the Progressive Jews called themselves "advanced Israelites of the Mosaic faith," almost no reforms of the ritual or liturgy, which were so characteristic of the proponents of reform in Germany, were introduced during the initial period. Zilbersztejn writes that the synagogue was different "only in that the area around it was kept clean and in order. The worshippers behaved decently during prayer, which made the synagogue stand out from all other synagogues which, as is known, left much to be desired in that respect."[27]

In 1838, Abraham Meyer Goldschmidt, who was born in Krotoszyn, came to Warsaw. He received religious instruction in Breslau and completed his secular education in Berlin and Jena, where in 1840 he obtained a doctorate for his dissertation entitled *De Mosis Maimonidis philosophia theologica*.[28] According to Zilbersztejn, he arrived in Warsaw at the age of twenty-four,[29] having previously been a tutor in the house of a Krakow merchant by the name of Adler.[30] His first post in Warsaw was also as a private tutor, in the house of Mejer Bershon, where he preached sermons on Saturdays. Goldschmidt's enthusiasm was instrumental in accelerating the decision to build the new, temporary synagogue, in which he would be the preacher.[31] Goldschmidt influenced some members of the synagogue, especially

---

[26] See Guterman, "The Origin of the Great Synagogue in Warsaw on Tłomackie Street"; Guterman, *Me-hitbolelut la-leumiyut: perakim be-toldot bet ha-keneset ha-gadol ha-sinagogah be-Varshah*, to learn more about the history of the Great Synagogue in Warsaw.

[27] Zilbersztejn, *Postępowa synagoga na Daniłowiczowskiej w Warszawie*, 8.

[28] For more about this, see Universitätsarchiv Jena, M 292, Bl., 244–256, 286–287.

[29] This appears to be in error; he would have been 26, not 24, in 1838. See Zilbersztejn, *Postępowa synagoga na Daniłowiczowskiej w Warszawie*, 9.

[30] It was most likely Jakub Adler.

[31] Nussbaum, *Szkice historyczne z życia Żydow w Warszawie*, 94–95. For more about Rabbi Dr. Abraham M. Goldschmidt, see Brocke, *Biographisches Handbuch der Rabbiner, Teil 1. Die Rabbiner der Emanzipationszeit in den deutchen, böhmischen und großpolnischen Ländern*, vol. 1, 375–376, which also contains an extensive bibliography of books about him.

Dr. Ludwik Berg,[32] with his sermons on the need for reform. Another important person interested in reform was Louis Wolfsohn, whose house was used for reformists' meetings and discussions. On Passover, April 1, 1838, Dr. Goldschmidt gave a lecture at his home in which he talked about the need for religious reform. His speech must have made quite an impression, because the following day he was invited to the synagogue to give a similar lecture. His speech struck a chord among the listeners and members of the Committee to such an extent that he was asked to give more lectures—for Shavuot, Rosh Hashanah, and Yom Kippur. These lectures evolved into a series of periodic sermons, which became a tradition and a permanent feature of services in the synagogue at Daniłowiczowska Street. In his sermons, preached in German, Goldschmidt tried to emphasize the need for reforms. The first visible change took place in 1840, when choral singing during services was introduced.[33]

Zilbersztejn writes that the first reform service took place on Shavuot in 1843; the preacher, Rabbi Goldschmidt, dressed in a white vestment, delivered a sermon from the pulpit, and the prayers were accompanied by choral singing of boys from the Rabbinical School.[34] Unfortunately, we do not know whether any liturgical innovations or shortened forms were introduced at the time.

After the death of its founder, Flatau, the synagogue was managed by a gabbai who was chosen from among the members of the synagogue.[35] In 1844 the first Committee was appointed in connection with the construction of the new synagogue. It was to be re-elected every three years, and its first members were Izaak Simon Rosen—president, Adam Epstein—vice-president, Stanisław Salinger—treasurer, Jan Glücksberg, Ludwik Kronenberg, and Dr. Abraham M. Goldschmidt. At the beginning Goldschmidt only took the minutes and had an

---

[32] Of whom Goldschmidt said: "Dr. L. Berg has done so much in his previous sphere of activity in Schwerin that he is still very fondly remembered and his name is associated with the beginnings of progressive religious advancement." Quoted after Zilbersztejn, *Postępowa synagoga na Daniłowiczowskiej w Warszawie*, 9.

[33] Ibid., 10.

[34] Ibid., 11. See also Juljan Berg, *Historia założenia chórów synagogalnych w Warszawie przy ul. Daniłowiczowskiej* (Warsaw 1903).

[35] Sara Zilbersztejn, *Postępowa synagoga na Daniłowiczowskiej w Warszawie*, 8.

advisory role, but in 1847, in recognition of his work, he became a full member with the right to vote. The alternate members were: Dr. A. Bernhard, M. Flatau, and H. Merzbach. Mathias Rosen[36] became another member of the Committee in 1845. He was the chairman of the Synagogue Supervisory Board[37] from 1841, despite his progressive and reformist views, and chairman of the Supervisory Board of Jewish Elementary Schools between 1842 and 1865. In addition, he held a number of important functions in Polish and Jewish charitable, social, and political organizations.[38] Another member of the Committee, Adam Epstein, was also active on the Supervisory Board of Jewish Elementary Schools, which he headed after Rosen had left.[39] The financial and social status of the Committee's members was such that a relatively small group of members of the Synagogue at Daniłowiczowska Street was very influential in the Synagogue Supervisory Board and government circles. This meant that ideas for reform were passed on to other milieux as well, and had an impact on other social groups.

After the new synagogue was built in 1849 at 615 Daniłowiczowska Street, the Committee and the owners of the land on which it was built, who ceded it to the community, raised the delicate issue of the autonomy of the synagogue and its removal from the jurisdiction of the Synagogue Supervisory Board. They formulated the conditions of such independence as follows:

> The status of the building shall be regulated and it should belong to the legal entity, i. e. the Synagogue.
> The Synagogue shall be called the "Synagogue of German Israelites."
> The acquired property, which is intended for a "prayer house," shall be equal to other synagogues—free from taxes and other burdens.

---

[36] For more about the changes in the Committee, see ibid., 13.

[37] He was chairman in 1841–1844 and 1856–1858.

[38] For more about Mathias Rosen, see R. Sejfer, *Mathias Rosen*, ŻIH Archives, Master's Theses, and Nussbaum, *Szkice historyczne z życia Żydów w Warszawie*, 213–228, passim.

[39] Zilbersztejn, *Postępowa synagoga na Daniłowiczowskiej w Warszawie*, 18.

Authority shall be vested in the Committee, elected from among the members of the Synagogue, without any interference of the Synagogue Supervisory Board.[40]

The reasoning behind disassociating this synagogue from all other synagogues by naming it the "Synagogue of German Israelites" was not so much to emphasize the origin of its members, as they already identified with Polish culture more than with German, as it was to draw attention to the distinctness of its rituals and liturgy. Another important issue was breaking away from the Synagogue Supervisory Board, in which Orthodox and traditional Jews had the majority. This kind of striving for independence and isolation was typical of progressive, reform communities. Jewish congregations in the United States and reform synagogues in some German towns had such autonomy, but unfortunately it often led to divisions in the Jewish community. Progressive communities on Polish territory also fought for this type of self-rule, for instance in Krakow, but legislation restricted attempts of this sort in Galicia.[41]

Breaking free from the governance of the Synagogue Supervisory Board was not an easy task, and the issue of autonomy was brought to the attention of the authorities in 1852. However, government commissions differed in their opinions and could not decide whether agreeing to the terms of the progressives would contribute to the spreading of heresy and sectarianism, so they turned to the Administrative Council of the Kingdom, where the case came to a standstill for a number of years. Before the final decision could be made, it was considered crucial that the following problems be solved: "Can there be more than one Jewish congregation in one place? Can there be "a separate minister referred to as rabbi with appropriate spiritual service" appointed for such a congregation? Can there be a separate Synagogue Supervisory Board appointed for such a congregation?"[42]

---

[40] The Archives of the Synagogue at Tłomackie, Files of the Committee of the Synagogue (Akta Komitetu Synagogi), 1858, quoted after Zilbersztejn, *Postępowa synagoga na Daniłowiczowskiej w Warszawie*, 19.

[41] Kozińska-Witt, *Stowarzyszenie Izraelitów Postępowych w Krakowie 1864–74*, 312.

[42] The Archive of the Synagogue at Tłomackie, Files of the Committee of the Synagogue (Akta Komitetu Synagogi), 1858, quoted after Zilbersztejn,

On 28 June 1855, after several years of efforts, the Administrative Council issued its final resolution, which read as follows[43]:

Dr M. JASTROW.

Jastrow in Warsaw (1).

"The Synagogue will be called "the Synagogue at Daniłowiczowska Street."" This name was a compromise, as there had been an earlier idea to call it "the Normal Synagogue," but that idea was rejected by the synagogue members themselves because other synagogues might then be considered "Abnormal," which would undoubtedly lead to conflicts.

"The Committee of the Synagogue shall henceforth fall within the jurisdiction of the Government Commission for Internal and Religious Affairs," becoming independent from the Synagogue Supervisory Board.

The Synagogue shall be exempt from taxes; payments shall only be made for residential premises.

The manner in which services are conducted shall be at the board's discretion; however, this authorization may not change or offend the existing order.

Postępowa synagoga na Daniłowiczowskiej w Warszawie, 20. See also the explanation of these issues in Nussbaum, *Szkice historyczne z życia Żydów w Warszawie*, 100.

[43] These resolutions are quoted after Zilbersztejn, *Postępowa synagoga na Daniłowiczowskiej w Warszawie*, 21.

At the same time, the issue of the synagogue's rabbi was raised. The applicants decided, though, that an official rabbi was not needed. What was needed was an educated minister who would hold the title of preacher, not rabbi. It is worth adding here that the preacher's remit is mostly restricted to the internal religious affairs of a synagogue and does not impinge on the powers of a rabbi. This was an attempt to avoid conflicts with official rabbis.

During Jastrow's first year in office, in May 1859, new members of the Committee of the Synagogue were elected, with Adam Epstein as president; Mathias Rosen as vice-president; Henryk Natanson as the seating supervisor in the synagogue; Dr. Adolf Bernhard; Henryk L. Toeplitz as the person responsible for inventory and staff; Jakub Centnerszwer, who supervised seats in the synagogue, and who was superseded by Herman Meyer in 1862; Bernard Kohen as treasurer; Samuel Orgelbrand in charge of administration; and Dr. Ludwik Natanson, who was replaced by Samuel Konitz in 1862; and additionally Dr. Marcus Jastrow with a casting vote and Jakub Elsenberg as secretary.[44]

These conditions were already in place and regulated when Jastrow took up his post as preacher in the synagogue at Daniłowiczowska Street, which was attended by 400 people at "pre-Saturday" services in January 1860.[45]

Jastrow the Preacher

As noted in the article "Nasza służba Boża,"[46] the statement that at the time in question "what is needed is religiosity, not confessionalism" was the motto of both Goldschmidt's and Jastrow's work. Their

---

[44] ŻIH Archives, *Bericht über Entstehung, Entwickelung und Tendenz der Synagoge Daniłowiczowskastrasse 615*, 31. For more on individual members of the Committee, see Zilbersztejn, *Postępowa synagoga na Daniłowiczowskiej w Warszawie*, 45–51.

[45] AGAD, CWW call no. 1731, 680. Efforts were already being made at that time to build a new synagogue, which was eventually completed in 1878 (the Great Synagogue at Tłomackie).

[46] "Nasza służba Boża," *Izraelita* 1875, no. 8, 9. See also Zilbersztejn, *Postępowa synagoga na Daniłowiczowskiej w Warszawie*, 22.

synagogue was to be completely different from other places of worship in Warsaw. At first there were only esthetic changes, confined to paying more attention to order during services. Further reforms, though, led to an even greater differentiation of this synagogue from others in Warsaw. These included the introduction of choral music with piano accompaniment into the liturgy (the choir members were students of the Rabbinical School), beginning in 1870 a harmonium as well,[47] and sermons preached in German—and in Jastrow's time, beginning in 1859, in Polish. Indeed, it was sermons that were the symbol of reform and progress in the synagogue service during that period.

Goldschmidt, who introduced sermons in the synagogue at Daniłowiczowska, initially preached them only on festivals, but at the Committee's request he later also started preaching once a month on Saturdays. Unfortunately, none of his sermons has survived. With Jastrow's arrival and takeover as preacher, sermons were delivered every two weeks beginning on August 1858. Zilbersztejn writes, "the synagogue preacher also delivered sermons from the pulpit at the Rabbinical School every four weeks—every Saturday following the sermon in the synagogue."[48] It seems, however, that sermons were only preached there until 1852, when a "Polish synagogue" was founded at Nalewki Street and the teacher from the Rabbinical School, Izaak Kramsztyk, became the preacher there.[49] Nothing is known about the content of Marcus Jastrow's sermons at the Rabbinical School.

In the letter from the Committee of the Synagogue to Mr. Muchanow of January 1860 regarding a request for permission to build a new, bigger synagogue, the congregation was described as having two characteristic features—choral singing and explication of the weekly Torah readings during uplifting sermons.[50]

---

[47] See the history of the choir in that synagogue in Juljan Berg, *Historia założenia chórów synagogalnych*, and Zilbersztejn, *Postępowa synagoga na Daniłowiczowskiej w Warszawie*, 23–24.

[48] Zilbersztejn, *Postępowa synagoga na Daniłowiczowskiej w Warszawie*, 24, note 3.

[49] See for instance Izaak Kramsztyk, *Kazania*, vol. 1–2, (Krakow: Gebethner, 1892).

[50] AGAD, CWW call no. 1731, 678–679. It was also added that: "This organization of the Service, which does not violate the commonly accepted ritual in any way, has found a growing number of supporters… " It must be assumed, though, that such a caveat was necessary to obtain the authorities'

Chapter 2. Jastrow in Warsaw, 1858–1862

The form of the sermons was established. The first part comprised prayers relating to the passages read from the Torah and the second concerned issues of religiosity, moral improvement of synagogue members, and current events and synagogue-related matters. Jastrow's sermons, most of which were lost or confiscated during his imprisonment in the Warsaw Citadel, complied with these new rules.

Only two collections of sermons were published—one in German (including two sermons) and one in Polish (including eight sermons)[51]—while a section of one further sermon has survived in the National Ossoliński Institute (*Zakład Narodowy im. Ossolińskich*) in Wrocław.[52] The sermons in German were delivered in Warsaw during Shavuot in 5620 (1860) and were published at the request of synagogue members. Their publication was possible due to a trip made by Jastrow to Prussia and Bohemia,[53] which attests to the fact that he maintained lively contacts with his friends in Germany throughout his time in Warsaw.[54]

The sermons have a typical construction. At the beginning there is a quote in Hebrew from a passage of the *haftarah*, and this is

---

permission to build a synagogue. A similar statement appears in Hilary Nussbaum's request for support for the Polish synagogue at Nalewki Street. "This synagogue, so frequently mentioned, is not distinguished by any reform of prayer or religious rituals, apart from choral prayer and sermons in Polish... " AGAD, CWW call no. 1731, 665.

[51] Marcus Jastrow, *Israels Auserwählung. Zwei Predigten am ersten und zweiten Tage des Wochenfestes (Schabuot) 5620 in der Synagoge zu Warschau (genannt: Synagoga przy ulicy Daniłowiczowskiej) gehalten und auf dringendes Bitten vieler Gemeinde-Mitglieder herausgegeben von Prediger Dr. M. Jastrow* (Berlin: Louis Gerschel, 1860), and Jastrow, *Kazania miane podczas ostatnich wypadkow w Warszawie r. 1861 przez Dra M. Jastrowa kaznodzieje Synagogi przy ulicy Danielewiczowskiej* (Poznań: Ludwik Merzbach, 1862).

[52] *Dokończenie mowy Jastrowa mianej na ulicy Daniłowiczowskiej w bóżnicy* 1.3.1861, Zakład Narodowy im. Ossolińskich, manuscript, call no. 13079/II, 26–28. Perhaps it is a section of a translation of a sermon, because *Jutrzenka* claims that Jastrow delivered his first sermon in Polish on March 9, 1861. *Jutrzenka* 13, September 25, 1861, 99.

[53] Marcus Jastrow, *Israels Auserwählung*, 1*

[54] Ibid., IV. The fact that the introduction was dated 11 Av 5620, and the location was given as Franzensbad (a health spa in the present-day Czech Republic), where he probably was at the time, may suggest that Jastrow was not well at the time.

followed by commentary with references to the current situation of the Jews. The text also contains biblical passages in Hebrew. As the sermons were delivered on the first and second days of Shavuot, it should not come as a surprise that their main theme was the choosing of Israel and the giving of the Torah. The central question was whether the choosing of Israel was a reason for the Jews to elevate themselves above other nations.

> We know that accusations are made against us in Israel and elsewhere because of this idea—that we supposedly grant ourselves priority before all others, as if the idea of chosenness were inevitably connected with pride and contempt for other nations. We know that, for this reason, even in Israel some whisper their *Ata Bechartanu* thanksgiving prayer, giving thanks for the choosing of Israel, only with half of their mouth, with a smile and a shrug; while others—it cannot be denied—look down proudly from the height of this chosenness on those who do not belong to the chosen people, and they are also sons of Israel, the chosen nation.[55]

The question of the place of Jews in the world, their being chosen, and their expectations related to it—the Messiah and the return to the Land of Israel—was one of the main theological issues debated by the proponents and opponents of the reform of Judaism in the nineteenth century.[56]

For Jastrow, the idea of chosenness was a historical fact confirmed in the history of the Jewish nation from "pre-times' until the present day. He believed that for this reason the Jews had the right to feel proud about it, though they should not claim any benefits from this fact, nor should they be haughty and consider themselves better than other people and nations, because it was God who chose Israel. Jastrow wrote, "there is a significant difference between a man's own experience and someone else's, between what we are given to rationally and clearly discover and what is imposed on us to be accepted

---

[55] Jastrow, *Israels Auserwählung*, 8.
[56] More about this later in the book.

without any basis or reason."[57] "This is precisely the peak of the Israelite faith, that it does not shackle the mind. This is why the Ten Words of Revelation[58] start with the words "I am the Lord your God, who brought you out of the land of Egypt'[59]; and not with: "I am your eternal God, who created heaven and earth," because God's command wishes to ensure its basis by referring to what may be seen and experienced."[60]

The above words are at once a eulogy and a suggestion to the Jews that they turn to their history, and study and research it. Jastrow believed that Jews can feel proud when they study their past, but at the same time they should remember why they were chosen by God, "to bear testimony to a clear recognition of God; to be the light of a pure path."[61] According to Jastrow, the choosing of the Jews was inextricably bound up with the mission of carrying God's light for the nations—light whose "loving father's eye looks at all of its residents."[62] Jews should not despise anyone, not even "Edom, for he is your brother."[63]

Jastrow believed that Israel's "priority" in the promise of existence and continuity stems from its chosenness, the covenant, and the mission. "Israel has never used or claimed priority in front of other nations; and the divine teachings did not award it any other priority than imposing more of the obligations which surround life, or, if you prefer, restrict life with reminder signs and symbols, the priority of being a kingdom of priests and a holy nation."[64]

---

[57] Jastrow, *Israels Auserwählung*, 9.
[58] The Ten Commandments.
[59] Exodus XX, 2.
[60] Jastrow, *Israels Auserwählung*, 10.
[61] Ibid., 13.
[62] Ibid., 20–21.
[63] Ibid., 16. In the Jewish tradition, Edom is identified with Christianity and, since the Middle Ages, especially with the Catholic Church. For more, see Gershon Cohen, "Essau as Symbol in Early Medieval Thought" in *Jewish Medieval and Renaissance Studies*, ed. Alexander Altman (Cambridge, MA: Harvard University Press, 1967), 19–48.
[64] Jastrow, *Israels Auserwählung*, 21.

At the end of that sermon, Jastrow states that the dissolution of Israel's existence as a nation and the beginning of the persecutions came after the downfall of the kingdom of David.

> Therefore, the only privilege Israel claimed was to be allowed to call itself the children of God, destined to serve Him, called to carry His faith through the countries. That was its consolation in all the suffering endured because of its faith; it was Israel's support during all the assaults intended to unsettle it in its steadfast faithfulness. Is this arrogant elevated pride due to being chosen by God? [...] Before God, there is no difference between people, denominations, conditions, or genders; whether one is an Israelite or a pagan, man or woman, if they completed the service, they will be rewarded for it.[65]

This fragment clearly demonstrates the influence of the Haskalah and reform ideas which reduced the Jews to followers of the Mosaic religion whose goal in Jastrow's time was to become Poles, Germans, and other citizens of the countries in which they lived. Also, Jastrow's vision of the mission of the Jews in the world, connected with their chosenness, shows characteristics of the progressive theology of the time.[66]

The sermons included in the second collection mentioned above[67] are written in Polish, and they all date from March and April 1861. Some of them are in the form of prayers, or are preceded by a prayer consisting of biblical passages, mostly Psalms. These sermons contain fewer theological references, and almost all of them were writ-

---

[65] Ibid., 23–24.

[66] Cf. Frankel's views on this topic.

[67] Jastrow, *Kazania*. The titles of the individual sermons are as follows: 1) *Prayer and sermon delivered during the memorial service on 27. Adar (March 9, 1861) for the souls of the victims fallen on February 27 of this year*, 11–23; 2) *Sermon delivered on the first day of Passover 5621 (March 26, 1861)*, 25–37; 3) *First sermon delivered after April 8, on Saturday, April 20, 1861*, 39–49; 4) *Sermon delivered on Saturday, the weekly portion of Parshat Korach 5621 (on June 8, 1861)*, 51–60; 5) *Memorial prayer said during the memorial service for the soul of the late Joachim Lelewel on June 10, 1861*, 61–66; 6) *Sermon delivered on Saturday (...), July 6, 1861*, 67–77; 7) *Sermon delivered on the day of Atonement (Yom Kippur) 5622, on September 14, 1861*, 79–95; 8), 8) *Sermon delivered on the first day of Sukkot of 5622 (September 19, 1861)*, 97–108.

ten in response to a specific historical event of that period, as the title of the whole collection, *Sermons Delivered During the Recent Events in Warsaw in 1861*, suggests. The sermons are the only surviving book publication in Polish signed by Jastrow. The book was prepared for publication after Jastrow's later banishment from Warsaw, when he was in Breslau for a few months, as will be discussed shortly. He completed the foreword on May 10, 1862.

We can say with certainty that these are not all of the sermons that Jastrow delivered and published, but, as he wrote himself, "The traces of my words preached in God's House have been burned by my judges, but I hope that they did not wipe them from the hearts of my listeners."[68]

Changes in the Liturgy

In Judaism, liturgy is the sphere which often demarcates Orthodoxy. Any attempts at changing it have ended in conflicts and accusations of heresy. Given the lack of dogmas and official theology in Judaism, it is liturgy that upholds adherence to tradition. Curses were often pronounced, for example on Hasidim, because of accusations of changes to the liturgy.[69] In the case of the Warsaw reformers, the conflict was not as serious for many reasons, mostly because the progressives had a lot of influence in the Synagogue Supervisory Board, as well as in business and government circles.

---

[68] Jastrow, *Kazania*, 9. In view of the references to historical events, the content of the "Polish" sermons will be examined in the next subchapter.

[69] For instance, the curse proclaimed on the followers of Hasidism in the Old Synagogue in the Kazimierz district of Krakow clearly reads, "The curse shall be pronounced on those who wish to build a separate altar, change the text of prayers set by the rabbis and approved by the Krakow Rabbi Moses Isserles, introduce different melodies, grimace during prayer, etc. After all, our fathers never told us of anyone wanting to change a word, or even half a word, in the prayers. But now—for our great sins—innovators have come into existence who do not know the Talmud, young and spiritually poor, and they have decided to build their own altar, change old texts, create separate groups for prayer… " See Michał Galas, "Chasydyzm—od herezji do ultraortodoksji," in *Czas chasydów. Time of the Hasidim* (Krakow: Muzeum Historyczne Miasta Krakowa, 2005), 19.

We do not have much information on the alterations introduced in the liturgy in progressive synagogues in Warsaw and in the Polish territory in general. Even Michael A. Meyer, the prominent historian of Reform Judaism, notes that it is difficult to talk about the development of the movement in Central and Eastern Europe, as there is little information on the innovations introduced into the liturgy and theology.[70] Indeed, it is difficult to write about changes to the liturgy, not because there were none, but because of the lack of sources. Many studies contain information about "Polish" progressives adopting the model of the Viennese community, which had been introduced by Isaac Noah Mannheimer and was referred to as "the Viennese rite,"[71] which is characterized by a moderate approach toward reform. With regard to the Synagogue at Daniłowiczowska Street, we must again for the most part trust and rely on Zilbersztejn's work for information.

One of the first attempts to bring about change in the Synagogue at Daniłowiczowska Street, apart from the aforementioned order during services, was an effort to shorten the service by removing from the liturgy some of the *piyyutim* for Rosh Hashanah, which were considered to be a medieval influence. A *mahzor* compiled by Mannheim for the Viennese community and printed in 1840 was later adopted as the official prayer book of the Synagogue, though not without doubts and debates.[72]

As discussed previously, Jastrow's predecessor, Abraham Goldschmidt, did not leave any writings from his Warsaw period, apart from a short description and history of the synagogue,[73] but when he arrived in Leipzig, he was faced with the need to compile a prayer book for the members of his synagogue. The prayer book he prepared, which was classified as a reform prayer book, was published in 1874.[74] Mannheimer's prayer book was much more moderate

---

[70] Meyer, *The German Model of Religious Reform and Russian Jewry*, 278–279.

[71] For more about the influence of Mannheimer and Sachs' reform in the Polish lands, see Bałaban, *Historia lwowskiej synagogi postępowej*, 3–5.

[72] See Ellenson, "The Mannheimer Prayerbooks," 64.

[73] ŻIH Archives, *Bericht über Entstehung, Entwickelung und Tendenz der Synagoge Daniłowiczowskastrasse 615*, 3–27.

[74] *Sefer ha-Avodah — Israelitisches Gebetbuch für die öffentliche Andacht des ganzen Jahres, zunächst für die israelitische Gemeinde zu Leipzig*, vol. II, Leipzig 1874; *Sefer ha-Awoda — Israelitisches Gebetbuch für die öffentliche Andacht, zunächst*

in terms of the changes introduced in it, however, and was often called "traditional" or "conservative."

However, Jastrow had different models for the reforms he introduced. His master and tutor in this regard was Rabbi Michael Sachs, and so it is not surprising that he tried to draft a Polish translation of Sachs's prayer book, though with a certain wariness. In his correspondence with Izydor Monasch, the son of one of the best-known Jewish pressmen and publishers of the nineteenth century, Ber Loebel Monasch of Krotoszyn[75], Jastrow wrote:

> In regard to the siddur, one has already been published in a poor Polish translation[76] but it is not selling very well. Jews prefer the German translation to the Polish one. In their view, the latter has connotations with Catholicism. If you find a good translator, an educated Pole, to translate Sachs' translation well, it would be worthwhile, although the financial result [of such an undertaking] may be doubtful.[77]

---

für die israelitische Gemeinde zu Leipzig, hrsg. A.M. Goldschmidt, vol. I, Leipzig 1876. For more, see Petuchowski, *Prayerbook Reform in Europe*, 8–9, 175–178.

[75] For more about Ber Loebel Monasch and his family, see *Bar Loebel Monasch 1801–1879, Lebenserinnerungen. Memoirs. Pamiętnik*, introduction, compilation, and the critical edition of the German original and Polish translation by Rafał Witkowski, English translation by Peter Fraenkel (Poznań: Towarzystwo Miłośników i Badaczy Ziemi Krotoszyńskiej, 2004). It also contains an extensive bibliography of the Monasch family and their publishing business. Ber Loebel Monasch was also the father-in-law of Heinrich Graetz. Jastrow was a friend of Izydor Monasch and his wife from Breslau, see AJA, SC no. 5686, [28]. After some failed business deals, Izydor Monasch left for the United States, where he founded the Monasch Lithograph Company of Minneapolis, Minnesota.

[76] He probably meant *Modlitwy dla Izraelitów na dni zwyczajne i uroczyste, wraz z przekładem polskim przez H[enryka] Liebkinda* (Warsaw: J. Rothwand, 1846), though Ezechiel Hog's collection of prayers, *Modlitwy Izraelitów* (Warsaw, 1822) was published previously.

[77] AJA, SC no. 5686, Warsaw 2.26.1859 [26].

Nevertheless, in the introduction to the 1861 edition of *Techinot*,[78] Jastrow changes his stance, suggesting that it was necessary for Polish translations of prayer books to be printed:

> How commendable and consistent with the spirit of the time the pursuit of the author of this book is, I feel, requires no further analysis and evidence. It has long been customary in Israel for women to use, both at home and in synagogue, and in addition to the ancient, liturgical Hebrew prayer books and other prayer books the "Techinot," in a language available to them, in which they could find prayers appropriate for their needs. More recent times have produced similar books, written in the spirit of past times and customs, in almost all European languages. However, as far as I know, there has only been one booklet of this sort in Polish;[79] therefore, we should welcome this one the more cheerfully that it contains prayers written in accordance with the spirit and principles of our Religion, in words full of inspiration for the heart, giving women that much needed nowadays intellectual guidance. May this prayer book, then, find its way to every Jewish home in which cultivation of the religious spirit has not yet been forgotten.

I will take this opportunity to express my wish that this book be the first of many religious works in the Polish language for use at home.[80]

It is clearly visible that from the moment Jastrow started to preach sermons in Polish and began feeling more confident in that language, he promoted the idea of publishing religious works in the vernacular for the use of the members of his synagogue, and also for wider Jewish and Polish audiences.

---

[78] *Techynoth. Modlitwy dla Polek wyznania Mojżeszowego przez Rozalię z Felixów M. S[aulsową]*, (Warsaw: Henryk Natanson,1861), VI, 210. [Introduction] Dr. M. Jastrow, V–VI. See also *Jutrzenka* Y. 1, 1861, no. 2, 13–14, 16.

[79] Again, what is probably meant is *Modlitwy dla Izraelitów na dni zwyczajne i uroczyste, wraz z przekładem polskim przez H[enryka] Liebkinda*.

[80] Marcus Jastrow, "Introduction" in *Techynoth. Modlitwy dla Polek wyznania Mojżeszowego przez Rozalię z Felixów M. S[aulsową]*, V–VI.

Certain more subtle changes were also introduced in the Synagogue at Daniłowiczowska Street. One of the most important modifications was the recitation of the prayer mentioning the souls of the dead, *Hazkarat neshamot*, only three times a year: on the eighth day of Passover, the second day of Shavuot, and the eighth day of Sukkot, also called Shemini Atzeret.[81] During the services, the choir sang the memorial song *Yizkor* and the preacher recited the prayer for the souls of the dead, though only mentioning the names of those who had rendered distinguished service to the synagogue, mostly former members of the Committee. After that, the cantor would recite the *El Male Rachamim* prayer in Hebrew. There were pauses between the above-mentioned prayers for individual prayers for the souls of deceased relatives.[82] In 1858 Jastrow introduced further changes to this ritual, ordering the cantor to recite the *El Male Rachamim* prayer separately for men and women.

Another modification introduced by Jastrow was in the language of the prayer for the government, *Hanotayn Teshuah*,[83] which was initially recited in Hebrew at the Daniłowiczowska Synagogue. Jastrow changed it first to German and later to Polish.[84]

In the early days of the synagogue, every member was called up to read the Torah (*Aliyah l'Torah*). Later, though, the *maftir* (repetition of the concluding verses of a reading on Sabbaths or holy days) was no longer read by the person called to the Torah Instead it was read by the *baal koreh*—the master of the reading, a person who could read Hebrew. The *maftir* could also be read by the preacher himself, who translated the recited passage from the *haftarah* (books of the Prophets) into German. We do not know whether the *haftarah* was later also translated into Polish, but everything suggests that it might have been. The only exception was *Maftir Yonah*, which was not translated but was read in the original on Yom Kippur.[85] The call to the Torah

---

[81] Rather than four, as in the Ashkenazi rite. The prayer left out was that on Yom Kippur. See Macy Nulman, *The Encyclopedia of Jewish Prayer* (Northvale, NJ—London: Aronson, 1996), 380–381.

[82] Cf. Zilbersztejn, *Postępowa synagoga na Daniłowiczowskiej w Warszawie*, 25.

[83] For more, see Nulman, *The Encyclopedia of Jewish Prayer*, 155–156.

[84] Zilbersztejn, *Postępowa synagoga na Daniłowiczowskiej w Warszawie*, 25.

[85] Ibid., 25–26.

was discontinued in Jastrow's time, probably due to a decline in the number of people who could read Hebrew. One of the important parts of the liturgy was the section of prayers for women after childbirth, for newborns, and for newlyweds.[86]

One of the most solemn services in the Synagogue at Daniłowiczowska was the marriage ceremony, as described by Sara Zilbersztejn:

> The closest relatives of the bride and groom would gather in the capping room. The preacher would pick up the veil to cover the head of the bride, and choral singing would begin, accompanied by a harmonium. Immediately afterward, the groom would go to the synagogue with his male relatives, followed by the bride with her female relatives, and they took their designated seats. After the Mincha prayer, the newlyweds were led under the canopy, and choral singing would begin again, followed by the preacher's speech, and the nuptials. After reciting the Aleinu, the newlyweds would leave the synagogue with their guests.[87]

New regulations were introduced in the synagogue, as they were in most progressive synagogues, to maintain order during services. These regulations, announced by the Committee of the Synagogue, were borrowed from the 1850 statute of the synagogue in Dresden, and they were very similar to those in other progressive synagogues in Europe and America in that period. The Warsaw Synagogue regulations were as follows[88]:

> 1. Those present in the synagogue are advised to avoid as far as possible doing anything that could derogate the sacredness of the place and the solemnity of prayer, such as murmuring, talking, praying loudly, and changing seats during the service or sermon.
> 2. It is forbidden to allow children under the age of 5 in the synagogue.

---

[86]   Ibid., 26.

[87]   Ibid.

[88]   Quoted after Zilbersztejn, *Postępowa synagoga na Daniłowiczowskiej w Warszawie*, 26.

3. Two persons may not sit in one seat, even with the owner's permission.
4. Those called up to the Torah scroll are obliged to wear black hats.
5. After the sermon has begun, the door shall be closed and no one shall be allowed to enter or leave during the sermon.
6. Members of the Committee are entrusted with ensuring that these regulations are adhered to, and they have the right to adjudicate immediately on arising issues. Everyone present is required to comply strictly with their instructions. Any defiance will involve consequences up to exclusion from the synagogue congregation.

Jastrow in Warsaw (2).

Jastrow's work as a preacher won him popularity in many Jewish circles, and apparently even some Christians (among them the well-known writer Eliza Orzeszkowa) listened to his sermons.[89] The publicity brought increasing numbers of new members to the synagogue, and in recognition of Jastrow's service his salary was raised to 1,100 silver rubles per annum. In an accompanying report, it was noted that "Our appreciation of our preacher's service to the community is so ubiquitous that the Committee's expression of gratitude is merely a faint echo of the voice of the community."[90]

Education and Culture

Education and culture were the two spheres in which Jastrow particularly wanted to become involved in Warsaw. He considered them to be among the most important issues to the members of his synagogue, and to Warsaw Jews in general. As he wrote after leaving Warsaw, "Propagation of learning and culture—that is progress, and for that I was offered a large field in Warsaw, which I worked to the best of my abilities."[91] Education, learning, and "learning Israel" were the main issues he raised in his sermons. It is not surprising, therefore, that he achieved his greatest successes in this field.

Under the terms of his contract, Jastrow was also to manage the religious school alongside the synagogue. With the qualifications and experience gained when he was a teacher in Berlin, he eagerly began his work in Warsaw.

The Statute of the synagogue, which was drawn up pursuant to the decision of the Administrative Council of the Kingdom of June 28, 1855, stated that there was to be "a religious school for Jewish pupils attending Christian schools"[92] alongside the synagogue—it was

---

[89] Cała, *Asymilacja...*, 221, footnote 5.

[90] Report of the Committee of the Synagogue for 1860/1861, quoted after Zilbersztejn, *Postępowa synagoga na Daniłowiczowskiej w Warszawie*, 29.

[91] Jastrow, *Antwort an Herrn I.M. Wise in Cincinnati auf dessen Aufsatz, betitelt*, 9–10.

[92] AGAD, CWW call no. 1731, 737–738; Zibersztejn, *Postępowa synagoga na Daniłowiczowskiej w Warszawie*, 36. Cf. Borzymińska, *Szkolnictwo żydowskie w Warszawie*, 77.

intended as an evening school similar to a Talmud Torah school, though with a modified curriculum. Additionally, in June 1859, the Committee of the Synagogue submitted an application to the Administrator of the Warsaw Education District for the approval of the school and for the issue of an order for Jewish pupils to attend the school.[93] Jastrow, who wanted to activate the donation mentioned in the document of 1855, prepared a "program of religious instruction," which was attached to the letter of January 23, 1861, to the High Government Commission of Internal and Spiritual Affairs.[94]

The religious school near the synagogue was established on December 1, 1859,[95] though it officially opened a little later. It was initially located in the administrative offices of the synagogue, and at first it was a boys' school only. When rooms in the rear wing were adapted for the school, a class was added for girls. Education lasted three years for boys and two years for girls.[96] Moreover, the Commission issued a positive evaluation of Jastrow just a few weeks before his participation in the demonstrations that will be discussed later:

> The Government Commission notes that Preacher Jastrow, to whom the Committee of the Synagogue intends to entrust the management of the School, is a Prussian subject. He received his education in a Posen gymnasium and the University of Berlin, worked as a teacher of Mosaic Religion in Berlin, and his

---

[93] Zilbersztejn, *Postępowa synagoga na Daniłowiczowskiej w Warszawie*, 36.

[94] AGAD, CWW call no. 1731, 738. The letter reads as follows: "The Committee of the Synagogue, wishing to implement [...] an upbringing for young people in accordance with the tenets of Religion, the foremost of all learning. [The Committee] honorably requests that the High Government Commission for Internal Affairs vouchsafe a permit to establish a Religious School alongside the Synagogue, in accordance with the abovementioned decision of the Supreme Administrative Council. The High Commission shall kindly see from the attached syllabus of religious classes in the establishment to be opened, prepared by our Preacher, Doctor Jastrow, who will superintend the establishment, whether the actions of the Committee are compliant with the spirit and intentions of the High Government."

[95] ŻIH Archives, *Bericht über Entstehung, Entwickelung und Tendenz der Synagoge Daniłowiczowskastrasse 615*, 32.

[96] AGAD, CWW call no. 1731, 741. Cf. Zilbersztejn, *Postępowa synagoga na Daniłowiczowskiej w Warszawie*, 36.

conduct in Prussia, both moral and political, was good. He has been in Warsaw since August 10, 1858, on a passport from his Government and he was appointed Preacher of the local synagogue with the permission of the Gov. Com. 2.23.[18]61.[97]

Pursuant to Jastrow's contract and the Statute of the synagogue, the preacher was obliged to superintend the school and give lectures on Judaism. Jakub Elsenberg was to teach basic Hebrew and assist Jastrow.[98] The school enjoyed popularity from the beginning and, surprising as it may seem, most pupils came from impoverished families who had problems paying the school fees. This may shatter the image of the synagogue as a congregation of the wealthy bourgeois and intelligentsia among Warsaw Jews. The details of the fees paid by the students suggest that there were originally about 80 students, only half of whom paid tuition.[99]

The confirmation ceremony for male and female pupils of the school took place on May 26, 1860.[100] The ceremony proper was preceded by an examination.[101] Special invitations were printed, with the following schedule of events:

1. *Mah tovu* song[102] and Mincha prayer
2. Choral singing (Isaiah 44:1–6)

---

[97] AGAD, CWW call no. 1731, 741–742. The document was also signed by P. Muchanow.

[98] Apart from working as an assistant teacher, Jakub Elsenberg was also secretary of the Committee of the Synagogue. See *Zdanie sprawy z działań Komitetu Synagogi przy ulicy Daniłowiczowskiej za rok 1859/60, mianowicie od dnia 1 maja 1859r. do dnia 1 sierpnia 1860r.* (Warsaw, 1860), 5.

[99] Minutes of the meetings of the Committee of the Synagogue (June 1, 1860); quoted after Zilbersztejn, *Postępowa synagoga na Daniłowiczowskiej w Warszawie*, 36.

[100] The first confirmation of girls in Warsaw took place in 1843 in the Rabbinical School synagogue, and it was described as "a great step of the civilization of Israelites in the Country." The occasion was honored with the striking of a commemorative medal. See AGAD, CWW call no. 1464, 2–3. Cf. Szacki, *Yidishe bildungspolitik*, 138.

[101] Zilbersztejn, *Postępowa synagoga na Daniłowiczowskiej w Warszawie*, 29.

[102] A prayer based on sections of Numbers 24:5 and Psalms 5:8, 26:8, 95:6, 69:14, usually recited upon entering the synagogue before morning prayers.

Chapter 2. Jastrow in Warsaw, 1858–1862

3. Preacher's speech
4. Confirmants' examination and prayer recited by a male and female student
5. Psalm 119:9–12 (choral singing)
6. Preacher's speech
7. *Aleinu* and *Adon olam* singing[103]

The ceremony was a very important event at the synagogue, and Jastrow was officially thanked for conducting it by President Adam Epstein and the Committee.[104] Holding a bar mitzvah and bat mitzvah together was also something which might have been received as a serious innovation in the synagogue, and it cannot have gone unnoticed in the wider Jewish community of Warsaw. A ceremony of the same type conducted by Rabbi Abraham Kohn in 1846 in Lviv was interpreted as an attempt to Christianize Judaism and eventually led to the death of Rabbi Kohn and his daughter died with him two years later. It has long been held that they were poisoned by an advocate of Orthodox Judaism, but recent research has called this into question.[105] Even though Warsaw was a more tolerant city, the ceremony conducted by Jastrow must have had an influence on the future of the school. The fact that the number of students fell to 30 in 1860 (the year of the ceremony) can undoubtedly be attributed to this event.[106] The decline in the number of students led to financial problems and the suspension of classes for over four years. The school was only re-opened under Jastrow's successor, Izaak Cylkow.[107]

---

[103] Files of the Committee, 1858; quoted after Zilbersztejn, *Postępowa synagoga na Daniłowiczowskiej w Warszawie*, 37.

[104] "On behalf of the Committee, the President thanked Dr. Jastrow during the meeting of June 1, 1860, for the examination and confirmation of male and female pupils of the religious school on the 2nd Day of Sabbath. Thanks to Dr. Jastrow's efforts, the religious school has been operating since December 1, 1859." ŻIH Archives, *Bericht über Entstehung, Entwickelung und Tendenz der Synagoge Daniłowiczowskastrasse 615*, 32.

[105] For more, see Bałaban, *Historia lwowskiej synagogi postępowej*, 47–48.

[106] "Ze sprawozdania Komitetu Synagogi przy ulicy Daniłowiczowskiej, za r. 1860," *Jutrzenka* no. 13, 1861 (9.25), 99; *Zdanie sprawy działań Komitetu Synagogi przy ulicy Daniłowiczowskiej*, 4. Cf. Zilbersztejn, *Postępowa synagoga na Daniłowiczowskiej w Warszawie*, 37.

[107] For more about the school's financial problems and future, see Zilbersztejn, *Postępowa synagoga na Daniłowiczowskiej w Warszawie*, 37–41 oraz

In 1860 a library was established alongside the synagogue. In accordance with the suggestion of Ludwik Natanson, its aim was to collect books on Jewish history, prayer books, copies of the Bible, and other liturgical works in various languages. We do not know how many books were collected or to what extent this idea was supported by others, but the library was certainly a predecessor of the Main Judaic Library established in 1881 alongside the Great Synagogue.[108]

The Lomdei Torah Society

Jastrow's arrival in Warsaw caused a small revolution in the sphere of higher education. Hopes vested in the education of progressive rabbis at the Rabbinical School were not bringing about the desired results. Despite administrative orders, graduates had trouble finding employment and winning authority. For that reason, the Lomdei Torah society[109] was established in 1858 alongside the Synagogue at Daniłowiczowska Street. The society was independent of the Committee of the Synagogue and had its own regulations.[110] It was founded on the initiative of Dr. Adolf Bernhard, Ignacy Bernstein, Hilary Nussbaum, Moses Wolfshon, and Rabbi Dr. Marcus Jastrow.

Each preacher was to become a member of Lomdei Torah as a term of his employment. The society helped talented youth—graduates of the Rabbinical School or the Main School—who wanted to obtain further education at secular and Jewish theological universities outside of the Kingdom of Poland, mainly in Berlin and Breslau, so that "by sending them to foreign rabbis for a short period of time in order to educate themselves further in theology and gain some experience in preaching, with permission they could speak in this synagogue from time to time as debutants."[111]

Borzymińska, *Szkolnictwo żydowskie w Warszawie*, 77–78.

[108] For more, see Zilbersztejn, *Postępowa synagoga na Daniłowiczowskiej w Warszawie*, 44.

[109] Nussbaum, *Szkice historyczne z życia Żydów w Warszawie*, 104. Cf. Zilbersztejn writes that the society was only established in 1864. See Zilbersztejn, *Postępowa synagoga na Daniłowiczowskiej w Warszawie*, 42.

[110] See also AGAD, CWW, no. 1731, 664.

[111] Quoted after Borzymińska, *Szkolnictwo żydowskie w Warszawie*, 93.

Chapter 2. Jastrow in Warsaw, 1858–1862

Jastrow often was held up as a paradigm for potential candidates, and his model of teaching was copied. In any case, he did not avoid giving assistance. In its essence, the model of education for preachers and rabbis preferred by Jastrow and the society was intended as competition for the Rabbinical School, which was not successful in this sphere. It is highly probable that Jastrow himself was active as a teacher of that group of young people, the students of the Rabbinical School or the Main School. Eisenbach even writes that Jastrow organized a "private rabbinical school,"[112] though what he probably meant is the Lomdei Torah society.

In the beginning, the society numbered about 100 members, who each contributed six silver rubles a year.[113] The recipients of Lomdei Torah scholarships included Izaak Cylkow, graduate of the Rabbinical School and Jastrow's successor as preacher at the Synagogue at Daniłowiczowska Street;[114] Szymon Dankowicz, preacher at the Tempel Synagogue in Kraków;[115] Rundbaken, who was later a rabbi in Cincinnati;[116] Józef Forelle; and Zygmunt Justman.[117]

Jastrow maintained a good relationship with the lecturers at the Jewish Theological Seminary in Breslau, the main center of Positive-Historical Judaism, the precursor of Conservative Judaism.[118] It seems that thanks to his personal influence, it was possible to place a few

---

[112] Eisenbach, *Kwestia równouprawnienia Żydów w Królestwie Polskim*, 368.

[113] Nussbaum, *Szkice historyczne z życia Żydów w Warszawie*, 103.

[114] For more about Cylkow, see *Izaak Cylkow. Życie i dzieło*.

[115] For more about Dankowicz (Nussbaum writes "Dankiewicz"), see Alicja Maślak Maciejewska, *Życie i działalność Szymona Dankowicza (1834–1910)*; Kozińska-Witt, *Die Krakauer Jüdische Reformgemeinde*, index; Teofila Mahler, *Walka między ortodoksją a postępowcami w Krakowie w latach 1843–1863*, ŻIH Archive, Master's Theses, especially pp. 59–70; Nussbaum, *Szkice historyczne z dziejów Żydów w Warszawie*, 104.

[116] Nussbaum, *Szkice historyczne z życia Żydów w Warszawie*, 104.

[117] For more about these scholars, see Zilbersztejn, *Postępowa synagoga na Daniłowiczowskiej w Warszawie*, 43.

[118] This can be demonstrated by the fact that Jastrow wrote to Izydor Monasch on February 26, 1859, asking him not to send a program written by Zachariasz Frankel of Breslau Seminary by post, as it could be confiscated by the censor. AJA, SC no. 5686, 2.26.1859, Warsaw [28]. This indicates that otherwise it would have been sent and, thus, that Jastrow was connected with the author.

theology candidates, his protégés, in the Seminary. They were probably also supported by the Lomdei Torah society. On September 1, 1861, Zachariasz Frankel, the director of the Breslau Seminary, sent Jastrow a progress report on the students from Warsaw, at the same time asking him to see to the payment of outstanding fees for teachers' salaries.[119] Unfortunately we do not have any more information on the number of students from Warsaw or their studies in Breslau at that time.[120]

Perhaps prompted by the letter from Frankel, Jastrow mentioned the Lomdei Torah society in his sermon delivered for Yom Kippur on September 14, 1861. He wrote the following:

> On the same day last year, I talked to you about the need to send talented but poor young men to those centers of education where the Teaching of Israel is lectured in the spirit of our time, i. e. in the spirit of real academic research, so that we can soon boast local teachers in synagogues and schools who can spread education and a real sense of duty to the community in the vernacular language. Thank God! My words did not resonate fruitlessly. A small society[121] has been established with that aim and we expect fruit from the seeds we sowed.[122]

At the end of the sermon, Jastrow issued the congregation an appeal to allocate a fraction of their wealth to the promotion of education and the dissemination of knowledge. He also boasted that a women's charity which looked after girls had been founded.[123]

---

[119] AJA, SC no. 5686, 9.01.1861, Breslau [29].

[120] Marcus Brann writes that between 1854 and 1903 there were 11 students from Russia in the Seminary in Breslau (which could mean that they were from the Kingdom of Poland). See Brann, *Geschichte des jüdisch-theologischen Seminars*, 135.

[121] Probably Lomdei Torah.

[122] Marcus Jastrow, "Kazanie miane w Dzień Ubłagania (Jom Kippur) 5622 r. dnia 14 Września 1861 r.," in his *Kazania*, 89.

[123] Ibid., 89–90.

The Salon: Among Young People

Jastrow endorsed other models of education as well. He leveraged his popularity to influence the views of people not necessarily connected with the Synagogue. He had a particular concern for and interest in youth, and therefore he eagerly agreed to be in charge of the self-study group, also referred to as the salon of young Jewish intelligentsia, whose members gathered in Henryk Toeplitz's house at Daniłowiczowska Street.[124] Before the group under Jastrow's spiritual guidance formed, Toeplitz had hosted meetings of influential members of the Warsaw Jewish community, such as the Natanson brothers, Aleksander Lesser, Mikołaj Epstein, Maksymilian Fajans, Aleksander Paprocki, Izydor Brünner, Daniel Neufeld, Jastrow himself, and graduates of the Rabbinical School.[125]

The self-study group was probably established in 1859, and it comprised around 50 members, most of whom were students of the Rabbinical School, other universities, and secondary schools, but there were also clerks, salesmen, and craftsmen, who later played important roles in their own circles. Some of those who participated in the meetings were Adolf Jakub Cohn, Bernard Goldman, Jerzy Goldman, Aleksander Lowenthal, Gustaw Paprocki, Stanisław Thalgrün, Stanisław Rotwand, Henryk Wohl, Maksymilian Unszlicht, Leon Wagenfisz, Stanisław Kramsztyk, Aleksander Kraushar,[126] Szymon Dankowicz,[127] and many others who were referred to by their first names only.[128] The leader of the group, Jastrow, "took upon himself

---

[124] The salon was established by Teodor Toeplitz. For more about nineteenth-century Warsaw salons, see Helena Michałowska, *Salony artystyczno-literackie w Warszawie w 1832–1860* (Warsaw: PWN, 1974); for information about Jewish salons, see Eisenbach, *Emancypacja Żydów*, 278–282.

[125] Eisenbach, *Kwestia równouprawnienia Żydów w Królestwie Polskim*, 311–312; idem, *Emancypacja Żydów*, 281.

[126] For more about Kraushar, see, e. g., Michał Galas, "Aleksander Kraushar als Erforscher des Frankismus," *Judaica. Beiträge zum Verstehen des Judentums*, 1 (1999): 42–53.

[127] Szymon Dankowicz, a student of the Medical School at the time, was also a very active member of the group. See Aleksander Kraushar, *Kartki z pamiętnika Alkara*, vol. II (Krakow: Gebethner, 1913), 27.

[128] Eisenbach, *Kwestia równouprawnienia Żydów w Królestwie Polskim*, 312; Eisenbach, *Emancypacja Żydów*, 420.

the moral protectorate […], and with the weight of his name endowed the group with the quality of an educational institution."[129] The main objective of these meetings was to learn about and discuss the political situation at the time in Poland and worldwide. Other important subjects were the effort to polonize the Jewish community through the study of Polish history and literature, and issues relating to the history and culture of the Jews, with which Jastrow was particularly familiar.

During one of the first meetings, when memories of "the Jewish war" and the antisemitic articles in *Gazeta Warszawska* from 1859[130] were still vivid, a lecture was given on the attitudes of Polish writers toward the Jews, which bemoaned the fact that that the Jews were mostly depicted negatively in Polish literature. Aleksander Kraushar, who was present during the lecture, recalled that Jastrow claimed that the Jews were partly to blame for that state of affairs.

> How on earth do you expect Polish writers, who know very few Jews, and only know them as much as the immediate (and, it must be admitted, not very appealing) surroundings have enabled them to observe, to have a good opinion of Jews when Jews themselves, or at least their more enlightened class, know their less spiritual co-religionists so little, so little effort do they make to learn about their past, present, and desires for the future. You, lucky that due to random circumstances and without contributing thereto in any way you have reached the margin and experienced the benefits of superficial civilization, put all your pride and worth into shrugging off the solidary responsibility for the ignorance, superstitions, and absenteeism of your younger brethren in faith… A measure of worth and merit in your eyes is to keep as much distance as possible from your co-religionists, leave them in the lurch… You do not found schools, do not train leaders of education, do not know your past, traditions, or customs, the history of your own tribe. In your community, the largest in the country, "the idea of starting a special

---

[129] Aleksander Kraushar, "Kartki z niedawnej przeszłości," in *Książka jubileuszowa dla uczczenia pięćdziesięcioletniej działalności literackiej J.I. Kraszewskiego* (Warsaw: J. Unger, 1880), 508—extensive excerpts of Kraushar's memoirs are included in the appendix; cf. Szacki, *Yidishe bildungspolitik*, 247–250.

[130] For more about this, see Kazimierz Bartoszewicz, *Wojna żydowska w roku 1859. (Początki asymilacji i antysemityzmu)*, (Krakow: Gebethner, 1913).

journal to influence the Jews and reduce prejudice against them in the society that surrounds them has not even been born."[131]

Jastrow saw a need to fight against such prejudice also through self-education and reform of the Jews. He believed that a change was possible and necessary, but it should be made alongside reform of the Jews, who would become full-fledged citizens of their country through their own change. And then, Jastrow claimed, all prejudice would wane and relations with other citizens would become proper.[132]

Jastrow's complaints that there was no Jewish magazine in the vernacular in which Jews could present their views and opinions and spur Polish interest in them contributed to the establishment of a Polish-language periodical, *Jutrzenka. Tygodnik dla Izraelitów Polskich*, which was published by Daniel Neufeld between 1861 and 1863.

It is very likely that it was during these debates on the need to promote knowledge among the Jews, especially about their history and culture, that Jastrow proposed to translate into Polish and publish Heinrich Graetz's *History of the Jews*. This would be of dual importance to Jastrow: first, it would make a recent Jewish academic achievement, *Wissenschaft des Judentums*, available to the Polish reader; and second, it would be a way for Jastrow to repay Graetz for his intercession and recommendation when Jastrow was applying for work as a preacher in Warsaw. The translation of the initial volumes (volumes three and four) into Polish was to have been published in January 1864, but the January uprising and Jastrow's vicissitudes prevented that enterprise.[133]

Jastrow did not limit himself to working only with this group of university students, though. He suggested in his postulates that Jewish youth should train in various occupations so that they could integrate into Polish society more rapidly. Hence, it is not surprising that he was also in charge of an education campaign in the Fraternity

---

[131] Kraushar, *Kartki z niedawnej przeszłości*, 509.

[132] Ibid.

[133] The publication had been announced, though it is not known what stage the translation work was at. See "Hirsch Graetz, *Historya Żydów*, vol. III and IV. Przekład przez Jastrowa, w Warszawie (zapowiedziany r. 1864)," in Karol Estreicher, *Bibliografia polska XIX stulecia. Cz. 1* (Krakow 1872–1882), vol. 2, 75; Karol Estreicher, *Bibliografia polska XIX stulecia. Cz. 2* (Krakow 1885–1890), vol. 9, 221.

of Commercial Clerks (Bractwo Subiektów Handlowych), which had 139 members—Jewish commerce and trade workers—in 1860. Jastrow reportedly even published a special pamphlet for this group in Polish, entitled *Praca, wiedza, postęp*[134] (Work, Knowledge, Advancement), promoting Jewish-Polish integration and brotherhood.

When discussing plans for a Jewish education reform, Jastrow postulated the introduction of elementary vocational training based on teaching trade, engineering, and the German language. He also frequently raised the issue of increasing the number of occupations available to Jews.[135]

Educational Reform

Education in his synagogue was not the only field in which Jastrow was active. From the moment of his arrival in Warsaw, he spoke out about issues related to the status of Jews in Warsaw and the Kingdom of Poland. His first book, laying out the tenets of reform for the Jews of the Kingdom, was published as early as 1859.[136] He later presented his own drafts for reforms (especially of education), sometimes anonymously. We learn from Zofia Borzymińska's research[137] that Jastrow was the author of a memorandum on education and Jewish schools,

---

[134] Only Lucjan Marek mentions this publication. See Lucjan Marek, "Początki ruchu zawodowego wśród pracowników handlowych w Warszawie, 1856–1881," *Biuletyn ŻIH* 58 (1966): 89. Cf. Eisenbach, *Kwestia równouprawnienia Żydów w Królestwie Polskim*, 316.

[135] "Wychowanie publiczne—O szkołach wyznania mojżeszowego. (Wyjątek z memoriału podanego do KRWRiOP w 1861 r.)," *Dziennik Powszechny*, nos. 125 and 126 (1862): 507, 511; Cf. Borzymińska, *Szkolnictwo żydowskie w Warszawie*, 143.

[136] [Marcus Jastrow], *Beleuchtung eines ministeriellen Gutachtens über die Lage der Juden im Königreich Polen. Veranlasst durch Kaiserlichen Willen und bureaukratische Willkühr* (Hamburg: Hoffmann und Cempe, 1859), published anonymously.

[137] Borzymińska writes, "In June 1862, *Dziennik Powszechny* published a memorandum received a year earlier by KRWRiOP (the Government Committee for Religious Denominations and Public Enlightenment). The author's name was not disclosed in the publication; however, a comparative analysis of various materials indicates that it was Marcus Jastrow." Borzymińska, *Szkolnictwo żydowskie w Warszawie*, 114.

which was sent to the Government Committee for Denominations and Public Enlightenment in 1861 and published in *Dziennik Powszechny*[138] in 1862. It is possible that this memorandum was connected with Aleksander Wielkopolski's call for comments on the planned school reform.[139]

Jastrow wrote that the curriculum in the schools that Jewish children attended at the time was more religious than academic, and that what it lacked most was teaching of the Polish language. Jastrow was eager to talk to anyone in order to draw them into the coalition of reformers of Jewish education. He even met with *tsadik* Izaak Meir Alter of Góra Kalwaria for this purpose.[140]

Despite Jastrow's commitment, few children of Jewish descent were sent to Christian schools, especially in the west of the Kingdom. The only problem he saw was the fact that Jewish children attended school on Saturday. The ideal solution, according to Jastrow, would have been for Jewish children to attend state schools and gain their knowledge of Jewish religion and history in Jewish schools, such as the one he ran at the Synagogue at Daniłowiczowska Street.[141]

Jastrow postulated that denominational elementary schools should first prepare pupils for general national schools and then exist as evening schools, like the school alongside the Synagogue at Daniłowiczowska Street, limiting their curricula to religious classes. Jastrow also called for making elementary school attendance compulsory.[142] In any case, this was in line with his watchword that "Jews needed to be led from their abnormal current situation to a normal

---

[138] "O szkołach wyznania mojżeszowego (Wyjątek z memoriału podanego do KRWRiOP w 1861 r.)," *Dziennik Powszechny*, nos. 125–126 (1862): 507, 511. See more about this document in Szacki, *Yidishe bildungspolitik*, 144–145; Aron Sawicki, "Szkoła Rabinów w Warszawie (1826–1863)," *Miesięcznik Żydowski*, 1933 no. 3, 272.

[139] Eisenbach writes that 38 papers were received, including Jakub Tugendhold's, Daniel Neufeld's, Mathias Rosen's, and Izaak Kramsztyk's, not to mention Jastrow's. Eisenbach, *Kwestia równouprawnienia Żydów w Królestwie Polskim*, 363. Cf. Stefania Sempołowska, *Pisma*, vol. I (Warsaw: Państwowe Zakłady Wydawnictw Szkolnych, 1960), 148.

[140] Gelber, "Dr Mordechai (Markus) Jastrow," 12. Cf. Wodziński, *Oświecenie żydowskie w Królestwie Polskim*, 162.

[141] "Wychowanie publiczne," 511.

[142] Ibid.

position—they needed to be made Poles of the Mosaic faith" first, and only then would they become "useful to the country."[143] In light of this view, Jastrow's stance was that turning Jews into "Poles of the Mosaic faith" was a process of educating and shaping a new type of Jewish citizen. On the other hand, the process assumed a certain change in the attitudes in Polish society, which Jastrow wooed so keenly, toward the Jews. To Jastrow, the process of becoming "Poles of the Mosaic faith" was inextricably bound up with the improvement of social relations with the Poles, but he also anticipated that it needed time—something that radical supporters of integration through assimilation, such as Henryk Natanson or Mathias Rosen, probably did not agree with.[144]

In his memorandum which was discussed above, Jastrow spoke out against the existence of the Rabbinical School, as he thought that this form of school was no longer viable. He believed that secular education could be received from elementary and secondary schools, while theological instruction was available at reputable universities in Germany, or could be obtained by studying, like Jastrow, under the supervision of prominent rabbis, which was common practice in Germany at the time.

The Rabbinical School was another issue important to Jastrow. His opinion of this institution was rather critical. He noted that while it was meant to educate rabbis, not a single rabbi came out of the school in Jastrow's time, and only a small number of religious studies teachers. For this state of affairs Jastrow blamed the erroneous presumption that the educated and learned would be chosen to be rabbis in uneducated communities. In his view, this attested to lack of knowledge about "the post of a rabbi and his attitude to the community," as he held that a rabbi was a man of confidence in the community to whom people turn for advice and answers to their questions. A rabbi gains his authority only through being elected by the community, and communities choose rabbis that are most suitable for them. Jastrow maintained that educated rabbis would not be able to find adequate employment unless the general condition of Jewish education changed. He gave the example of the rabbinical schools in Vilna

---

[143] AGAD, CWW, call no. 1732, 38, 40; quotes from Borzymińska, *Szkolnictwo żydowskie w Warszawie*, 117.

[144] For more about various Jewish education projects, see Borzymińska, *Szkolnictwo żydowskie w Warszawie*, 105–168.

and Zhytomyr, where the situation was similar,[145] and went on to suggest that the Rabbinical School could have served as a Jewish secondary school, but that after the reform of 1857, "the benefits of that institution as a sort of Jewish gymnasium in the general education of the Jews were lost."[146]

Antony Polonsky writes that with regard to the reform of the Rabbinical School, Wielkopolski "was less influenced by Tugendhold and the Synagogue Supervisory Board than by the preacher of the Synagogue at Daniłowiczowska Street, Dr. Marcus Jastrow."[147]

Jastrow's project is an important record of the history of Jewish education in Warsaw, as it contains statements and detailed information regarding numbers of schools and pupils in earlier decades. Nevertheless, what Jastrow communicated in this document and his many other declarations was that the reform of education should be combined with the granting of equal rights to the Jews. Education was only to be the means to achieve a goal. Jastrow believed that denominational elementary schools for Jews should exist for some period of time, but that their curriculum should be changed to one that would accelerate the process of "civilizing" the Jews. He was hoping that "if all Israelites of one generation go through institutions that are able to broaden their knowledge, the whole of the next generation will attend general Christian schools."[148]

Polish-Jewish Relations and Reform Ideas in Polish Sermons

Jastrow arrived in Warsaw following a very turbulent period, immediately after the so-called "Polish-Jewish war,"[149] and tried to acquaint himself with the general situation of the Jews in the Kingdom of

---

[145] About those institutions, see Dohrn, "The Rabbinical Schools as Institutions of Socialization in Tsarist Russia, 1847–1873"; Malamed, "The Zhitomir Rabbinical School: New Materials and Perspectives."

[146] "Wychowanie publiczne," 511.

[147] Antony Polonsky, "Warszawska Szkoła Rabinów: orędowniczka narodowej integracji w Królestwie Polskim," in *Duchowość żydowska w Polsce*, 306.

[148] "Wychowanie publiczne," 511

[149] For more, see Bartoszewicz, *Wojna żydowska w roku 1859*.

Poland. Having ties with progressive circles, he wanted the Jews to receive full civil rights as quickly as possible.[150] Thus, it does not come as a surprise that his first published book dealt with that very issue. It was an anonymous review of Jewish rights in the Kingdom, based on a report by the Internal Affairs Committee for the Administrative Council, entitled *Beleuchtung eines ministeriellen Gutachtens über die Lage der Juden im Königreich Polen*. It was published in Hamburg in 1859 — about a year after Jastrow's arrival in Warsaw.[151] As was pointed out by Artur Eisenbach, the book is analogous to Ludwik O. Lubliner's piece published a year later in French.[152]

Rabbi Jacob S. Raisin[153] asked Jastrow directly whether he was the author of *Beleuchtung eines ministeriellen Gutachtens über die Lage der Juden im Königreich Polen*, and Jastrow not only answered in the affirmative, but he told Raisin about his involvement in conspiracy.

> I, being a perfect stranger in Poland at that time (I came to Warsaw in 1858), had to get the advice of natives, and from week to week we had meetings to that effect, and for similar purposes, — all this in secret, at the risk of liberty if not life, for a sojourn in some fortress or in Siberia is not conducive to

---

[150] For attempts to reform the status of the Jews in the Kingdom and related discussions, see, e. g., Artur Eisenbach, *Z dziejów ludności żydowskiej w Polsce w XVIII i XIX wieku* (Warsaw: PIW, 1983),189–215.

[151] [Jastrow], *Beleuchtung eines ministeriellen Gutachtens über die Lage der Juden im Königreich Polen*. It contains a German translation of *Przegląd istniejących w Królestwie Polskim postanowień w porównaniu z obowiązującymi w tym względzie zasadami w Cesarstwie tudzież uwagi o stosowności lub niestosowności obecnego urządzenia Żydow w Królestwie* ("A review of the existing regulations in the Kingdom of Poland juxtaposed with the binding regulations in the Empire, and comments on the propriety or impropriety of the current situation of the Jews in the Kingdom"). The original may be found in AGAD KRSW call no. 6632, 81–151 (quoted after Eisenbach, *Z dziejów ludności żydowskiej w Polsce*, 327). Unfortunately, this piece is not attributed to Jastrow in many Polish libraries.

[152] Ludwig O. Lubliner, *De la condition politique et civile de Juifs dans le Royaume de Pologne: examen critique d'un rapport adressé en l'année 1858 à l'empereur*, (Brussels 1860). See Eisenbach, *Z dziejów ludności żydowskiej w Polsce*, 199–200.

[153] Raisin was the author of an interesting book, *The Haskalah Movement in Russia*.

health. Thus I translated my report and made my annotations, as you see.[154]

In his book, Jastrow limited himself to comments on the situation of the Jews in the Kingdom, which he included in the introduction and notes to individual chapters of the *Review*. These differ significantly from his later statements, particularly on Polish- and Christian-Jewish relations, for which he considered Prussia to be an exemplar. The stimulus for Jastrow's brave undertaking was the fact that all attempts to improve and regulate the legal situation of Jews in the Kingdom, or at least to adopt the regulations in force in Russia, came to naught in spite of the tsar's favorable attitude. Neither Sir Moses Montefiore's pressure, nor the memorandum of Ignacy Turkułł, nor articles in the foreign press, nor the actions of the Jewish Committee in Saint Petersburg brought any results because, according to Jastrow, administrative issues and "bureaucratic lawlessness' served to maintain the status quo, which was beneficial to the government officials.[155] Matters were different in Prussia, where, Jastrow claimed, government officials "created an impeccable, reliable, and strong state."[156] The lack of equal rights and access to government posts was connected with the Poles' aversion toward the Jews, which Jastrow felt was growing rather than decreasing during his early time in Warsaw.[157] He wrote: "Poles do not have much of a speculative sense by nature and due to failing to look at problems deeply are inclined to see Jews and Germans as dangerous competitors, and consider their thriftiness an ulcer sucking out the country's market, that should be extirpated if possible."[158] At the same time, in his opinion, the Jews had formerly

---

[154] AJA, SC no. 5686, Jastrow's letter to Raisin—see appendix for the whole letter.

[155] Cf. [Jastrow], *Beleuchtung eines ministeriellen Gutachtens über die Lage der Juden im Königreich Polen*, 2–3, and Eisenbach, *Z dziejów ludności żydowskiej w Polsce*, 190, 197–199.

[156] [Jastrow], *Beleuchtung eines ministeriellen Gutachtens über die Lage der Juden im Königreich Polen*, 4–5.

[157] Ibid., 8–9. It is worth noting that Jastrow used the term "Pole," which was very rare, as he later referred mainly to "brothers," "natives," "fellow countrymen," and "Christians' in his works.

[158] Ibid., 9.

enjoyed relative respect for the same reason—as they were the carriers not only of Polish trade and commerce, but also of the Polish bookselling market.[159] Jastrow described this situation mainly on the basis of his own observation, but also on the basis of the works of Wawrzyniec Surowiecki,[160] the brochure *Memoire sur la situation des Israelites en Pologne*,[161] and articles from the Western press published between 1856 and 1858.[162] The information and views of Jastrow evident in this introduction were undoubtedly connected with the atmosphere of the "Jewish war" which was being played out, mainly in the Warsaw press, that year.[163]

Jastrow paid particular attention to gaps in legislature that hindered the "civilization" of the Jews. He also stressed that the situation of the Jews in Poland at the time was far from what it was in Prussia, where Jewish elementary schools were established, as he noted, often against the will of the Jews themselves. The practice was different in Poland, where Jews were not given full rights due to not being "civilized," while, according to Jastrow, "in 450 provincial towns in Poland there [was] not a single elementary school in which poor Jewish children could learn the national language. Only in Warsaw [were] there four Jewish elementary schools for boys and two for girls."[164] On the other hand, Jastrow noted that the communities did not receive any financial return on the taxes paid by the Jews, which should have been used to pay for education—"Jewish elementary schools in Warsaw [did] not receive a single ruble of that money, only from community income."[165]

At the end of his introduction to *Review*, Jastrow made reference to the view that "the moral condition of the Jews is much worse than

---

[159] Ibid., 10.

[160] In particular Wawrzyniec Surowiecki, *O upadku przemysłu i miast w Polszcze* (Warsaw, 1810).

[161] *Memoire sur la situation des Israélites en Pologne*, Paris 1858.

[162] See Eisenbach, *Z dziejów ludności żydowskiej w Polsce*, 327 for a list of some of the publications about the situation of the Jews in Poland.

[163] See Bartoszewicz, *Wojna żydowska w roku 1859*.

[164] [Jastrow], *Beleuchtung eines ministeriellen Gutachtens über die Lage der Juden im Königreich Polen*, 16.

[165] Ibid., 18.

the moral condition of Christians." He believed those accusations to be false, because Jews were not crammed into "filthy streets," where they lived in poverty, "excluded from all opportunities to receive education," and denied access to farming and crafts, of their own will. According to Jastrow, it was not Judaism and its dogmas that were to blame for the situation, but rather the administrative authority. The reaction to the difficult situation of the Jews was Hasidism, which he believed would disappear when the standard of education among the Jews was raised:

> Although—we admit—under the force of long-term oppression Judaism has adopted a peculiarly mystical form among many of its Polish followers, it was originally free from mysticism, unlike any other religion. But firstly, it has always been the way that people who do not have a shelter on earth resort to a heaven that cannot be taken away from them; and this peculiarity of Judaism—mysticism, or Hasidism, as they refer to it here—will gradually disappear when it becomes deprived of its basis— repression and ignorance. Secondly, Hasidic fanaticism has not posed any more threat to the state than any other type of fanaticism of any other religion.[166]

Jastrow ended his introduction with an appeal calling on the tsar to recognize the impure intentions of the legislature, which were discussed in *Review*, and the wish for "truth, kindness, and compassion" to shine out for the Jews in Poland.[167]

---

[166] Ibid., 20–21. The attitude toward Hasidism evident here is typical of the worldview of progressive Prussian Jews. This fragment cannot have been known to the author of the book *Oświecenie żydowskie w Królestwie Polskim wobec chasydyzmu*, who attributed to Jastrow a generally positive attitude to Hasidism. Jastrow wrote directly about Hasidism in the passage quoted and possibly also in his review of the novel *Lejbe i Siora*, printed in *Jutrzenka* 3 (1861): 28. In his other works, he called for unity among the sons of Israel in the Kingdom of Poland. Cf. Wodziński, *Oświecenie żydowskie w Królestwie Polskim wobec chasydyzmu*, 154, 156, 161–165, 188, 190–191, 194, 201–203, 225. See also the review of Wodziński's book by Glenn Dynner in *Kwartalnik Historii Żydów*, 2007 (2).

[167] [Jastrow], *Beleuchtung eines ministeriellen Gutachtens über die Lage der Juden im Königreich Polen*, 22.

Further on in the book Jastrow made comments, in the form of notes, on various statements, in particular regarding the issue of how Jews in the Kingdom of Poland were treated worse than they were in the Empire, which to him evidently meant worse treatment by both the Kingdom's government and its Christian citizens. In the appendix, he included a list of professions to which Jews did not have access, restrictions on settlement and the buying of property, and specific tax burdens. This collective presentation of facts was designed to appeal to Tsar Alexander II, who in Jastrow's opinion was the only person able to untie the "Gordian knot" that was "the Jewish question in Poland."[168]

On analysis of Jastrow's book, the first after his arrival in Warsaw, it becomes clear that he was calling for an improvement to the situation of the Jews in Warsaw and the Kingdom of Poland from the very beginning. He was comparing the situation to that in Prussia, so he thought that the first step to "civilizing" the Jews should be taken by the government of the Kingdom or the tsar himself, in whom he clearly believed. For this reason, there are few examples in this book of the rhetoric known from his future works, in which he held the Jews jointly responsible for their fate and situation. On the other hand, we must acknowledge Jastrow's courage: even though his book was published anonymously in German in Hamburg, he must have been aware that if the authorities learned who was criticizing them so vehemently, he would be expelled from Poland very quickly. His authorship thus needed to be a well-kept secret.

However, the events during Jastrow's initial period in Warsaw did not close his eyes to other problems of the Jewish people residing in the Kingdom of Poland. His attitude toward Polish society changed as he learned the realities of the situations of Poles and Jews living under the Russian occupation. Once he had organized the religious life in his synagogue, he actively joined the discussion about the necessary reforms in the Jewish community which would lead the Jews out of their situation and guide them to equality. This postulate was to be accomplished through improvement of education, reforms—mainly religious—and above all, cooperation with Polish society. The main goal was to become "Poles of Mosaic persuasion." Such a standpoint openly suggested that Jastrow supported Poles in their pursuit of

---

[168] Ibid., 132.

regaining independence and driving out the Russian occupant. Thus, despite being aware of the many differences and problems dividing the Poles and the Jews, he spared no effort in working toward both convincing the Jews of the need to support the Poles and raising the Poles' interest in Jewish issues. He was also an excellent observer and a sapient witness of the social processes occurring at the time. Seeing that the fates of Poles and Jews had been interconnected for many centuries, he longed for the improvement of mutual relations and perception, believing that the feuds between the Poles and the Jews only served their mutual enemy, Russia. Jastrow dealt with most of these issues in his sermons collectively called *Kazania miane podczas ostatnich wypadków w Warszawie r.1861* (Sermons Delivered During the Recent Events in Warsaw in 1861).[169] He began the collection with a summary of his activity in the Kingdom.

> It has not been long—little over three years—that I have been lucky to plough the field of my work in the community called "the Synagogue at Danielewiczowska Street." Having come to Warsaw in 1858, I found division where there should have been unity, hatred instead of the love which could pull the nation out of the abyss of decay; I found prejudice and superstition where only correct judgment could have appeased evil; I found blindness instead of the light which could have been only salutary for the poor folk. These miserable people had been made the blind tool of the enemy for the persecution of those who were even more unhappy because they were denied even the solace of suffering in their own homeland and for their homeland; oppressed themselves, they could forget about the crushing yoke by oppressing the followers of another religion, though inhabitants of the same land ..., and the best way to do it was to awaken the vehement caste hatred which deprives man of his clarity of thought and his heart beat! And unbridled feuds and hatred were most convenient for the enemies; for they remembered well the old Roman maxim—*divide et impera*.[170]

---

169   Jastrow, *Kazania*.
170   Ibid., 3–4.

Despite such a grim beginning to his time in Warsaw, Jastrow tried to instill in his community members a love for the land and their "brethren, to whom they were connected by a common homeland," as well as to develop in them "a love of [their] native language and education," which was his duty as preacher.[171] His inspiration for this behavior was the Chief Rabbi of Warsaw, Ber Meisels, who since 1856 had been working to promote understanding between Jews and Poles, and with whom Jastrow was to share a prison cell in the Warsaw Citadel, as will be discussed shortly.[172] Jastrow had a great deal of respect for Meisels,[173] which he frequently stressed:

> Meisels supported me, or rather preceded me, in this work of reconciliation ... and [it was his] lot ... to leave with me the place where love and unity were a sacred goal toward which he worked, and where love and unity are the great memento he left behind...[174]

It was thanks to their joint efforts, Jastrow believed, that Polish-Jewish fraternization was achieved within a few years, in spite of very

---

[171] Ibid., 4–5.

[172] For more about Meisels' work, see Franciszek Kupfer, *Ber Meisels i jego udział w walkach wyzwoleńczych narodu polskiego (1846, 1848, 1863–1864)* (Warsaw: ŻIH, 1953); Michał Galas, "Rabbi Ber Meisels i jego działalność w Warszawie," in *Żydzi szczekocińscy. Osoby, miejsca, pamięć*, eds. Michał Galas i Mirosław Skrzypczyk (Krakow—Budapest: Wydawnictwo Austeria, 2008), 157–169.

[173] After Meisels' death, Jastrow published his memories of him in the American press: Marcus Jastrow, "Bear Meisels, Oberrabbiner zu Warschau. Ein Lebensbild auf historischen Hintergrunde nach einiger Anschauung entworfen," *Hebrew Leader*, April-June 1870 (1870: vol. 15 no. 25 [4.01], no. 26 [4.08], vol. 16 no. 1 [4.15], no. 2 [4.22], no. 3 [4.29], no. 4 [5.06], no. 5 [5.12], no. 6 [5.20], no. 7 [5.27], no. 8 [6.03], no. 9 [6.10], no. 10 [6.17], no. 11 [6.24]. This text was translated into Hebrew by Natan M. Gelber in *He-Avar*, no. 13 (1966): 210–222. In Polish, see Mordechaj (Marcus) Jastrow, "Ber Meisels naczelny rabin Warszawy i jego życie na tle wydarzeń historycznych," trans. Agata Paluch, in *Żydzi szczekocińscy. Osoby, miejsca, pamięć*, 231–256; some fragments were translated also into Polish in Kupfer, *Ber Meisels i jego udział w walkach wyzwoleńczych*, 139–143.

[174] Mejer Bałaban, "Żydzi w powstaniu 1863," *Przegląd Historyczny* XXXIV: (1938): 10, quoted after Kupfer, *Ber Meisels i jego udział w walkach wyzwoleńczych*, 75–76.

Chapter 2. Jastrow in Warsaw, 1858–1862

difficult beginnings. When Jastrow came to Warsaw, relations between the two communities were characterized by excessive nationalism, fanaticism, and the discriminatory legal status of the Jews.[175] He tried to change this situation, with some degree of success, through "a covenant of love" for the common homeland, language, and culture. He wrote:

> I thought it my new duty to address my co-religionists, considered Poles, in the Polish language, and lead them into the house of the Israeli God for this treasure so dear to all who have not yet forgotten Poland's past, and have not doubted its resurrection.[176]

Another person Jastrow held in high esteem was Joachim Lelewel. After Lelewel's death, a memorial service was held in the Synagogue at Daniłowiczowska Street, during which Jastrow portrayed him as an example to follow in the building of "unity and fraternization of all the children of the country."[177] There were Poles, too, who spoke positively of the work of Jastrow and other rabbis. In her letter to Bibianna Moraczewska, Narcyza Żmichowska wrote that "there are Jews here who are well disposed" (among whom she included Jastrow).[178]

One such symbolic act of fraternization was the joint participation of Poles and Jews in a political manifestation during the funeral of five victims of the demonstration on Krakowskie Przedmieście on February 27, 1861. Jastrow and Meisels were among those who took part in it, and Jastrow's presence was immortalized in the famous paintings by Aleksander Lesser and Henryk Pillati depicting the event. It is worth noting that the funeral took place on Saturday, March 2, which makes the rabbis' participation even more significant.[179]

---

[175] Ibid., 140.

[176] Jastrow, *Kazania*, 7.

[177] Jastrow, *Modlitwa odprawiona podczas Nabożeństwa żałobnego za duszę ś. p. Joachima Lelewela, dnia 10 Czerwca 1861 r.*, in Jastrow, *Kazania*, 61–66.

[178] Narcyza Żmichowska, *Pisma Gabryelli* (Warsaw: Jan Jaworski, 1861), vol. II, 177. Cf. Eisenbach, *Kwestia równouprawnienia Żydów w Królestwie Polskim*, 339.

[179] Similarly, Rabbis Mannheimer and Sachs took part in the funerals of demonstrators and victims of the revolution of 1848.

Jastrow's first sermon in the collection we have described above[180] is dedicated to the souls of those who died on February 27. It is preceded by a prayer in which Jastrow lists the victims' names— Marceli Kurczewski, Zdzisław Rutkowski, Michał Arcichiewicz, Karol Brendel, and Filip Adamkiewicz—and calls them co-brethren. He prays for them in the following words: "Merciful Father, hear our wishes, answer our prayers for eternal salvation of their souls... "[181] Such affirmation of the unity of the fate of Christians and Jews in both earthly and eternal life was Jastrow's contribution to the Polish-Jewish fraternization in that period, and possibly even a positive exception in the long history of Jewish-Christian relations in the Polish lands before the nineteenth century.

Jastrow also stressed in the sermon that a fundamental doctrine of Judaism was the equality of all people. He called the miseries of the existing divisions not only the fault of people, but God's will.

> God is the righteous Judge of the world and He degraded this country in his unsurpassed wisdom, the country of our fathers in which we have lived for centuries, our homeland, through division and bifurcation of those who could be happy in unity. But likewise He will lift our country as we have given such great and memorable proof of our return to God and His commandment of brotherly love; when our country has shown the whole world, openly, under the tent of the sky, an example of union and fraternization of all its sons so rare in history, of wonderful reconciliation of all the divided children of one mother.[182]

Jastrow believed that people, Jews and Christians alike, could maintain this state of fraternity through brotherly love and tolerance, that there should be faith in "the ineffaceable nucleus of a noble and good element in man."[183] He considered Abraham an example of real tolerance. The idea of equality and the "reflection" of God in every

---

[180] It is entitled "Modlitwa i kazanie miane podczas nabożeństwa żałobnego odprawionego w d. 27. Adar (9 Marca 1861) za dusze ofiar poległych dnia 27. Lutego t. r.," in Jastrow, *Kazania*, 13–23.

[181] Jastrow, *Kazania*, 16.

[182] Ibid., 18.

[183] Ibid., 21.

man was born in reform circles in the nineteenth century and became the basis for contemporary interfaith dialogue.[184]

However, according to Jastrow it was necessary to tend this state of fraternity, tolerance, and love in order to rid oneself of imperfections and learn to correct mistakes. To him, the remedies for these shortcomings were mainly education and learning—pillars very close to Jastrow, though to him completely underdeveloped in the community of Warsaw Jews:

> Brothers in Israel, the time has come to teach and educate our children more than ever, to show the gratitude of our hearts to the country, with actions and sacrifice. For hospitality? No! Rather for the love with which the country welcomes us; and may educating the mind be our gratitude.[185] For as wise men say, "where the mind learns, God is, and His Temple, and the Ark of His covenant, and repetition of the truth revealed on Mount Sinai." (Berakhot 33a)[186]

According to Jastrow, the progress of all people (one of the main categories of the Reform movement in Judaism) depended on learning and knowledge that led to discoveries of God and brotherly love. Education, however, should not facilitate withdrawal from Judaism: on the contrary, when Jastrow spoke about education he also meant the study of Jewish history and Jewish tradition. The purpose of studying one's own tradition was to help find one's roots and the deep meaning of the rich Jewish religious tradition. Jastrow believed that examining ancient rituals would reveal the deepest essence of the Torah, which may seem empty and inexplicable to the uneducated and unversed.[187] In his opinion, the past was "our strength," which

---

[184] This was also noticed in the United States, where Jastrow was considered a pioneer of interfaith dialogue. See Yaakov Ariel, "American Judaism and Interfaith Dialogue," in *The Cambridge Companion to American Judaism*, ed. Dana Evan Kaplan (Cambridge: Cambridge University Press, 2005), 327.

[185] Jastrow, *Kazania*, 22. We will find similar content in the section of sermon in the Ossolineum. Zakład Narodowy im. Ossolińskich, manuscript, fo. 13079/II, 26–28.

[186] Quoted after Jastrow, *Kazania*, 22.

[187] Ibid., 30.

"brightened the present times, and whoever rejected the past would not have the motivation to sacrifice themselves for the future and the whole community."[188] An important point of his philosophy was that, "…All instruction, when it is real and not feigned, leads man to God."[189] Jastrow tried to put these words into action and, despite the fact that he was very busy in Warsaw, made an effort to find the time for academic work. During his office, he wrote two articles and one review, all of which were published in *Monatsschrit für Geschichte und Wissenschaft des Judenthums*.[190]

In the sermon delivered on the first day of Passover 5621 (1861), Jastrow stressed that in "our country," where the Jews had found hospitality a long time previously, "the light of love has also now risen toward us," and he hoped that all prejudice and stereotypes regarding the Jews and their religion would soon disappear. He noted that there was a change taking place among the Poles, who were allowing the Jews to "co-participate in deciding on the fate of the country."[191] Jastrow linked this participation in the country's fate with the responsibility and patriotism of Poles of the Mosaic faith. This is particularly visible in his statements after the bloody events of April 1861, in which he said that he had noticed an improvement in attitudes toward the Jews. He believed it was important to unite merchant guilds and allow Jews to join craft guilds.

> Not long ago, there was such darkness between us—the children of Israel—and our fellow countrymen, that we could not see or recognize each other! Blindness was dividing those who should have been connected by one land and one love, one desire and one goal.[192]

---

[188] Ibid., 74–77.

[189] Jastrow, "Kazanie miane w pierwszy dzień Święta Szałasów (Sukot) r. 5622 (dnia 19 Września 1861 r.)," in his *Kazania*, 107.

[190] Marcus Jastrow, "Das Zusammenwirken Easra's und Nehemia's," *MGWJ* VII (1858): 72–80; Marcus Jastrow, "Erklärung des vierunddreissigsten Kapitels im Jecheskeel," *MGWJ* X (1861): 111–117; and Marcus Jastrow, "Saisset über die Philosophie der Juden" [review], *MGWJ* XI (1862): 204–205.

[191] Jastrow, *Kazania*, 35.

[192] Ibid., 57.

According to Jastrow, fraternization was a victory of "light and truth." Appreciative of these changes, he asked what Jews could offer in return, and ascertained that the only thing they could do was "suffer together with their brethren," with the Christian citizens of Warsaw.[193]

Jastrow stressed again that in order for the Jews to be able to participate fully in the life of the country, access had to be obtained to "the door of real learning," which was closed to them. Even those who understood and used the Polish language did so in spite of many obstacles, and mainly through hard work. Jastrow believed that universal education should be received by all Jews, "because no community deserves to exist without the strength of character, education, and learning; it will not live to prosperity."[194] Jastrow also reiterated that "friends [of the Jews]" were pointing out the Israelites' need for a new type of education and upbringing, appropriate for the spirit of the time, in order to reform and revive. Such education should be aimed mainly at youth. He remarked, though, that the new type of education was not and could not be contrary to the Teachings of Israel, "whose light has spread to all nations." Instead, he said, "let us build an edifice full of light, an edifice of knowledge and learning based on our Teaching."[195] To Jastrow, there was no contradiction between traditional religion—"the teachings of Israel"—and the achievements of the modern world. What is more, he actually encouraged his listeners to actively participate in the world through education and social, cultural, and work relations. Jastrow considered everyone who opposed those views an enemy of the true faith of Israel:

> Anyone who says that the spirit of education is not compatible with the spirit of our ancient Teachings, and that for that reason one must renounce all progress, truly may not know that he harbors a woeful disregard for our Teachings under the cover of piety and religion. Whoever is afraid that the light of knowledge and education will eradicate the light of his faith, instead

---

[193] Jastrow, "Pierwsze po 8 Kwietnia kazanie miane w Sobotę dnia 20 Kwietnia 1861," in ibid., 45–46.
[194] Ibid., 49.
[195] Ibid., 58–59.

of being a defender of and warrior for faith, is, perhaps inadvertently, its dangerous enemy.[196]

The Yom Kippur sermon delivered by Jastrow in 1861 is of particular significance to the issue of the impact of the Reform movement and its ideology.[197] In this sermon, he unequivocally stressed the equality of all people called to build the City of God. He believed that every nation, society, and individual is entrusted with carrying out a certain part of this plan. He remarked, however, that humanity still had a lot to do before its work could be considered complete. Humanity was thus treated by Jastrow as God's tool, carrying His light. Neither in this sermon nor in any other is there any reference to a personal Messiah, who was replaced with messianic times in Reform Judaism.[198]

Another interesting issue is the lack of references to the Temple in Jerusalem, which is so crucial for the symbolism of Yom Kippur. Jastrow used a typical Reform term for the synagogue—God's temple. I shall quote an abstract from this sermon, as it raises very important issues:

> Today, having rejected the everyday dress of our sensual life and dressed in a festive robe of purity, as the high priest once did, we enter the *Kodesh Hakodeshim* on the holiday of the temple of our hearts. Today, we return to the knowledge that we are God's ministers, chosen by Him to fight prejudice, error, falsehood, and lies wherever they prevail; to spread pure knowledge of the One and Only. Today, we celebrate the day of atonement with all our fellow brothers when we enter God's temple with a joyous feeling of forgiveness for everyone who has ever hurt us either with words or actions; today, we once again hallow the great brotherly covenant with humanity, which is only one, as is the One God that rules it. Today, we feel closer than ever

---

[196] Ibid., 60. Wodziński sees references to Hasidim here, but this remark made by Jastrow was probably directed at the broader milieu of traditional Jews. See Wodziński, *Oświecenie żydowskie*, 188.

[197] Jastrow, "Kazanie miane w Dzień Ublagania (Jom Kippur) 5622 r. dnia 14 Września 1861 r.," in his *Kazania*, 79–95.

[198] See the example platforms of Reform Judaism in Michael A. Meyer and W. Gunther Plaut, *The Reform Judaism Reader: North American Documents* (New York: UAHC Press, 2001).

to the City of God, to whose realization the whole of humanity is called; today we feel more profoundly than ever that every nation, every society, and every individual has been entrusted with a part of that incredible role. ...Much labor remains for humanity, as its work has not yet been completed.[199]

In his next sermon, prepared for Sukkot, Jastrow refers to the synagogue as "God's Temple," deserving of "age-old" dignity and solemnity, which should stem from the internal need to respect "the tabernacle of prayer and instruction."[200] He also touches upon the important issue of equality before God of all people living in one land:

> True happiness and the tabernacle of joy before God are to be found under the cover of equality of all, under care for the master and the servant, the local and the foreign, the Levite and the orphan and the widow.[201]

This may also be related to Jastrow's rejection of the idea of rebuilding the Temple in Jerusalem.

Jastrow the Revolutionary

The year 1861 was a landmark for Jastrow in terms of his patriotic activity and his work in the cause of Polish-Jewish fraternization. After the funeral of the five victims of the demonstration on Krakowskie Przedmieście, Jastrow continually spoke out against the Russian occupation and the barbaric treatment of Poles and Jews alike. The idea of fraternization and the unity of the fates of the two nations became the subject of almost all of his sermons and publications in the press. Unfortunately, however, many of them were lost or confiscated by the censors and the authorities. For this reason, his work entitled *Die Vorläufer des polnischen Aufstandes. Beiträge zur Geschichte des Königreichs*

---

[199] Jastrow, "Kazanie miane w Dzień Ubłagania (Jom Kippur) 5622," in his *Kazania*, 86–87.

[200] Jastrow, "Kazanie miane w pierwszy dzień Święta Szałasów (Sukot)," in ibid., 99.

[201] Ibid., 103.

Polen von 1855 bis 1863 is very valuable.[202] Jastrow's articles, which were published anonymously in the Berlin *National-Zeitung*,[203] constitute the basis of the book. Those articles, Jastrow wrote in the introduction, received "much praise" from both Polish and Jewish readers. He regarded the volume as an aid for future researchers of these events, but through it he also "wanted to [...] communicate to German society information about the little-known and often negatively judged internal relations in Poland."[204] Jastrow did not limit his activity to working toward Polish-Jewish fraternization, though. He also wanted his actions to win the support of the German public, and thus often used the expression "we Germans."[205]

Jastrow's book is not only in effect a history of the Kingdom of Poland from 1831 until 1863, supported by his extensive knowledge; it is also a story of his involvement and views of the events he described. Thus, it is a sort of diary of a witness of those times, and as such it is of more interest to us.

To Jastrow the events preceding the January Uprising, especially those of 1861, were a "spiritual uprising." In his opinion, the Poles' hatred of the Jews and the Germans was based on nationalism, not religion. While the Germans assimilated, the Jews remained enemies. What is new in this later work is Jastrow's view that there were certain mistakes made by the Jews which contributed to their bad reputation. According to him, an example of such a mistake was the Jews' attitude during the November Uprising, when they "supported the Russian army with deliveries and espionage. [...] The reason and consequence created a vicious circle. The Jews became Russian spies because they were persecuted by the Poles, and they were persecuted by the Poles because they were Russian spies."[206] In return, not only did Tsar Nicholas I not grant the Jews equal rights, but he also tightened the laws against them and began conscripting Jews into the Russian

---

[202] [Marcus Jastrow], *Die Vorläufer des polnischen Aufstandes. Beiträge zur Geschichte des Königreichs Polen von 1855 bis 1863* (Leipzig: Otto Wigand, 1864).

[203] See *National-Zeitung*, Berlin, June-November 1863.

[204] [Marcus Jastrow], *Die Vorläufer des polnischen Aufstandes*, II–III.

[205] Ibid., see, for example, 45.

[206] Ibid., 25–26.

army. That situation was experienced by many Jews, and according to Jastrow the change of their stance visible after 1861, despite the "Jewish war" of 1858, fueled by the government and censorship, was a consequence of that experience.[207]

Jastrow attributed the change of the overall spiritual situation in Poland to prominent Polish exiles, particularly Mickiewicz, Lelewel, Słowacki, Krasiński, and Mochnacki, as well as their ability to speak to young people, bourgeois, and tradesmen.[208] He had a positive opinion of the role of the clergy and the Church—not as a religion, but as a place where patriotic ideas could flourish. He wrote,

> Never was Poland less bigoted and less intolerant than when all of its prayer houses of all denominations reverberated with patriotic speeches and nationalistic songs, and when Catholic processions and pilgrimages were accompanied with political emblems.[209]

To Jastrow, this spiritual passion had an obvious religious, but not denominational, basis. He noted that the first patriotic demonstration in August 1860 was of a religious nature and was connected with the death of the widowed wife of General Józef L. Sowiński, who was killed in 1831. Thereafter, churches began organizing services for the anniversary of Tadeusz Kościuszko's death (October 15) and the anniversary of the outbreak of the November Uprising (November 29). According to Jastrow, such ceremonies and demonstrations affected the lower strata of society. In his book, he devoted much attention to the days preceding the tragic demonstration of February 27, 1861, which he witnessed himself:

> [On February 27] the procession set off from the Old Town and increased in size as passers-by joined it. The singing alternated with calls for unity and fraternization of all estates and denominations, and the Catholic character of the procession disappeared as increasing numbers of people, including both Protestants and Israelites, voluntarily heeded the call to join. To

---

[207] Ibid., 27–28.
[208] Ibid., 46–47.
[209] Ibid., 50.

the surprise of the governor, the group marched past his residential castle and finally reached Krakowskie Przedmieście and the Warsaw Boulevard. The crowd came upon a closed-off street there, so they neatly turned into a side street and continued the procession, leaving the soldiers behind. It then accidently encountered a funeral procession, which swelled the crowd and, at the same time, irritated the soldiers, who obstructed the cortege. They broke the cross being carried ahead of the coffin, and assaulted the priest who was leading the funeral. Even the leaders of the nation could not have found a better way to ignite the passion of the crowd. Stones were thrown at the soldiers, who responded with fire, and five people fell. The crowd did not step back, as if they were awaiting more casualties.

When it comes to courage for martyrdom, where it is necessary for the national cause and its manifestation to sacrifice one's life without reluctance or even consideration of the benefits, a Pole may only be compared to the first Christians, who found the greatest delight of the soul and merit in dying for their cause. Passive martyrdom becomes a certain obsession in the Polish nation when its nationalist or religious feelings are awakened. Martyrdom ceases to be a means and becomes an end in itself. In such cases, nationality and religion mix in the simple man's mind; Poland becomes a lamb to the slaughter, crucified for humanity, etc. This martyromania can explain the fact that Warsaw and other Polish cities saw blood, the blood of the defenseless, flowing in the streets, before the outbreak of the armed uprising. A Russian soldier shoots even when there is no need—at the defenseless. The Polish obsession with martyrdom allows the agitated to face death proudly. On April 8 [1861], when the Russian troops were moving from the castle and firing at the five streets leading out of there, I saw a woman praying on her knees in front of the Bernardine church, about 20 steps away from the rifle bores. One bullet hit her in that position and blood stains were visible in front of the church even the following day. …

Five dead bodies with open wounds were carried by the respectful crowd; the military leader removed his helmet. The crowd approached the French and British consulates, the casualties were shown to the representatives of the Western empires, and the consuls exchanged a few sentences. The aim of inspiring the compassion of the West was for the West to raise its voice not only against Saint Petersburg, but also against Europe, because

Chapter 2. Jastrow in Warsaw, 1858–1862

Henryk Pillati, *Pogrzeb pięciu ofiar manifestacji w Warszawie w 1861 roku* [Funeral of five victims of the demonstration in Warsaw in 1861]. Jastrow is seen standing behind the Catholic priests.

Aleksander Lesser, *Pogrzeb pięciu ofiar manifestacji w Warszawie w roku 1861* [Funeral of five victims of the demonstration in Warsaw in 1861]. Jastrow is standing next to Rabbi Meisels.

the voice of Europe meant more in Saint Petersburg than millions of subjects did.

The crowd felt directed by a strong, though invisible, hand, and gained trust in themselves and their cause. A peculiar joyous awareness fell on all the residents of Warsaw. The mourning of the deaths of five innocent victims was displaced by the hopeful conviction that their blood would break the tightly closed barricades of bureaucracy and pave the way for the voice of a people governed by despotism to reach the throne and heart of the tsar. In that conviction, the people of Warsaw adopted a calm, dignified demeanor, which would have brought honor to a free nation, but was astounding in the case of a nation oppressed for so long. No concourse, no screams—nothing disturbed the peace of the day.[210]

According to Jastrow, the funeral itself was a non-denominational, even ecumenical event, of which he provided a detailed description. It is worth remembering that Jastrow himself was present at the funeral, as depicted in the previously mentioned two paintings.[211] He described it as follows:

...: n the early morning of March 2, thousands of people [marched] in grave solemnity to the Holy Cross Church on Krakowskie Przedmieście, where five coffins were placed the evening before, after having been displayed in premises accessible to the public. ...The door was opened at 10 a. m., and the archbishop came out with the bishops. Then, despite the pressing crowd, the five black coffins, with white nails spelling the names of the victims, were carried out in profound silence. The coffins were decorated with crowns of thorns and palm fronds, and carried by representatives of various social strata, according to a set program.

Guilds with their standards, charitable organizations, and educational institutions queued up beforehand, and everyone set off when the sound of the bells announced that the funeral procession was setting out to the lugubriously decorated city.

---

[210] Ibid., 61–63.

[211] See the paintings of Aleksander Lesser and Henryk Pillati.

Chapter 2. Jastrow in Warsaw, 1858–1862

The elite of the Catholic clergy and the highest clergymen and preachers of both Evangelical Reformed churches walked immediately ahead of the coffins; Jewish rabbis with their heads covered walked behind the coffins, in accordance with their tradition, led by members of the funeral committee. Further back, members of the Agricultural Association, the only representatives of the state, walked in closed ranks in the middle of the street. On pavements and squares along the streets on the route of the procession stood the citizens of Warsaw, squeezed together and displaying signs of mourning on their hats and sleeves, as well as people of all estates, genders, and denominations who had come in from surrounding areas. [...]

The procession moved without any disturbance, often along narrow streets between houses draped with black or black and white rugs; behind the closed windows, one could see figures of women bent in profound sadness.

The city's character, with its clear-cut social gradation, changed completely due to the overwhelming sense of mourning, which was at the same time a celebration of victory.[212]

Not only does Jastrow highlight the patriotic dimension of the event but he also, or perhaps above all, describes the Polish attitude toward the Jews. He notes that Poles—even those who would have shouted anti-Jewish slogans not too long beforehand—were clearly glad that the Jews participated in the ceremony. Jastrow wrote that their attitude might have been defined as overzealous "fraternization" then, but "[t]oday, they sheltered a Jewish child lost in the crowd to cheer it up and take it to a safe place. One would pre-empt another with politeness toward "the Old Testament brethren," as if they wanted to sweeten previous wrongdoing to the oppressed."[213] The manifestation the funeral became was the first instance in Polish history of clergymen of all denominations meeting at a grave and attending a funeral ceremony in their liturgical vestments, in accordance with their rituals.[214]

---

[212] [Marcus Jastrow], *Die Vorläufer des polnischen Aufstandes*, 71–72.

[213] Ibid., 73.

[214] Jastrow wrote: "One of the most talented historical painters of Poland took it upon himself to picture that moment in a large painting in order to show proper appreciation of the events, as this would be the most pronounced expression of denominational reconciliation; future turbulence prevented

Jastrow saw the event as an inspiration to implement fraternization between all estates and denominations—first in Warsaw and then in the whole Kingdom of Poland and the lands of the partitioned Poland. That special atmosphere was intensified during the funeral services on March 9,[215] which were organized in Catholic and Protestant churches and in synagogues. The major themes of those services were fraternity, concord, peace, and order.

> During the early euphoria about the movements, and before there was statutory representation of the nation's interest, it took words and grand demonstrations often devoid of inner truth to proclaim fraternization, and that required pulpits and churches of all denominations, which at the same time represented different or at least not yet completely united ethnicities.[216]

Patriotic services continued for several more months.[217] According to Jastrow, that "moral" and spiritual movement not only had a positive effect in the Kingdom of Poland and in the Polish lands, but it was also noticed abroad—particularly in Germany, where it commanded respect and sympathy. The atmosphere of euphoria ended after 40 days (beginning February 27), a number based on biblical events. Jastrow compared the events and the spirit of freedom of that period to the events of 1848 in Prussia (when he was a student at a gymnasium in Poznań): "Anyone among us who sat at a desk in a German school in 1848 can probably still remember that the political movement was trying to infiltrate the gymnasiums too."[218]

Jastow devotes the following chapters to a detailed presentation of the internal situation in the Kingdom of Poland between April and August. He almost completely passes over the issue of Polish-

---

him from finishing and publishing the painting." (Ibid., 73). This was probably written about Aleksander Lesser, who completed his painting only in 1867, a year after Jastrow had left Warsaw.

[215] On the eighth day following the funeral itself.
[216] [Marcus Jastrow], *Die Vorläufer des polnischen Aufstandes*, 75.
[217] Ibid., 139.
[218] Ibid., 122.

Jewish relations, focusing instead on the underground activity of contemporary formations. He seemed to have favored the Black Party, as it was ideologically closer to him in seeking "enlightenment of the nation." He also profiles a secret pamphlet encouraging participation in the election, which could be used to introduce reforms in the spirit of mutual understanding and reconciliation.

> Nothing—says the secret pamphlet about these elections—is needed more by this country at the moment than unity and concord; this is what we must all strive for, because only this can revive us. At a moment as important as this, that with which the majority is in accord is the rule for all; whoever breaks rank recklessly will lead the country to undoing. Therefore we are calling all who love their fatherland not to allow themselves, in their fever of enthusiasm, to turn away from what society currently considers beneficial. We are talking about the district and municipal council elections. Participation in these elections and their fair conduct, so that men of civic courage, intelligence, and energy are chosen, is the duty of every decent citizen. It is not about adopting or rejecting reforms, as council elections are in themselves not reform, but about coming to a point from which we can attain reforms adequate to the needs of the country, and it is this point that we must make use of. Do not be deceived by appeals that are not well thought out, even though they stem from love for the fatherland and other noble motives. The country needs above all organization, mutual understanding, reconciliation, and similar work, even if in different directions.
>
> Even though municipal councils are not characterized by great effectiveness in their scope of work, they may become meaningful if we choose men who love their country and can, with strong will and hard work, bravely represent its needs and wishes. Let us therefore strive for the elections to actually take place, and for a situation in which we do not need to be ashamed of our elects and we can count on them. This is not the time for protests and words; we need actions, organization, and work. The more difficult the future, the more effort must be put into working it out. Unity and concord for the fatherland are of utmost importance.[219]

---

[219] Ibid., 144–145.

Another important event to which Jastrow pointed was the funeral of Archbishop Antoni Melchior Fijałkowski, who participated in the funeral of the five victims of the incident of February 27 and actively worked toward Polish-Jewish fraternization. Jastrow went to the main office of the archbishop with Rabbi Meisels on October 9 to pay homage to the deceased.[220] The funeral took place on October 5, and it too became a political and religious manifestation of the union of all estates and denominations.

Jastrow's extensive knowledge of the internal affairs of individual formations suggests that he had already been involved in conspiracy at that stage. He understood the importance of education for the anticipated reforms and noticed that education was thriving especially in the provinces, despite Muchanow's bans and the lack of Wielkopolski's new draft reform. Jastrow wrote that there was growing enthusiasm for learning in all towns, even among those who would previously only have indulged in pleasure:

> In a word—through work and education the Polish nation wished to attain an honorable place among the nations of Europe, which will finally, as a ripe fruit, bring it freedom. And in such an atmosphere, the city of Warsaw, and then the whole Kingdom of Poland, were surprised with the implementation of martial law on the morning of October 14, the day before Kościuszko's Day.[221]

Marital law did not stop services in the spirit of patriotism from taking place on October 15. These ended, however, in the participants being beaten and arrested, while Russian soldiers profaned and desecrated churches. Jastrow wrote that "the countenance of Warsaw was intimidating that day"; several thousand men were arrested and taken to the Citadel.[222] All the Catholic churches in Warsaw were

---

[220] There was a mention of his death in *Jutrzenka*, no. 16, October 18, 1861: 1. Earlier, on September 19, Meisels ordered all Warsaw synagogues to hold prayers for Archbishop Fijałkowski's health. Such a service most likely took place in the synagogue at Daniłowiczowska Street. *Jutrzenka*, no. 14, 1861: 116.

[221] [Jastrow], *Die Vorläufer*, 150.

[222] Ibid., 152–153. Chwalba quotes 1,500 people. See Andrzej Chwalba, *Historia Polski 1795–1918* (Krakow: Wydawnictwo Literackie, 2000), 327.

closed, ostensibly in protest but mostly to prevent further profanation. Likewise, the rabbis and representatives of the Jewish community closed synagogues and prayer houses, though they did so with the approval of the chief inspector of the police.[223] Three Jewish clergymen did not, however, avoid being arrested and taken to the Warsaw Citadel. Rabbis Meisels, Kramsztyk, and Jastrow were convicted for "active involvement in the closing of synagogues, and rebellious sermons."[224] The pretext for the arrests was the ostentatious closure of churches and synagogues, and their participation in religious and political demonstrations. According to Jastrow, though, the real reason was the integration of Catholics, Protestants, and Jews, which symbolized spiritual unity, freedom of religion, and the equality of worshippers before the law as a manifesto of the nation's will—something that Jastrow believed irritated the government the most. Thus the authorities wanted to extract from the prisoners how that interreligious alliance came into existence. Each of the arrested clergymen had to answer many questions in writing, most of them related to that issue. Through such reports, the authorities intended to learn the names of the organizers and instigators of the movement. Jastrow gave some examples of the questions: "Why did the Jews not call for the government's help if they felt persecuted by the fanatic prejudice of their Christian compatriots? What did Israelites and Protestants count on from fraternization with the Catholic majority? In what manner did fraternization occur, and who was particularly active in the process?"[225] Some prisoners, such as Rabbi Meisels, refused to submit written reports, though he advised the much younger Jastrow to write something and even helped him decide on the content. Jastrow and Meisels were together for the majority of their imprisonment in the Citadel. Their relationship grew stronger there, and his friendship with Meisels affected Jastrow's whole life.[226] During their time in prison, the apartments of the prisoners were searched, and all written

---

[223] [Jastrow], *Die Vorläufer*, 153.

[224] Ibid., 163.

[225] Ibid., 162.

[226] For more about his imprisonment in the Citadel, see A. Eisenbach and D. Fajnhauz, eds., *Żydzi a powstanie styczniowe. Materiały i dokumenty* (Warsaw: ŻIH, 1963), 196–199, passim; see also Jastrow's memoirs about Meisels, Jastrow, *Bear Meisels*.

and printed material was confiscated. Jastrow lost his records, correspondence, and the majority of his.

Jastrow's account of the search of Meisel's apartment is very interesting:

> Every little piece of paper confiscated at a detainee's house that seemed to point to fraternization became the subject of meticulous scrutiny. The translator in the court-martial, a person with a bad reputation, Jakub Tugendhold,[227] in his report on Rabbi Meisels' Hebrew documents, made note of an empty envelope which accidentally got between those documents. The seal on the envelope allegedly had a cross in the middle, and the translator concluded that this attested to the fact that the sender of the letter which no longer existed was a Catholic priest. What could a Catholic priest correspond with an Israelite colleague about if not fraternization of the religions?!
>
> The rabbi was to testify in the court-martial about the content and sender of the letter which was once in the empty envelope—neither of which he could remember—and he probably would have been forced to remember by being held on remand for longer, had he not luckily discovered that the supposed symbol of Christianity in fact belonged to the son of Mercury and was an anchor.[228]

Jastrow was arrested on the night of November 9, 1861, and taken to the Warsaw Citadel, where he was detained in a single cell for 23 days. He was allowed to move to Rabbi Meisels' cell for Hanukah, and he stayed there until the end of his imprisonment on February 12, 1862.[229] Like the other rabbis, Jastrow was convicted for taking an

---

[227] Tugendhold did not enjoy a good reputation. Bartoszewicz wrote about him that, "In another respect, as an unquestioning minion of the government, Tugendhold left behind mediocre memories," Bartoszewicz, *Wojna żydowska*, 3. For more about Tugendhold's work as an advocate of the Haskalah and director of the Rabbinical School in Warsaw, see Wodziński, *Oświecenie żydowskie*, 52–82; Wodziński, "Jakub Tugendhold and the First Mascilic Defense of Hasidism," *Gal Ed*, no. 18 (2001): 13–41.

[228] [Jastrow], *Die Vorläufer*, 162.

[229] See AJA, SC no. 5686 [27]. Jastrow wrote about his imprisonment in the Citadel with Meisels in his memoirs after Meisels' death, Jastrow, *Bear*

active part in the closing of the synagogues and for giving "rebellious patriotic sermons."[230] The three rabbis were not the only ones imprisoned or exiled to Siberia. Jastrow listed other names too—Schlenker, Krajewski, Ehrenberg, Feinkind, and Rotwand—but mentioned as well that hundreds of clergymen of many denominations faced the same fate, and pointed to the partiality and lawlessness of the courts.[231] Jewish participation in the preparations for the January Uprising and the uprising itself has been the subject of many studies.[232]

Jastrow suffered a great deal from being separated from his family, the more so as he was by then a father of twins, Wilhelm and Moritz.[233] Concern for his family was one of his primary motives in his subsequent activity. He was also upset about the confiscation of his sermons and letters. Szacki wrote that after Meisels' arrest, over a thousand letters were confiscated from his home, many of which were Jastrow's, Meisels", and Kramsztyk's correspondence with Archbishop Fijałkowski.[234]

Jastrow's arrest provoked a reaction from many of his supporters, but particularly from friends and family. His wife Bertha received letters with questions about the reasons for his arrest and suggestions that

---

Meisels, cf. Kupfer, *Ber Meisels*, 139–143.

[230] [Jastrow], *Die Vorläufer*, 163.

[231] Ibid., 164–166.

[232] For more about the involvement of Jews in the events of 1861–1864, see *Żydzi a powstanie styczniowe*; Bałaban, "Duchowieństwo żydowskie w okresie powstania 1863 r.," *Głos Gminy Żydowskiej*, no. 1 (1938); Bałaban, "Żydzi w powstaniu 1863 (Próba bibliografii rozumowanej)," *Przegląd Historyczny*, no. 2 (1938): 564–599; Abraham Duker, "Jewish Paricipants in the Polish Insurrection of 1863," in *Studies and Essays in Honor of A.A. Neuman* (Philadelphia—Leiden: Brill, 1949), 144–153; E. Friedmann, "Żydzi w epoce powstania styczniowego." *Głos Gminy Żydowskiej*, no. 1 (1938); Natan M. Gelber, "Akt zbratania polsko-żydowskiego przed powstaniem styczniowym 1863–1864," in *Almanach żydowski na rok 5678* (Vienna, 1918); Natan M. Gelber, "Zur Geschichte der Judenfrage," *Zeitschrift für Osteuropäische Geschichte* (1914): 483–512; idem, *Die Juden und der polnische Aufstand 1863* (Vienna, 1923); Jakub Szacki, "Yidn in dem poylishn ufshtand fun 1863," in *Historishe Shriftn* 1 (1929): 423–468; Kupfer, *Ber Meisels*.

[233] From August 13, 1861.

[234] Jakub Szacki, *Geshikhte fun Yidn in Varshe* (New York: YIVO, 1948), vol. II, 234. See also AJA, SC no. 5686 [34].

the Prussian consul in Warsaw should be informed about the case.[235] Heinrich Graetz became involved in the attempts to free Jastrow by intervening in Berlin and writing to Rabbi Michael Sachs, asking him to use his influence.[236] Newspapers in Prussia and Galicia reported on the arrests of Jastrow, Meisels, and others. Divided opinions from other papers were quoted, especially in *Allgemeine Zeitung des Judenthums*. Some sympathized with the arrestees, suggesting only that their sermons were too openly pro-Polish, while others pointed out that the rabbis' actions violated the law of the Kingdom of Poland, and that they meddled too much in others' affairs. The articles overall had positive overtones about Jastrow's activity and the Jewish community.[237]

Both Jastrow and Meisels were released from prison and, as citizens of foreign countries, were expelled from the Kingdom of Poland, in distinction from those like Kramsztyk, were exiled to Siberia.

Jastrow went to Breslau, where he received help from his friends, especially Heinrich Graetz, Manuel Joël, Joseph Perles, and David Rosin—lecturers from the Jewish Theological Seminary. Jastrow took with him a fork and a knife as "mementos' from the Citadel,[238] and experienced health problems of both physical and mental natures as a result of his imprisonment. These lasted for several months and were exacerbated by concerns for his family, who stayed in Warsaw.[239] On the other hand, he was comforted by his popularity in Breslau. In a letter to his wife written February 17, he wrote, "This morning a deputation of young Poles called on me and handed me an address containing many signatures."[240] Other Poles also wanted to meet with him, even offering him accommodation and maintenance. One of these

---

[235] AJA, SC no. 5686 [30–32]; see also Gelber, *Dr Moredchai (Markus) Jastrow*, 14, and *AZJ*, 26.11.1861, no. 48, 695.

[236] AJA, SC no. 5686, 2.08.1862, Berlin [33].

[237] See e. g. *AZJ*, 26.11.1861, no. 48, 694–695.

[238] Jastrow arrived in Breslau on February 12, 1862, AJA, SC no. 5686 [33].

[239] Jastrow suffered from headaches and nosebleeds, as noted in AJA, SC no. 5686 [40]. In a letter to his wife, he wrote, "I still tremble when I see a soldier. Today I noticed with trembling and a smile that an officer sat next to me at the "Golden Goose." It is the nervous consequence. I hope you will soon write, rather pay for the postage than for the sleigh to the citadel." AJA, SC no. 5686, 2.13.1862 and 2.14.1862 [34, 35].

[240] AJA, SC no. 5686 [37].

was Jan Nepomucen Niemojowski, who invited Jastrow to his estate in Śliwniki, near Kalisz, and offered him lodging for as long as he wished.[241] He sent Jastrow the following letter:

> Dear honorable compatriot of the Mosaic faith! As you have been exiled from our country, where you did so much for the Fatherland, if you stay in Prussia for longer, may you accept a stay at my house and consider it your own until this star that has been shining for us, brightens up and enlightens a complete revival...[242]

Niemojowski also made a trip to Breslau in order to meet Jastrow, who intended to accept his invitation and go to Śliwniki with his family. However, due to a change of plans, Jastrow only sent Niemojowski a photograph of himself and his wife, thanking him sincerely for the invitation.[243]

In a letter to Jastrow, his wife described the unique atmosphere in Warsaw: "Marcus, if you knew the fame that you have attained here it would repay you for all your suffering. It is something that money cannot buy."[244] Jastrow's wife mentioned that the Committee of the Synagogue was still paying her his salary. Even though Jastrow received a number of offers to work as a preacher and teacher, for instance in Toruń, Magdeburg,[245] and Königsberg, and his friends (especially Graetz) advised him against returning to Warsaw, the Committee of the Synagogue in Warsaw did not terminate Jastrow's contract and continued to pay his salary as agreed.[246]

---

[241] Jan Nepomucen Niemojowski, *Wspomnienia*, ed. and with a foreword, commentaries, and index, by Stefan Pomarański (Warsaw: Pomarański, 1925), 518. He continued, "Aside from the pleasure and honor of hosting a man with such great service in our cause, I was thinking that maybe, with his help, we could positively influence our Jewish compatriots of Poznań, who unfortunately differ from the Polish Israelites in Congress Poland in all respects." Also 518–519.

[242] Niemojowski, *Wspomnienia*, 519–520.

[243] Ibid., 520.

[244] AJA, SC no. 5686, 2.15.1862 [35].

[245] AJA, SC no. 5686 [36]; Gelber, *Dr Mordechai (Markus) Jastrow*, 16.

[246] As reported by his wife from Warsaw AJA, SC no. 5686 [37].

At the end of March, Jastrow's wife moved from Warsaw to Breslau with the children, though he stayed in contact with the members of the Committee of the Synagogue and his friends in Warsaw. Most of the letters he received emphasized his achievements as a preacher in Warsaw, and all their authors asked him to return to Warsaw, where he was indispensable. When portraying the situation of the Jews in Warsaw, Herman Meyer noted that despite a certain improvement in their legal situation, their general advancement depended largely on the Jews themselves, and there was much to be done in order to turn 800,000 Jews into valued citizens. The "hydra of Hasidism" had to be combated, and Jastrow was needed for that in Warsaw.[247] Meyer's correspondence was also of a political nature. He wrote in July 1862 that the political situation was changing, and that he hoped Jastrow would return to Warsaw before long.[248] Much was being done in Warsaw to enable his return. Mojżesz Cohn wrote that the initial permission for Jastrow's and Meisels' return had been obtained, on condition that they acquire Russian citizenship, which of course was not acceptable to them.[249] The situation forced Jastrow to look for other employment.

Jastrow became a popular figure even outside of Warsaw, and not only in Jewish milieux. In the spring of 1862, he was elected a member of the United Polish Emigration Committee, along with T. Malinowski, L. Mazurkiewicz, W. Milowicz, Z. Waryłkiewicz, and J. Wysocki.[250]

With no hope of a return to Warsaw, Jastrow began to consider employment in Germany, an option supported by his family, particularly his brothers Isaak in Rogoźno and Herman in Rio de Janeiro. They stressed that the situation in the Kingdom of Poland had become significantly more complicated, and that he, as a non-Pole, should not interfere with Polish matters, as he could be sent to Siberia.[251]

---

[247] AJA, SC no. 5686, 6.19.1862 [42].

[248] Gelber, *Dr Mordechai (Markus) Jastrow*, 17.

[249] Ibid., 18.

[250] Stefan Kieniewicz, *Powstanie Styczniowe* (Warsaw: PWN 1983), 268.

[251] See Herman's letter from Rio de Janeiro of 11.06.1863, AJA, SC no. 5686, [75]; letter from Isaak Jastrow of 10.19.1862, AJA, SC no. 5686, [68].

Chapter 3

Mannheim

There are many blanks in the story of Jastrow's life after his departure from Warsaw.[1] We know that he was waiting for some sort of a decision from Warsaw after he was reunited with his family in Breslau. For many months he continued to receive letters with contradictory information, some of which claimed that the political situation was changing and he would be able to return before long, others warning that he should not think about going back yet as it would be too dangerous.[2] In the meantime, Jastrow settled in Colberg[3] with his wife and children and began searching for a position that would ensure he could provide for his family. He learned of a rabbinic vacancy in Mannheim and immediately expressed his interest in the post, despite his contract with the community in Warsaw. This caused consternation among the Committee of the Synagogue in Warsaw, as efforts were still being made to obtain permission for his return. However, Jastrow himself had no hope of returning to Warsaw. Abraham Geiger, who represented a different ideological camp at the time, was probably the one who suggested him to the community in Mannheim.[4]

On September 6, Jastrow delivered a trial sermon in the synagogue in Mannheim. On the same day, the press reported that

---

[1]   Most information available is gleaned from copies of his correspondence in the possession of the American Jewish Archives, and this should be treated with some skepticism.

[2]   See fragments of Jastrow's correspondence with his friends from Warsaw between February and August 1862, AJA, SC no. 5686 [37–47]. Cf. Information from Warsaw included in AZJ, 08.26.1862, 493; and AZJ, 09.23.1862, 557, which contains contradictory details about the possibility of Jastrow's return.

[3]   There were a number of towns called Colberg, but here the name may refer to Kołobrzeg (German Kolberg) or Colberg near Berlin.

[4]   Heinrich Graetz disliked Geiger intensely and believed that he must have presented Jastrow in a bad light, see AJA, SC no. 5686, 07.28.1862 [46]. Cf. Gelber, *Dr Mordechai (Markus) Jastrow*, 18.

Dr. Jastrow's sermon filled the synagogue to the rafters. He was advertised as a former Warsaw rabbi known for his participation in the recent events in that city. His fame must have reached Mannheim too, for his listeners included not only members of the Mannheim community but also "numerous members of Christian denominations." The subject of his sermon was "the ethical and philosophical interpretation of the law of the Old Testament," which, according to Jastrow, should be understood not as an absolute external obligation, but rather as an appeal to the spiritual nature and will of man. He held that law was an ethical necessity.[5] Jastrow also discussed the history of his community and the Jews in Warsaw in the context of contemporary events. The author of the newspaper articles stressed that with his sermon Jastrow lived up to his reputation as an excellent preacher with substantial knowledge who presented his views with liberalism and civil courage, emphasizing in particular the tasks to be undertaken by the contemporary Jewish teacher of religion. It was predicted that Jastrow would be elected as the new rabbi.[6]

Jastrow had the same sense, and wrote to his wife that his election was highly probable: "Everyone has gone mad about me and I took a liking to the people here. They are very warm-hearted and open, like Poles."[7]

In the meantime, Jastrow received several letters from Warsaw, some of which were from Luis Mayer and Mojżesz Cohn. They contained, once again, contradictory information as to whether it would be possible for him to return to Warsaw in the near future.[8] Therefore, he accepted the post of *Stadtrabbbiner* in Mannheim with an annual salary of around 1,200 thaler.[9]

Jastrow received congratulations on his election as rabbi of Mannheim from Heinrich Graetz, Zacharias Frankel from Breslau,[10] and

---

[5] *Mannheimer Journal*, September 6, 1862.

[6] *Mannheimer Journal*, September 6, 1862, and September 7, 1862.

[7] Quoted after Gelber, *Dr Mordechai (Markus) Jastrow*, 19.

[8] AJA, SC no. 5686, [46–47].

[9] AJA, SC no. 5686, [49], letter to his wife. Cf. Gelber, *Dr Mordechai (Markus) Jastrow*, 19.

[10] See AJA, SC no. 5686, [54], and Heinrich Graetz, *Tagebuch und Briefe*, ed. Reuven Michael (Tübingen: Mohr, 1977), 237.

his family from Rogoźno[11] on September 15, a few days after the news of the election of a new *Stadtrabbiner* was published in local newspapers.[12] But even before Jastrow's investiture, which was planned for the beginning of October,[13] he received letters from Warsaw in which Mojżesz Cohn confirmed that the situation had improved enough for Jastrow to be able to return. Cohn thought Jastrow should do so, invoking the tsar's resolution granting Jastrow and Meisels permission to return to the Kingdom of Poland:

> His Imperial Majesty, Grand Duke Viceroy of the Kingdom, notified His Majesty, the Head of the Administrative Government, in a rescript of 17/29 August [1862],… that the Israelites Ber Meisels and Marcus Jastrow, foreign subjects exiled abroad for political crimes, have been granted permission by His Imperial Majesty to return to the Kingdom and that appropriate regulation has been issued for their passports to be validated for their return so that they are allowed to cross the border.[14]

Cohn wrote that Jastrow should return to Warsaw not only because his contract was still binding, but most importantly because the Warsaw synagogue could not function without him. He added that if there were any misunderstanding, Jastrow should write to the Synagogue Committee.[15] Rabbi Meisels also sent Jastrow a letter, though not directly but via his brother-in-law, Dawid Posner. He reminded

---

[11] AJA, SC no. 5686, 10.19.1862, [68], letter from Isaak Jastrow: "The relatives express their pleasure at J."s location at Mannheim. "The condition of the Jews in Poland is at present a most miserable one. In recent times a great hatred has arisen between the Poles, particularly the noblemen, and the Jews. The former are incensed at the fact that the Jews have made such advances in Poland through the trend of circumstances, whereas the newly reforms have done very little for the Poles.'"

[12] See *Mannheimer Journal*, September 13, 1862, 3, and *Mannheimer Anzeiger*, September 14, 1862.

[13] *Mannheimer Anzeiger*, October 12, 1862, reports that Jastrow arrived in Mannheim with his family on October 1, though some sources claim it was September 30.

[14] AGAD, CWW, file 1732, 38–39.

[15] AJA, SC no. 5686, 09.27.1862, [55–56]. Cf. Gelber, *Dr Mordechai (Markus) Jastrow*, 19.

Jastrow of his responsibility for his post of preacher in Warsaw and told him how many people were waiting for his return and the completion of his mission.[16] All these appeals placed Jastrow in a quandary about whether to choose the post in Mannheim, which would provide security for his family and an opportunity for him to make a career in Germany, or follow his heart and return to Warsaw.

Jastrow initially chose the appointment in Mannheim, moving there with his family on September 30, 1862, and living in the home of Jonas Meir at E2, Apartment 15.[17] The members of the Mannheim community gave Jastrow a warm welcome, portraying him not only as a courageous hero of the recent events in Warsaw but also as an advocate of religious reform, which had not yet been introduced in Mannheim.[18] They vested much hope in him with regard to the introduction of innovations. As may be expected, though, not everybody was thrilled by the idea, and opposition to him emerged almost immediately. Following his appointment, an article appeared in one of the Heidelberg newspapers highlighting Jastrow's radical views and suggesting that he wanted to shorten the fasting period on Yom Kippur from 24 to 12 hours. Jastrow's denial was published on October 9, 1862. He emphasized that abolishing or shortening the fasting period during the most important Jewish holiday was unthinkable.[19] However, this situation demonstrates that the enthusiastic opinion of Jastrow was not shared by all of the Jews in Mannheim and Baden, where the majority were traditionalists.[20]

The extent to which the conflict in Mannheim affected Jastrow's future attitude and actions is unclear. Perhaps finding himself in a quandary caused him to initiate a correspondence with the Committee of the Synagogue in Warsaw at the beginning of October

---

[16] AJA, SC no. 5686, 10.05.1862, [57–58]. Cf. Gelber, *Dr Mordechai (Markus) Jastrow*, 19.

[17] His wife Bertha and sons Moritz and Wilhelm, born on August 13, 1861, in Warsaw, were registered at the same address. See Stadtarchive Mannheim, Familienbogen (Polizeipräsidium Zug. —/ 1862).

[18] Central Archives for the History of the Jewish People, Jerusalem, P. 38, Brief aus Erfurt vom 30. Sept. 1862, 38.

[19] *Mannheimer Anziger*, October 9, 1862.

[20] Adolf Lewin, *Geschichte der badischen Juden seit der Regierung Karl Friedrichs (1738–1909)* (Karlsruhe: Kommissionsverlag G. Braun, 1909).

with the purpose of renegotiating the terms and conditions of his contract so that he would not lose his livelihood if he was banished from Warsaw again.[21] In September he had received another letter intimating that he ought not to affiliate with the Mannheim community but to return to Warsaw. Jastrow's explanation and his new conditions of return were presented during a general meeting of the synagogue members on October 12. His terms were accepted, though by a small majority.[22] Moses Orgelbrant, a member of the committee, traveled to Mannheim to inform Jastrow of its decision and try to convince him to return.[23]

Due to these new circumstances, Jastrow turned to the court of arbitration in Karlsruhe on October 20 in order to determine whether he was contractually obliged to return to Warsaw or stay in Mannheim. The judges were Rabbi Benjamin Willstätter, the publisher and bookseller Adolf Bielefeld, and the lawyer Dr. Jakob Guttmann.[24] They concluded that Jastrow "did not have any moral obligation to return to Warsaw after the amnesty and he was thus entitled to accept the offered post in Mannheim".[25] Jastrow then wrote an open letter to the Council of the Synagogue in Mannheim, in which he outlined the situation and his dilemma.[26] The letter is one of Jastrow's most moving manifestos of his attachment to the community in Warsaw.

---

[21] The Committee of the Synagogue had already sent Jastrow a letter about his return on September 2, but Jastrow did not reply to it. He may never have received it. *Jutrzenka*, no. 19, September 25, 1862: 393.

[22] "During the general meeting of the members of the Synagogue on October 12, 1862 ... the details of the case of Dr. Jastrow (who accepted an appointment as Preacher and Senior Rabbi in Mannheim) were presented. After the exposition of the terms on which Dr. Jastrow would agree to return to the pulpit in Warsaw, a vote took place and the result was in favor of Jastrow's return by a majority of 51 to 46." ŻIH Archives, *Bericht ...*, 33. Cf. *Jutrzenka*, no. 19, September 25, 1862: 393.

[23] *Jutrzenka*, no. 19, September 25, 1862: 393.

[24] *Mannheimer Anzeiger*, October 31, 1862. Cf. Lewin, *Geschichte der badischen Juden*, 298–299, 338, 322.

[25] Marcus Jastrow, *Offenes Schreiben an den Grossh. Synagogenrath in Mannheim* (Mannheim, 1862), 7.

[26] Ibid. The letter is dated November 2, 1862, and its complete contents may be found in the appendix.

On receiving the arbitration verdict, my inner spiritual light grew stronger and led me to believe that I was at a stage of dangerous self-deception, believing that I could cut those many threads which bound me to my brothers in faith in the country that has become even dearer to me through the suffering. I understood that by parting with my beloved community with a bleeding heart in the best interests of my family, I was causing greater harm with that sacrifice, as I was sacrificing myself. I have understood that my heart must bleed, my strength must weaken. Only after the seeming separation did I realize where the homeland for my spiritual strength lies and where the land in which it is rooted.

Finally, after a difficult battle, I decided to come forward with a declaration to the Honorable Council of the Synagogue and the general public that my duty to save myself orders me to return to Warsaw to my previous activity.[27]

Jastrow went back to Warsaw, "following his calling"[28] in November 1862.[29] He was truly irreplaceable there, combining the skills and knowledge of an educated preacher able to deliver passionate sermons in Polish with his teaching and organizational talents.

His *Open Letter…* is a very important and hitherto largely unknown source of information on the history of the Jews in Mannheim.[30] The fact that Jastrow's name does not appear in any studies of the Jewish community of Mannheim may be explained by the short period of time he spent there—between September and November 1862.[31] Only brief notes about his arrival, his work in, and his departure from the town may be found in the previously mentioned short articles in the local newspapers of the period. However,

---

[27] Ibid., 8–9.

[28] See also AZJ, 11.18.1862, 675.

[29] He reassumed the office of preacher in Warsaw on 11.18.1862. See *Jutrzenka*, no. 19, September 25, 1862: 393.

[30] Michał Galas, "Einmal Warschau—Mannheim und zurück. Rabbiner Marcus Mordechaj Jastrow zum hundertsten Todestag," *Jüdaica. Beiträge zum Verstehen des Judentums* 4 (2003): 289–298—includes the full original version of Jastrow's letter to the Council of the Synagogue in Mannheim.

[31] See, e. g., the list of rabbis in Mannheim in Volker Keller, *Jüdisches Leben in Mannheim* (Mannheim: Edition Quadrat, 1995), 72–77.

these few pieces of information combine to give a general picture of Jastrow's activity as a reformer and preacher who cared about the moral and spiritual condition of his co-religionists. His sudden interruption of his career in Mannheim did not have a positive effect on his future contacts with that community.

Synagogue in Mannheim, nineteenth century.

Chapter 4
Return to Warsaw, 1862–1863

Marcus Jastrow's return to Warsaw was made possible with the authorization of the tsar and through the efforts of the Committee of the Synagogue at Daniłowiczowska. It caused a big stir not only in Mannheim, but also among the Jewish and Polish population of the Prussian Partition, and naturally in Warsaw. After his banishment, Jastrow had returned to his native Rogoźno and Poznań for some time during the spring of 1862. He was already such a popular figure by then that non-Jewish Poles were also seeking his support. As reported by *Allgemeine Zeitung des Judenthums,* the Poles wanted to invite Jastrow to a demonstration in Poznań in April, while representatives of the Polish Party in Rogoźno wished to put him up as their candidate in the election to obtain the votes of the Jewish electorate.[1] Thus there was presumably also a demonstration of support for Jastrow's return.

Jastrow probably left Mannheim on November 11. Upon his arrival in Warsaw, he was greeted enthusiastically not only by the members of his synagogue but also by the Jewish and Polish residents of the city. An example of this cross-denominational euphoria was a poem entitled *"Rabin"* (Rabbi), written especially for the occasion by Mieczysław Romanowski.[2]

---

[1] *AZJ*, May 6, 1862, 243.

[2] Mieczysław Romanowski (1834–1863) was a participant in the January uprising and died in the battle of Józefów. See the poem by Mieczysław Romanowski, "Rabin," in *Żydzi w Polsce. Antologia literacka*, ed. Henryk Markiewicz (Krakow: Universitas, 1997), 244. There are more literary references hailing Jastrow, one of which is the poem by Artur Oppman (1867–1931), "Berek Jawor": " ... Pan dobrodziej Majzelsa pamięta? Pan dobrodziej nie widział Jastrowa? ..." ("Do you remember Meisels, good sir? Have you not seen Jastrow, good sir?"), Artur Oppman, "Berek Jawor," in *Księga wierszy pisarzy polskich 19-go wieku*, ed. Julian Tuwim (Warsaw: PIW, 1954), 483. See Magdalena Opalski and Israel Bartal, *Poles and Jews: A Failed Brotherhood* (Hanover–London: University Press of New England, 1992), 43, 62, 143.

In spite of the enthusiastic welcome in Warsaw, we know little about Jastrow's preaching and patriotic actions during that period. The police undoubtedly kept a close watch on him. As a person previously banished for political activity, he was not allowed to express or publish his opinions freely. However, we know from his letter to Jacob S. Raisin[3] that he conspired and was politically involved during his stay in Warsaw.[4]

Jastrow returned to his preaching and teaching work in the Lomdei Torah society and the rabbinical school with redoubled enthusiasm. He also wrote articles for *Jutrzenka* and other journals, though he did not always sign them with his name. One of his texts from that period seems to be relevant to our subject matter—a review of the first volume of the Torah as translated by Daniel Neufeld, entitled *Pięcioksiąg Mojżesza dla Żydów-Polaków* (The Pentateuch for Jews—Poles).[5] Jastrow enthusiastically welcomed the translation of the first volume of the Bible into Polish, stating that there had previously been no adequate Polish edition which would introduce Polish Jews to the arcana of the local language and education the way as Mendelssohn's Bible had for German Jews. Jastrow hoped that the translation would "significantly contribute to ending the battle between education and fanaticism."[6] Neufeld's *Pięcioksiąg* consists of three sections—a foreword, the translation proper, and the translator's notes. Jastrow commented mostly on the first and last parts, and left the translation to be assessed by others "more privy to the nature of the spirit of the Polish

---

[3] Quoted above, AJA, SC no. 5686.

[4] It is likely that Jastrow's name could not be printed due to censorship, as his name does not appear in the Jewish press after 1864. In Aleksander Kraushar, "Kartki z niedawnej przeszłości," in *Książka jubileuszowa dla uczczenia pięćdziesięcioletniej działalności literackiej J.I. Kraszewskiego*, 508, only the initial J. appears.

[5] *Pięcioksiąg Mojżesza dla Żydów-Polaków*, vol. I. *Księga Rodzaju, Genesis (Bereszyt)*. […] (Or Torah) *Światło Zakonu; Uwagi i objaśnienia gramatyczne, leksykograficzne, historyczne, geograficzne i obrządkowo religijne, do tłumaczenia polskiego Pięcioksięgu Mojżesza*, transl. from Hebrew and edited by Daniel Neufeld (Warsaw, 1863).

[6] Marcus Jastrow, "[Review of] *Pięcioksiąg Mojżesza dla Żydów-Polaków*. Vol. I, transl. from Hebrew and edited by Daniel Neufeld," *Jutrzenka*, no. 21, May 22, 1863: 204–205.

language than [him]."[7] With regard to the ancillary sections, Jastrow criticized Neufeld for his ignorance of Jewish history in writing that the Jews in Poland were descended from Jews exiled from Spain.[8] But the most important polemic concerns the issue of the attitude to the law. Neufeld wrote in the foreword that the Books of Moses, the Torah (*Księgi Mojżeszowe*) incorporates "police, hygienic, legal, religious, etc. regulations."[9] As a moderate reformer, Jastrow believed that the foundation of law and regulations "is the Israelite religion," which encompasses the entirety of man's relationship with God, his fellow man, and every other creature. He thus held that Neufeld's words should read: "There are religious regulations closely connected with the police, hygiene, the law, etc."[10] Further on, Jastrow used the term "symbolic religious regulations, such as dietary, circumcision, and other similar laws,"[11] which Neufeld rebutted, as he believed that the dietary laws and principles of circumcision were not symbols but real laws comprising many chapters in the Talmud. He claimed that they could not be compared to "those known as the commemorative laws," which related to the celebration of holy days or the wearing of *tefillin*.[12]

Jastrow's review is a significant example of the theological polemic about attitudes to the law and the Talmud that was very typical of the Reformers of that period in Germany but rare in the Polish lands. In this case, Jastrow and Neufeld—the two antagonists—suspected one another of seeking to overthrow the authority of religious law based on the Bible and the Talmud, though we can see their propensity to make concessions with regard to the customary local law, *minhagim*, which they refer to as "commemorative law."

---

[7] Ibid., 205.

[8] In his response to Jastrow's article, Neufeld retorted that there were Spanish and Italian Jews living in Zamość, and that the Hasidim follow the Sephardic rite. Daniel Neufeld, "Odpowiedź," *Jutrzenka*, no. 21, May 22, 1863: 208. To Jastrow, this was evidence of Neufeld's ignorance.

[9] Jastrow, "[Review of] *Pięcioksięgu Mojżesza dla Żydów-Polaków*," 206.

[10] Ibid.

[11] Ibid.

[12] Neufeld, "Odpowiedź," *Jutrzenka*, no. 21, May 22, 1863, 209.

Chapter 4. Return to Warsaw, 1862–1863

Jastrow's family obligations increased at the time of the January uprising, as his son Joseph was born in Warsaw on January 30, 1863.[13] Jastrow also had an accident in February, after which he needed to convalesce, but its circumstances are unknown.[14] He left for treatment in Vevey, Switzerland, and from there he corresponded with Dr. Leopold Ladeburg, who was trying to convince him to return to the Mannheim community, which had been very impressed with him. When Jastrow continued to refuse, Ladeburg asked him to choose his successor from among the other candidates who had applied for the position.[15] Jastrow suggested Dr. Bernhard Friedmann, a disciple of Geiger's, who ultimately served as rabbi in Mannheim until 1879 and introduced further reforms in that community.[16]

Following a brief stay in Warsaw,[17] Jastrow traveled to Colberg again with his family.[18] During his absence, something undefined happened in Warsaw that upset him, probably a representation of him in a negative light. However, Mojżesz Cohn wrote to him that "the person who wanted to damage his image is not credible, so no one will listen to them."[19]

Rumors about Jastrow's activity must have been widespread, as the Prussian authorities confiscated his passport when he decided to return to Warsaw, preventing him from crossing the border. This came as a shock to Jastrow, though the view in Warsaw was that it might have been another excuse of his in order to not have to return and expose himself to persecution by the Russian authorities. Cohn even wrote that it was not received well that Jastrow was not coming back, and that it was his duty to be there for Rosh Hashanah: "For you do not work for a specific person, but to earn respect for yourself, and a good

---

[13] Joseph Jastrow (1863–1944) was later a well-known professor of psychology at the University of Wisconsin–Madison.

[14] See AJA, SC no. 5686, 2.03.1863 and 2.13.1863, 63.

[15] There were five candidates. See Gelber, *Dr Mordechai (Markus) Jastrow*, 19.

[16] For more about Bernhard Friedmann, see *Biographisches Handbuch der Rabbiner*, Teil 1, 347.

[17] We know that he was in Warsaw on May 14, as he dated his review of Neufeld's translation of the Bible on that day.

[18] AJA, SC no. 5686 [65].

[19] Gelber, *Dr Mordechai (Markus) Jastrow*, 21.

reputation for your friends."[20] Despite the efforts of his friends from Berlin, Breslau, and Warsaw, Jastrow was unable to recover his passport and return to his synagogue at Daniłowiczowska Street. Having received an official refusal to issue him a passport, he informed the members of the Committee of the Synagogue—Herman Meyer, Mojżesz Cohn, Józef Cohn, Adam Epstein, and Henryk Natanson—with whom he corresponded extensively, mostly about the tragic fates of their friends who had been sent to Siberia and the future of Poland. Some of the letters probably did not reach their intended recipients, due to Jastrow's name being written on the envelope. By that time, both the Russian and Prussian authorities were interested in him, and so letters to him were subsequently addressed to Mr. S.W. Errant in Berlin.[21]

In the meantime, Jastrow received news that Abraham Geiger had left his post as Reform rabbi in Breslau, and he was encouraged to apply for the vacancy. However, he wished to avoid the situation he had been faced with in Mannheim, so he decided against it. Another reason for his decision was the fact that his friend from school and university, Manuel Joël, had applied for the job. Joel was ultimately appointed.[22]

With no prospect of going back to Warsaw, Jastrow had all of his belongings, including his furniture[23] but not his documents, letters, or sermons,[24] moved to Berlin in October 1863. He maintained

---

[20] Quoted after ibid.

[21] AJA, SC no. 5686, 69. Cf. AJA, SC no. 5686, 67. M. Cohn's letter of September 24, 1863, from Warsaw, "describes how in a talk with Adam Epstein the latter told him he had written to Jastrow and was surprised at not having received a reply. "I asked him how he addressed the letter, and when he told me it was directly addressed to you I comforted him with the fact by reminding him in all probability the letter never reached you but was confiscated by the Post authorities.""

[22] See, e.g., Leszek Ziątkowski, *Dzieje Żydów we Wrocławiu* (Wrocław: Wydawnictwo Dolnośląskie, 2000), 80; Maciej Łagiewski, *Wrocławscy Żydzi 1850–1944* (Wrocław: Muzeum Historyczne, 1997), photo 83.

[23] Gelber, *Dr Mordechai (Markus) Jastrow*, 21–22.

[24] It is not known whether these ever reached him. The only letters mentioned in the archival materials found in the US are from the time when Jastrow was in Warsaw. See also AJA, SC no. 5686, 77. On December 13, 1963, M. Cohn wrote Jastrow that he wanted to give his papers to Cohn's nephew, who was travelling to Berlin, but the nephew was too afraid, as

regular contact with the members of the synagogue, who reported on the difficult situation in Warsaw and informed him of the arrests of his colleagues and friends, among them Izaak Kramsztyk and Daniel Neufeld. They often added that Jastrow's accident was a godsend, preventing him from being arrested and exiled to Siberia.[25] Some of the members of the Synagogue Committee, including Adam Epstein and Henryk Natanson, left Warsaw for Breslau. Jastrow corresponded with Natanson about whether the Russification of Poland was possible after the failure of the uprising. Natanson thought that it was not, since Polish culture was higher than Russian, though he was concerned about the Jews submitting to Russification as they had submitted to Germanization in the Prussian Partition. He was hoping this would not be the case in the Kingdom of Poland, precisely owing to Jastrow's considerable work: "It is for you to take a leading part in the development of culture among the Polish Jews, and to culture them means under present conditions to make them loyal Polish citizens, for culture is synonymous with turning one's back on Russia."[26]

Nevertheless, Jastrow did not want to take risks, and having been warned by his family and friends from Warsaw and Breslau[27], he dismissed the thought of going back to the Kingdom and instead plunged into academic work and writing. He wrote for a number of German newspapers, including *Allgemeine Zeitung des Judenthums*[28]

---

there were inspections at the borders and his luggage might be checked. Cohn promised that he would try to find someone who would agree to take Jastrow's documents.

[25] J. Cohn's letter of October 24, 1863, may attest to that. "Last night there was another wholesale fishing. You may be happy that you are far away or else you would [have] probably fallen into the net. God help you as us." AJA, SC no. 5686, 69. Also see AJA, SC no. 5686, 10.30.1863, 72.

[26] AJA, SC no. 5686, 70–71. Natanson's letter of October 29, 1863, from Breslau.

[27] His brother Herman wrote to him from Rio de Janeiro, saying that he had read that the secretary of the Jewish Congregation in Warsaw and four members of that Congregation had been exiled to Siberia. He asked Jastrow if he was still considering his return in spite of such danger. AJA, SC no. 5686, 11.6.1863, 75.

[28] This sometimes ended in disputes with the editor, Ludwik Philippson. For an example of their correspondence, see AJA, SC no. 5686, 3.24.1864, 82; 3.25.1864, 83.

and began working on academic publications on Jewish history from the period of the Second Temple.

The first and primary reviewer of Jastrow's works was Heinrich Graetz, to whom Jastrow sent all his publications, asking for an opinion. Graetz wrote at the time that Jastrow should devote himself to literary work, as he had a clear and eloquent writing style.[29]

In April of 1864 Jastrow was informed of a rabbinic vacancy in Worms—one of the most respected Jewish communities in Germany due to the honor paid to the medieval sage Rashi,[30] who had studied there for some time. Conducting services and delivering sermons in Rashi's synagogue must have been appealing to Jastrow, but he was still dependent on the Warsaw Synagogue Committee, which continued to pay his salary. However, when he learned that there were proceedings against him for his alleged assistance in writing patriotic poems (the court in Warsaw even addressed a petition to the Prussian authorities to attend to the case),[31] it became clear to him that he could not wait for the situation in the Kingdom to improve, as any crossing of the border could result in his arrest. He therefore decided to apply for the position of rabbi in Worms. This had been anticipated in Warsaw, so M. Cohn wrote to him: "You are now going to Worms and for the present we have lost you, a great and enormous loss to us."[32] In his letter to Jastrow, Herman Meyer stressed their joint work: "In the meantime no matter in what part of the earth you may dwell you belong to us. You have worked for us and with us; you have given us many exalted moments and enjoyed them with us and finally you have suffered for us and with us. This is a strong three-fold point between us."[33]

Jastrow submitted an official request to the Synagogue Committee for the dissolution of his contract, to which he received

---

[29] See AJA, SC no. 5686, 6.22.1864, 87.

[30] Rashi's full name was Rabbi Shlomo Itzhaki (1040–1105). See Esra Shereshevsky, *Rashi: The Man and his World* (Northvale, NJ—London: Aronson, 1996).

[31] Cohn informed Jastrow of this from Warsaw, see AJA, SC no. 5686, 6.03.1864, 85. Cf. Gelber, *Dr Mordechai (Markus) Jastrow*, 23.

[32] See AJA, SC no. 5686, 6.03.1864, 85. Cf. Gelber, *Dr Mordechai (Markus) Jastrow*, 23.

[33] Herman Meyer's letter from Warsaw, AJA, SC no. 5686, 6.22.1864, 87–88.

a positive reply.³⁴ He stopped receiving his salary at the beginning of July, and on July 11 he got an official letter from Worms informing him that he had been chosen as the new rabbi and preacher of that congregation.³⁵ He bade Warsaw farewell forever, but maintained close contacts with his numerous friends for a long time thereafter. On August 8, 1864, he sent a farewell letter to Józef Ignacy Kraszewski, sending him his regards.³⁶

---

34 AJA, SC no. 5686, 6.21.1864, 87.
35 He only needed to send the required documents; see AJA, SC no. 5686, 7.11.1864, 89.
36 Jagiellonian Library Archive, no. 6508 IV, correspondence of Józef Ignacy Kraszewski, series III, letters from 1863–1877, vol. 48, 68.

Chapter 5

Worms

Worms was a congregation with great traditions—it may even be said that it was the mother of all Ashkenazi communities and moreover of the Ashkenazi rite itself, contained in the *Worms Machzor*.[1] In Jastrow's time, however, the population of Worms was about 10,000, including approximately 800 Jews, and its years of glory were long gone.[2] Nonetheless, a rabbinic post in such a place was not only an honor, but also a challenge. As in Mannheim, the Jewish community in Worms was predominantly Orthodox, with few signs of reform.

The decision about Jastrow's appointment as the new rabbi of Worms was made very quickly—his reputation was evidently known even there. The contract of the congregation's previous preacher, Dr. Isidor Rosenfeld, who had served there between 1860 and 1864, was not extended.[3] Jastrow was appointed rabbi, and arrived in Worms with his family on August 16, 1864.[4] He probably signed a fixed-term contract, as was customary at the time.

Few documents remain from Jastrow's Worms period. The primary sources of information are Samson Rothschild's study, which profiles the officials of the Jewish community of Worms from the mid-eighteenth

---

[1] Fritz Reuter, *Warmaisa. 1000 Jahre Juden in Worms* (Frankfurt am Main: Jüdischer Verlag bei Athenäum, 1987), 100–128, bibl.; *The Worms Mahzor: The Jewish National & University Library in Jerusalem, Ms. Heb. 4º 781/1*, ed. Malachi Beit-Arie (Vaduz-Jerusalem: Jewish National University Library of the Hebrew University, 1985).

[2] See ibid., 220–227, for an extensive bibliography of the history of the Jews in Worms.

[3] For more about Isidor Rosenfeld, see Rothschild, *Beamte der Wormser jüdischen Gemeinde (Mitte des 18. Jahrhunderts bis zur Gegenwart)*, 31–32; *Biographischer Handbuch der Rabbiner*, Band 2, 750–751.

[4] Jastrow registered at his address his wife, his sons—Moritz, Wilhelm, and Joseph—and Augusta Wolffssohn (probably his wife's sister). See Stadtarchiv Worms, Abt. 5, no. 5759.

century to the beginning of the twentieth century[5] (Rothschild seems to have accessed archives subsequently destroyed during the Second World War), and a few documents in the city archive. According to the information we have, Jastrow's relations with the board of the community were disharmonious from the beginning. Jastrow, who by that time had the experience and authority of a distinguished rabbi and preacher, was not willing to comply with all the directives of the members of the board, which he considered to be too traditional. The first conflict was rather startling: Jastrow apparently refused to teach religious studies to Jewish pupils in the local town school. Following a long exchange of letters full of unpleasant epithets, in which Jastrow was reminded that teaching was his duty, he finally agreed to do so, though on one condition: that he would teach the pupils outside of the school, in a different building. He was also reluctant to agree to any interference in the curriculum he would teach.[6] Perhaps he had intended to establish a school alongside the synagogue, as in Warsaw, for which he would be solely responsible—it is difficult to imagine any other reason for the conflict.

Another controversy surrounded a ceremony organized by Jastrow, without prior consultation with the board, to celebrate the opening of a new quarter in the cemetery.[7] However, the most consternation was caused, according to Samson Rothschild, when Jastrow introduced changes to *minhag Worms*—a rite established in the Middle Ages, contained in the *Worms Machzor* of 1272. According to the Worms *minhag*, "neither *Lechu Neranena*[8] nor *Lecha Dodi*[9] were sung on Friday evening." Apparently, the cantor L. Elkana once sang *Lecha Dodi* in Jastrow's presence, and the latter enjoyed it so much that from then on, Friday's Sabbath services began with *Boi Beshalom*. Samson Rothschild confirms in 1920 that this custom was continued in his time.[10] This was Jastrow's contribution to the "new Worms *minhag*" which was soon implemented in Rashi's synagogue.

---

[5]   Rothschild, *Beamte der Wormser jüdischen Gemeinde*.

[6]   Ibid., 34.

[7]   Ibid., 34–35.

[8]   Psalm 95.

[9]   The hymn is recited or sung. It was composed in the sixteenth century by a kabbalist, Rabbi Shlomo Alkabetz of Safed.

[10]   Rothschild, *Beamte der Wormser jüdischen Gemeinde*, 35.

However, these changes introduced by Jastrow were not the only ones; conflicts in the community did not abate, and some Orthodox members soon split with the congregation to build a new synagogue, known as the Levy'sche Synagogue.[11] Paradoxically, the proponents of progress and reform remained in Worms—an important place for the traditional Ashkenazi rite—and the Orthodox Jews had to look for a new location. In December 1865, Jastrow was accused in the *Rheinischer Herold* of having contacts with Freemasonry. This information—false, according to Jastrow—was also published in *Allgemeine Zeitung des Judenthums*.[12]

Despite all of these conflicts, however, Jastrow was very popular in Worms, and his sermons were particularly in demand, attracting many listeners every Sabbath. Soon after his arrival in town, he also organized a series of public lectures on ancient Jewish history. They took place in the "Worret'scher Saal," and were frequently attended by Christians too. The lectures, twelve in total, were published in 1865 under the title *Vier Jahrhunderte aus der Geschichte der Juden von der Zerstörung des Ersten Tempels bis zur Makkabäischen Tempelweihe*,[13] and they comprise Jastrow's first major academic publication. As always, before publishing Jastrow sent the manuscript to Heinrich Graetz, asking him for an opinion, which initially was not enthusiastic. Graetz wrote that he had read the lectures carefully and his "opinion [was] that [he had] no opinion about them."[14] He wrote that the lectures were generally interesting, especially where Jastrow drew parallels with contemporary Jewish history, but that he did not really know how a work prepared as a series of lectures would be received by experts and sophisticated readers. In addition, Graetz noted that certain parts of the lectures, particularly those referring to prophecy, might be considered heretical by Jastrow's neighbors Samson Raphael Hirsch and Marcus Lehman, advocates of neo-Orthodoxy. Graetz also pointed out a few factual mistakes and ended his letter with an admonition that, "when you go to print your work you must make clear that these are

---

[11] Reuter, *Warmaisa*, 164.

[12] *AZJ*, December 19, 1865, 788.

[13] Marcus Jastrow, *Vier Jahrhunderte aus der Geschichte der Juden von der Zerstörung des Ersten Tempels bis zur Makkabäischen Tempelweihe* (Heidelberg: Ernst Carlebach, 1865).

[14] Graetz, letter of March 28, 1865, AJA, SC no. 5686, 92.

lectures, for you will then be able to ask forgiveness for the occasional preacher's manner natural to a theologian."[15]

However, the review written by Graetz after the publication of the lectures was much less critical. He began by saying that readers needed to take into consideration the fact that the book was based on lectures and that the author did not always adhere to academic parameters. He stressed that there were also advantages to such an approach, as Jastrow often made comparisons between ancient times and the contemporary situation. Graetz particularly praised the chapter about the Book of Esther, in which Jastrow set forth his own interesting thoughts. Graetz recommended the book to all readers, both laymen and scholars.[16]

The publication was also noticed by Isaac Leeser, who reviewed it positively in *The Occident and American Jewish Advocate*. Moreover, in what Graetz had called parallels with modern history Leeser saw Jastrow's view of the reforms in Judaism and Israel's mission in the world. Jastrow wrote that it was the mission of Israel to disseminate faith in the one and only God among all people without discrimination. In his opinion, the equality and unity of all people depended only on their moral demeanor. Through Providence, which leads humanity to constant moral progress, everyone should ultimately recognize the one true God. Jastrow also believed that when love reached all people, there would be no more wars and peace would prevail, and that reforms in Judaism should follow the direction of internal spiritual development:

> It must have been not so long ago, or the time has not yet completely passed, when we Jews believed that we would win the respect of others and equality of rights by putting aside everything that could distinguish us as belonging to some other religious body, and by copying all of the customs of our neighbors. The desire for reform, often manifested in the granting to Judaism of a dignified external form, has often been confused with, or exchanged for, the need to imitate others; and we had to make many mistakes before we arrived at the conclusion that we need to reform ourselves from within on our own territory and renew our spirit, the spirit of Judaism.[17]

---

[15] AJA, SC no. 5686, 3.28.1865, 93.

[16] See MGWJ, 1866, 237–238.

[17] See *The Occident and American Jewish Advocate* 24 (1866): 470–471.

These two postulates—the mission of the Jews in the world, and reform not only in external matters but also in the spiritual sphere—accompanied Jastrow throughout his life. It is not surprising that having read Jastrow's work, Isaac Leeser recommended it for publication in the United States. The lectures were published in installments in the *Hebrew Leader*.[18]

Three children were born to Jastrow in Worms—the twins Carl Eduard and Johanna Maria in 1864,[19] and a daughter, Alice Esther,[20] in 1866.

In spite of his substantial popularity,[21] Jastrow did not feel comfortable in Worms for at least two reasons: conflicts in the congregation, and police surveillance. The police did not cease to be interested in Jastrow's past and they observed him incessantly.[22] For that reason, Jastrow was considering the newly vacated position of rabbi in Vienna in 1865,[23] but when he was offered a rabbinic position in Philadelphia he accepted it without much hesitation. Almost the whole Jewish community of Worms came to hear Jastrow's farewell speech. The meeting took place in the "Wilde Mann," room because the president of the congregation deliberately ordered renovation work to begin in the synagogue at the same time.[24]

---

[18] Articles comprising six of Jastrow's lectures were published under the title "Sechs Vorlesungen über die Geschichte der Juden von der Tempelweihe bis zum Tode Jochanan Hyrkana (164–106 v. Chr.)" in the *Hebrew Leader* between July 1867 and May 1868.

[19] On December 5, 1864. See Stadtarchiv Worms, Geburtsregister Worms 1864, Abt. 12, no. 372 and 373.

[20] On July 9, 1866. See Stadtarchiv Worms, Geburtsregister Worms 1866, Abt. 12, no. 277.

[21] Rothschild quoted a few anecdotes and wrote that Jastrow was renowned for his great sense of humor. "When there was a long period without rain in 1864 or 1865, an Orthodox member of the congregation turned to Jastrow reproachfully: "Why did you not order recitation of the Psalms in this difficult time? They were recited in the Bible." Jastrow asked, "Have you ever heard of it raining in the Bible?" Another time Jastrow visited Hochheim, near Worms, with a few men. When they sat down in a garden restaurant, Jastrow asked: "Do any Jews live here?" "No!" "I would like to be a rabbi here."" See Rothschild, *Beamte der Wormser jüdischen Gemeinde*, 35.

[22] Some police files on Jastrow survived in the archives: Stadtarchiv Worms, Abt. 13, No. 477.

[23] See AJA, SC no. 5686, 5.04.1865, 94.

[24] Rothschild, *Beamte der Wormser jüdischen Gemeinde*, 36.

Part II

The United States of America

Chapter 6

Congregation Rodeph Shalom

At the beginning of the nineteenth century, Philadelphia was one of the largest centers of Jewish life in the United States, though its Jewish population was smaller than it was by the end of that century. The Jewish population in the early years of the nineteenth century was less than 500, but it grew to 1,000 in 1830;[1] 1,800 around 1846; and almost 10,000 by the time Jastrow arrived in the 1860s.[2] And even though New York later boasted the largest Jewish population in America, Philadelphia Jews were still in the lead in developing an intellectual, spiritual, and social life that set the tone for and gave the vital spark to many Jewish organizations and associations.[3]

In the second half of the eighteenth century, there were already Ashkenazi Jews in Philadelphia, but Sephardic traditions were dominant. Sephardic and Ashkenazi Jews were members of Congregation Mikveh Israel, established around 1745 and officially founded in 1782. Conflicts regarding the rite of synagogue services began with the influx of new immigrants, mainly from German-speaking countries, who brought with them their traditional customs based on the *Minhag*

---

[1] Murray Friedman maintains that there were only approximately 500 Jews living in New York at the time. See "Introduction: The Making of a National Jewish Community," in *Jewish Life in Philadelphia 1830–1940*, ed. Murray Friedman (Philadelphia: Institute for the Study of Human Issues, 1983), 2. For more about the first centuries of Jewish presence in Philadelphia, see Edwin Wolf II and Maxwell Whitman, *The History of the Jews in Philadelphia from Colonial Times to the Age of Jackson* (Philadelphia: Jewish Publication Society of America, 1975), and Hyman P. Rosenbach, *History of the Jews in Philadelphia Prior to 1800* (Philadelphia: Edward Stern, 1883).

[2] Ibid. According to Robert Tabak, there were 15,000 Jews in Philadelphia in 1880, and as many as 70,000 in 1904. See "Orthodox Judaism in Transition," in *Jewish Life in Philadelphia 1830–1940*, 48.

[3] See Murray Friedman, ed., *When Philadelphia Was the Capital of Jewish America* (Philadelphia: Balch Institute Press; London: Associated University Presses, 1993), for the influence of the Jews of Philadelphia on the lives of American Jews.

Ashkenaz. In the mid-nineteenth century, half of the members of the congregation were immigrants from Bavaria and the Rhineland.[4] Due to differences between them, many German Jews decided to separate from Congregation Mikveh Israel in 1795 and found their own congregation. The Hebrew German Society Rodeph Shalom,[5] also known as the Congregation of German Jews, was established in 1802.[6] Rodeph Shalom comprised about 40 families of Ashkenazi origin, and was the first congregation in America to introduce the Ashkenazi rite.[7] It was stated at the very beginning of the congregation's first statute, dated 1810, that "prayers shall be performed according to the German and Dutch Rules and shall not be altered."[8] Until Jastrow arrived in 1866, Rodeph Shalom had functioned as a model German Orthodox congregation, and nothing portended change. The congregation had to move around frequently, but eventually settled in a former church building on Juliana Street.[9] Meanwhile, as the Jewish population increased, other congregations arose. Beside Mikveh Israel and Rodeph

---

[4] See AJA, SC no. 5686, 3.13.1866, 102.

[5] The congregation was known initially by its German name, "Rodef Sholem," and later as "Rodeph Shalom."

[6] Interestingly, the "deutsche Schul"—the "German synagogue," where Jastrow later worked—was established in the same year: 1802.

[7] Anndee Hochman, *Rodeph Shalom: Two Centuries of Seeking Peace* (Philadelphia, 1995), 3.

[8] Edward Davis, *The History of Rodeph Shalom Congregation Philadelphia: 1802–1926* (Philadelphia [1927]), 16. Cf. Hochman, *Rodeph Shalom*, 4–5.

[9] For more about the history of Congregation Rodeph Shalom, see also Henry Berkowitz, "Notes on the History of the Earliest German Jewish Congregation in America," *Publications of the American Jewish Historical Society* 9 (1901): 123–127; Kerry M. Olitzky, *The American Synagogue: A Historical Dictionary and Sourcebook* (Westport, CT: Greenwood Press, 1996), 313–316; Rodeph Shalom Collection, Philadelphia Jewish Archives, Balach Institute for Ethnic Studies, Philadelphia [no date]; Jeanette W. Rosenbaum, "Hebrew German Society Rodeph Shalom in the City and County of Philadelphia (1800–1950)," *PAJHS* XLI, no. 1–4 (1951–1952): 83–93; Douglas Kohn, *Two Paths of the Nineteenth-Century Synagogue Reform: Charleston and Philadelphia*, AJA, SC no. 6390; Herman Blumenthal and Elaine Blumenthal, *Rodeph Shalom … 166 Years of American Jewish Living*, AJA, SC no. 9648.

Shalom, there were also the German Congregation Beth El Emeth, the Ashkanazi Keneseth Israel, and Adath Jeshurun in 1866.[10]

Jastrow as the Rabbi and Preacher of Congregation Rodeph Shalom

It seems that the search for a new rabbi began as early as in 1865. Jastrow was approached around that time, and when he officially expressed his interest in the post of preacher in Philadelphia in April, he was immediately sent a contract, which was dated May 27, 1866. His first name was misspelt in the contract—it was written as Moses Jastrow. He was offered an annual salary of $4,000, which was a respectable figure at the time.[11]

Jastrow's arrival in Philadelphia was an important event not only for the members of Congregation Rodeph Shalom, who were just beginning a completely new chapter, but also for all of Philadelphia and American Jewry.[12] Edward Davis wrote that there was such great interest in Jastrow's arrival that several people in the crowd waiting for him at the harbor fell into the water. Similarly, so many people came to Jastrow's official welcome, to which representatives of all congregations were invited, that not everyone could fit into the space provided.[13]

Jastrow was welcomed not only as a great preacher and scholar; the congregation also remembered his participation in the struggle for

---

[10] For more about each of these congregations, see especially Henry Samuel Morais, *The Jews of Philadelphia: Their History from the Earliest Settlements to the Present Time* (Philadelphia: Levytype Co., 1894), 59–110.

[11] The original contract can be found in AJA, MC no. 517, box 2. The salary was later increased. Jastrow took up residence in Germantown, in the suburbs of Philadelphia.

[12] Bernhard Felsanthel of Chicago wrote about this to Abraham Geiger with pride. Geiger's response was, "This is a new element in Philadelphia— Jastrow is a talented preacher but he acts as if he was an Orthodox." Geiger's letter to Felsanthel of September 26, 1866, AJA, SC no. 3886.

[13] Davis, *The History of Rodeph Shalom Congregation Philadelphia*, 82. There was even a printed program for the welcome ceremony, *Programme der Einführungs-Feier, des Rev. Dr. Jastrow, Rabbiner der Rodef Sholem Gemeinde in Philadelphia, 14. September 1866*, AJA, MC no. 517, box 5.

Chapter 6. Congregation Rodeph Shalom

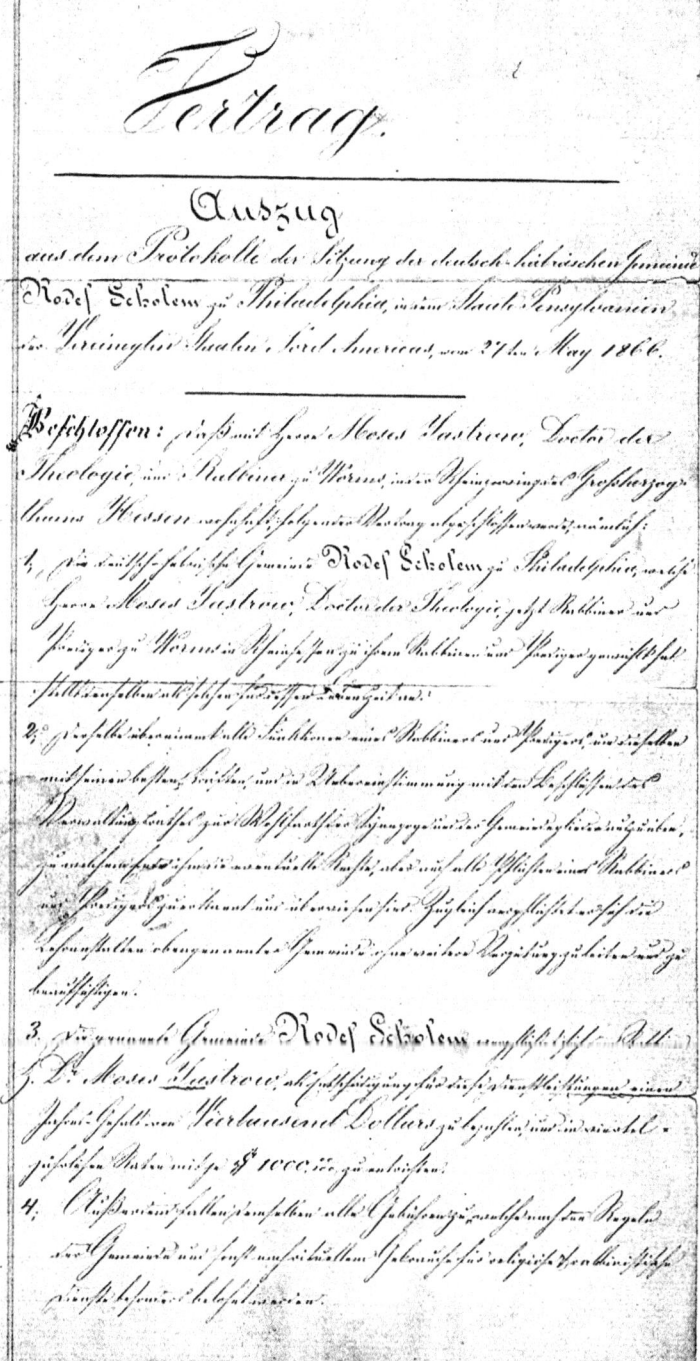

Jastrow's contract with Congregation Rodeph Shalom in Philadelphia.

Jastrow's contract with Congregation Rodeph Shalom in Philadelphia.

equal rights for the Jews in Poland, for which he had paid with his imprisonment and banishment.

His friend, Benjamin Szold of Baltimore, described Jastrow in Philadelphia in 1868 in the following words:

> Dr. M. Jastrow, who is only in the fourth decade of his life, has been known and respected in large circles in Europe for many years as a rabbi of outstanding knowledge and a true friend and defender of progress. Much incontrovertible evidence attests to

Front page of the program of Jastrow's welcome ceremony in Philadelphia, 1866.

this. Beside many articles published in a number of Jewish journals, he also enriched Jewish literature with excellent historical works.[14]

...And he portrayed his love for freedom in a beautiful light by openly joining the Polish national cause, to which, with his gripping eloquence, he also was able to convince the Warsaw community. He almost fell victim to his love of freedom, which

---

[14] He lists Jastrow, *Vier Jahrhunderte aus der Geschichte der Juden* and Jastrow, *Beleuchtung eines ministeriellen Gutachtens*; idem, *Die Vorläufer des polnischen Aufstandes*.

he professed in speeches and brochures. He endangered himself and his ideal rabbinic post in Warsaw by constantly calling on [his contemporaries] to shake off the Russian yoke; he put himself in danger of banishment, which the Russian government used for hot-blooded enthusiasts of freedom to dampen their enthusiasm. All the European newspapers at the time were full of articles about Dr. Jastrow's nationalist-liberalist activities. One French pictorial printed Jastrow's photograph among pictures of distinguished Polish men of freedom from earlier periods. A photograph of Jastrow framed with the aureole of fame of a true martyr. He exposed his freedom and existence to danger in fighting for the freedom of the oppressed nation against the violent rule of the Russian government. Happily he managed to evade imprisonment, banishment, and the loss of a very important post.[15]

Advocates of reform saw Jastrow as a backer who would contribute through his activity to the promotion of progress in America as much as in his own community. Isaac M. Wise, the editor of *Deborah*, was hoping that Jastrow would banish neo-Orthodox Jews from his congregation.[16]

Jastrow put his heart and soul into his work in the new congregation from the very beginning of his time in Philadelphia. He had an assistant rabbi, Jacob Frankel, whose role was referred to as *hazan* or, more often, as "reader." The new statutes of the congregation, prepared for the new rabbi in 1867, included the rights and duties of the rabbi and preacher. One of his most important duties was to deliver sermons in German—which was still the official language of the community—or in English every Sabbath and festival. Jastrow's sermons, some of which caused a lot of controversy, were extensively discussed in the press, though unfortunately few have survived.[17]

---

[15] Szold Benjamin, *Auch ein Wort über Jastrow und Hirsch* (Baltimore, 1868), 4–6.

[16] *Deborah*, October 26, 1868, 63.

[17] The most important sermons will be discussed later in the book. Other surviving sermons include Marcus Jastrow, *Predigt, gehalten am Danksagungs-Tage, (29. November 1866) von ... Rabbiner der Gemeinde Rodef Scholom zu Philadelphia* (Philadelphia [1866]); Marcus Jastrow, *Sermon Delivered in the Synagogue Rodef Shalom, Juliana Street on Thanksgiving Day, November 26th, 1868, by Rev. Dr. ..., published by the Congregation* (Philadelphia, 1868); Marcus Jastrow, "Simchath Torah," in *The American Jewish Pulpit, A Collection of Sermons by the Most Eminent American Rabbis* (Cincinnati, 1881), 31–39; Marcus Jastrow,

Jastrow's sermons, which were of a high standard, became a magnet attracting members of other congregations as well as Christians, though not all those who wished to attend could be admitted, due to the limited space in the synagogue.[18] This was probably the main reason for the decision to build a new, larger synagogue. Jastrow initially preached in German, but when the Board of the Congregation noted in 1869 a decline in interest in services among the youth, it was decided that Jastrow would be asked to preach in English at least once every four weeks. In addition, he was obliged to perform marriage ceremonies and funerals, and superintend children's education in the school run by the congregation. He was also required to perform other duties imposed by the Board.[19]

One of Jastrow's first suggestions bucking Orthodox customs was the suggestion to abolish the sales of positions and offices in the congregation. Subsequently he introduced gradual changes to existing rituals. In August 1867 Jastrow officiated over a confirmation service, probably of both boys and girls.[20]

At Jastrow's suggestion, in September 1867 the Board of the Congregation implemented a set of resolutions regulating proper behavior during services. They were not much different from the resolutions implemented in Jastrow's synagogue Warsaw. According to these bylaws, loitering in the synagogue before, during, and after services was prohibited. Anyone wearing a *tallit* had to put it on before entering the synagogue, and they were not allowed to remove it until the end of the service. The *tallit* needed to be clean and in good condition, and it was obligatory for those called to the Torah. Everyone was required to behave in a respectful manner in the synagogue, and

---

Der ganze Mensch, Rede gehalten Samstag, den 28. April 1888, in Rodef Shalom Synagoge in Philadelphia (Philadelphia, 1888); and Marcus Jastrow, *Turn Not to Folly Again, Sermon Delivered at the Synagogue Rodef Shalom, on Thanksgiving Day (Nov. 27, 1890)* (Philadelphia [1890]).

[18] *Deborah*, October 26, 1868, 63; December 7, 1866, 88. This was a relatively common phenomenon at the time—likewise, Jews went to Christian churches to listen to sermons and compare preachers to decide who was the best.

[19] Davis, *The History of Rodeph Shalom Congregation Philadelphia*, 83–84.

[20] See the program of the event, which took place on 9.21.1867, AJA, MC no. 517, box 5.

changing seats without the permission of the Committee was prohibited. Prayers were to be said in a low voice, according to the rabbi's instructions; reciting prayers loudly and conversing were not allowed. No one was permitted to enter or leave the synagogue during a service, and children under the age of six were not allowed to participate in services.[21]

Front page of the program of the opening of Congregation Rodeph Shalom's new synagogue, Philadelphia, 1870.

---

[21] *Rules of Order—Synagogen Ordnung*, 11.20.1867, AJA, MC no. 517, box. 5. Cf. Davis, *The History of Rodeph Shalom Congregation*, 84.

When the cornerstone of the new synagogue building at Broad and Mount Vernon Streets was laid in July 1869, a discussion about the liturgy in the new synagogue began, and there was a debate about the direction of the reforms. Jastrow suggested that the congregation should abolish the separate gallery for women, so that men and women could be seated on one level, though still on two separate sides. This idea was criticized by Isaac M. Wise, who did not consider it to be enough of a reform, as he regarded the family pews he introduced when in rabbinical office in Albany as a model reform.[22] Another idea of Jastrow's was the installation of an organ and the institution of a choir, which would later include non-Jewish members as well.[23] Sabbath service was anchored to a fixed time on Friday evening.[24]

The synagogue, designed by Frank Furness, was officially opened on September 9, 1870.[25] One of the inscriptions carved on the front wall of the synagogue was particularly emphatic: "My House shall be called the House of Prayer for all Nations."[26] The bylaws adopted here became a model for the regulations of other emerging congregations, and some newly established congregations even requested a copy of the bylaws of Rodeph Shalom.[27]

It seems that it was also Jastrow's suggestion to consider making reforms of the liturgy in order to encourage worshippers to attend services. A special committee with Jastrow as secretary was appointed to prepare a proposal for changes. The committee submitted the following report on November 12, 1870:

---

[22] Some publications claim that there were family pews in Rodeph Shalom. Perhaps they were introduced after the controversy with Wise. Cf. Morais, *The Jews of Philadelphia*, 76; Olitzky, *The American Synagogue*, 314; Malcolm H. Stern, "National Leaders of Their Time: Philadelphia's Reform Rabbis," in *Jewish Life in Philadelphia 1830–1940*, 183.

[23] Morais, *The Jews of Philadelphia*, 76.

[24] Davis, *Emergence of Conservative Judaism*, 143.

[25] The program for the ceremony was printed in English and German, see AJA, MC no. 517, box 5. Davis gives June 21, 1871, as the date of the opening of the synagogue; Davis, *The History of Rodeph Shalom Congregation*, 88.

[26] Morais, *The Jews of Philadelphia*, 75.

[27] For instance, congregations in Memphis and Montgomery. AJA, SC no. 5686, 10.16.1871; 06.1870.

At a meeting of the Committee on the adoption of a revised Prayer Book for the use the congregation it was Resolved

1. That the Committee recommend to the Board of Directors, the adoption of the Prayer Book edited in the year 1865, by Rev. Dr. Benjamin Szold, of Baltimore,[28] which Prayer Book will be revised by Dr. Jastrow in conference with the author and such Rabbis as they may choose for assistance.

2. Resolved that the Committee recommend that the reading of the Torah on Sabbath morning services be shortened by selecting from the weekly portion called Parashah, such a part as the Rabbi may choose for the occasion, the calling up however of seven persons will be retained as heretofore.

3. It was finally resolved that the Committee recommend to convene at an early day, all the members … of the congregation for the purpose of ratification of the above Resolutions.[29]

Only the first resolution was accepted, and Jastrow set about revising a prayer book for his congregation. The prayer book was published in German in 1871,[30] and in English two years later.[31] Jastrow fell foul of Wise for his choice of *Avodat Israel* as a prayer book, as Wise was promoting his own prayer book, *Minhag America*, at the time. It was too soon for further reforms, but the following year it was agreed that only one-third of the weekly portion would be read during services.[32]

---

[28] *Awodat Israel. Israelitisches Gebetbuch für den öffentlichen Gottesdienst im ganzen Jahre,* geordnet und übersetzt von Benjamin Szold, Rabbiner der Oheb Schalom-Gemeinde in Baltimore (Baltimore, 1865).

[29] Quote from Davis, *The History of Rodeph Shalom Congregation*, 86.

[30] *Awodat Israel. Israelitisches Gebetbuch für den öffentlichen Gottesdienst im ganzen Jahre,* geordnet und übersetzt von Benjamin Szold, Rabbiner der Oheb Schalom-Gemeinde in Baltimore, revidiert von M. Jastrow, Rabbiner der Rodef-Schalom Gemeinde zu Philadelphia und H. Hochheimer, Rabbiner der Oheb Israel zu Baltimore (Baltimore, 1871).

[31] *Avodat Israel: Israelitish Prayer Book, for all the Public Services of the Year,* Originally Arranged by Rev. Dr. Benjamin Szold of Baltimore, second edition (Hebrew and German) Revised by Rev. Drs. M. Jastrow of Philadelphia, and H. Hochheimer of Baltimore. Hebrew and English Edition, Ed. in Text and Typographical Arrangement Fully Corresponding with the Revised Hebrew-German Edition, by M. Jastrow, Rabbi of the Congregation Rodef Shalom (Philadelphia, 1873).

[32] Davis, *The History of Rodeph Shalom Congregation*, 87.

Jastrow was still in charge of the school, which had 80 students in 1875. The school house was not big enough to accommodate all of the students, and therefore larger rooms were rented at Jastrow's recommendation. Jastrow fell seriously ill in 1876, and he was replaced at the pulpit for a few months by Rabbis Benjamin Szold, Moses Mielziener, Henry Hochheimer, Adolph Huebsch, Emil G. Hirsch, and George Jacobs.[33]

From the beginning, Jastrow was active in the Board of Delegates of American Israelites—the first American nationwide Jewish organization.[34] He also organized a meeting of the representatives of the United Hebrew Charities in Philadelphia. By 1869, he was well known almost throughout the country through his numerous publications and involvement in many organizations. He was even invited to open a session of the House of Representatives in Washington with a prayer.[35]

With time, the further Americanization of the members of the congregation prepared the ground for reforms. New Hebrew-German, and later Hebrew-English, prayer books were introduced. Jastrow did not need to wait long for the results and, once recovered from his illness, he proposed further reforms. Knowledge of Hebrew decreased so much among the congregation that not everyone could read prayers and the relevant Torah portions. Asked if it was possible to abolish calling worshippers to the Torah, Jastrow answered that if anyone did not want to read with a *hazan* and did not know Hebrew, they should not be forced to do so. The practice of calling people up to the Torah was thereby discontinued in Rodeph Shalom, with the exception of bar mitzvahs.[36]

Jastrow brought up his children in the spirit of respect for tradition. All five of his surviving children[37] were active in a number of organizations and clubs affiliated with the congregation and in

---

[33] Ibid., 90.

[34] Max J. Kohler, "The Board of Delegates of American Israelites, 1859–1878," *PAJHS* 29 (1925): 75–135.

[35] Malcolm H. Stern, "National Leaders of Their Time: Philadelphia's Reform Rabbis," in *Jewish Life in Philadelphia 1830–1940*, 183.

[36] Davis, *The History of Rodeph Shalom Congregation*, 91–92.

[37] The Jastrows had seven children in total: Moritz (Morris), Wilhelm, Joseph, Karl, Alice, Nelli, and Annie, but two of their sons—Wilhelm and Karl—died at a young age.

Philadelphia. Moritz (Morris) in particular was prepared for a career as a rabbi, and went to the Congregation Rodeph Shalom religious school with his brother Joseph.[38] Morris studied at the seminary in Breslau between 1881 and 1884,[39] and at the universities in Breslau and Leipzig. He later devoted himself to an academic career, and became a professor of Semitic studies and a librarian at the University of Pennsylvania.[40] Joseph chose an academic career, too, and taught at the University of Wisconsin in Madison. He went on to become one of its most respected professors of psychology.[41]

In 1873 the Union of American Hebrew Congregations was founded, on Wise's initiative. It initially consisted of 34 congregations, mostly Reform-oriented.[42] Congregation Rodeph Shalom was invited to join the Union, which it did on Jastrow's recommendation.[43] The main goal of the Union of American Hebrew Congregations was to establish a new seminary training progressive rabbis, and the Hebrew

---

[38] They were also both active in the United Hebrew Charities; *Deborah*, February 27, 1890, 7–8.

[39] *Das Breslauer Seminar 1854–1938*, 420.

[40] Davis, *The History of Rodeph Shalom Congregation*, 94; Harold Wechsler, "Pulpit or Professoriate: The Case of Morris Jastrow," *American Jewish History* 74 (June 1985): 338–355.

[41] Joseph Jastrow, "Joseph Jastrow," in *A History of Psychology in Autobiography*, ed. Carl Murchison, vol. I (Washington, D.C.: American Psychological Association, 1930), 135–162; Arthur L. Blumenthal, "The Intrepid Joseph Jastrow" in *From Pioneers in Psychology*, ed. G.A. Kimble, M. Wertheimer, C. While, vol. I (Washington, D.C.: American Psychological Association, 1991); and Levin Alexandra Lee, "The Jastrows in Madison: A Chronicle of University Life, 1888–1900," *Wisconsin Magazine of History* 46, no. 4 (1963): 243–256.

[42] Before long, the Union of American Hebrew Congregations (UAHC) became the organizational branch of Reform Judaism and an organization bringing together Reform synagogues. For more, see *Reform Judaism in America*, 233–246, bibl. 295–337; Kohler, *The Board of Delegates of American Israelites*.

[43] Olitzky, *The American Synagogue*, 314. Davis claims that the issue was discussed by Jastrow in 1878, but by issue he probably means membership of the Hebrew Union College, the seminary established by the UAHC; see *The History of Rodeph Shalom Congregation*, 92.

Joseph Jastrow (1863–1944). Morris Jastrow (1861–1921).

Union College was established in Cincinnati in 1875.[44] However, Rodeph Shalom was not a member of the Union for long: Jastrow and other conservative rabbis from Philadelphia and New York criticized Wise and his camp for their excessively radical reforms and a lack of knowledge and consideration for the opinions of others. The turning-point in Jastrow's relations with the Cincinnati reformers was a banquet on July 11, 1883, organized to celebrate the annual meeting of the representatives of the Union of American Hebrew Congregations and the graduation of the first rabbinical class of the Hebrew Union College (among the graduates were Israel Aaron, Henry Berkowitz, Joseph Krauskopf, and David Philipson).[45] The banquet turned into a scandal and caused a rift among the reformers because non-kosher seafood—mussels,

---

[44] For more on the history of the Hebrew Union College, see David Philipson, "The History of the Hebrew Union College," *Hebrew Union College Jubilee Volume (1875–1925)* (Cincinnati, 1925), 1–71; Samuel S. Cohon, "The History of the Hebrew Union College," *PAJHS* XL, no. 1–4 (1950–51): 17–55.

[45] "The First Ordination and the Terefa Banquet 1883," *AJAJ* (November 1874): 129.

frogs' legs, and soft-shell crabs—was served.[46] Among the guests at this event, which is often referred to in historiography as "the Trefa Banquet," were Kaufmann Kohler and Gustav Gottheil of New York, Benjamin Szold of Baltimore, George Jacobs of Philadelphia,[47] and possibly Jastrow as well, but we do not know if he was one of the two rabbis who walked out of the banquet. Jastrow and a few of the other guests certainly broke off contact with the reformers from Cincinnati at that point. The incident became a point of reference by which moderate reformers manifested their disapproval of further law-breaking. They criticized Wise—the president of the Hebrew Union College at the time—and his supporters for their insufficient knowledge of religious issues and for setting a bad example for the students and future rabbis. On the other hand, Wise was unperturbed by the situation, and attacked the rabbis who ostracized him, writing in the *American Israelite* that they were "men of purely Jewish stomachs and unadulterated tastes," and that "Nobody has appointed those very orthodox critics, overseers of the kitchen or taskmasters of the stomach."[48] He believed strongly that one should not be concerned with food. The whole controversy lasted almost a year, and as a result of it Jastrow recommended to the Board that Congregation Rodeph Shalom should withdraw from the Union of American Hebrew Congregations. This was not an easy decision, however, as some of the members of the congregation had adopted Wise's reforms and they did not wish to abandon them. At a meeting of the Board on June 15, 1884, attention was called to the fact that the congregation joined the Union to support the Hebrew Union College—an American institution where young rabbis were to train in accordance with new, high standards—partly to eliminate the need to constantly bring in rabbis from Europe who did not understand the local conditions. Attention was also drawn to the inappropriate behavior of certain members, including Wise; and therefore it was decided that Congregation Rodeph Shalom would withdraw from the Union for some time, until everything was put back in order.

This seemingly insignificant conflict made both parties realize that they could no longer cooperate due to their different views

---

[46] For the complete menu, see John J. Appel, "The Trefa Banquet," *Commentary* (Feb. 1866): 75; Sarna, *American Judaism*, 146.

[47] See "The First Ordination and the Terefa Banquet 1883," 129.

[48] Quoted after Davis, *The History of Rodeph Shalom Congregation*, 96.

of the reform of Judaism.⁴⁹ Therefore, the "Trefa Banquet" and the rabbinical conference in Pittsburgh in 1885, where the principles of Reform Judaism were formulated (to create the so-called Pittsburgh Platform),⁵⁰ with which conservative reformers could not agree, marked the birth of Reform Judaism in the center of Cincinnati, and at the same time the beginning of Conservative Judaism.

After these events, Jastrow left the reformers' camp and adopted a more conservative stance. On March 7, 1886, he took part in a meeting at which the Jewish Theological Seminary Association was created, with the goal of establishing a seminary. On April 25, he recommended to the members of Congregation Rodeph Shalom that they join the Association. He argued that the newly created educational institution would provide proper training for future ministers—preachers and rabbis—and that the new movement needed such a rabbinical seminary.⁵¹ Congregation Rodeph Shalom joined the Jewish Theological Seminary Association in 1888.

The direction of reforms initiated by Jastrow in his congregation could not be halted. In 1886 a request was made to him to say more prayers on Yom Kippur in German and English instead of Hebrew, as Hebrew was no longer widely understood.

It seems that Jastrow maintained some contact with individuals in Poland, because in 1883 he received a gift, a silver tea service, from his friends in Warsaw to mark the twentieth anniversary of his departure from the Kingdom of Poland.⁵² In 1884 or 1885 Jastrow traveled to Europe, mainly for treatment in Karlsbad, but he also visited friends in Worms, Mannheim, Frankfurt, Leipzig, and Breslau, as well as family in Rogoźno.⁵³

In 1891, the twenty-fifth anniversary of Jastrow's service in Philadelphia was celebrated by many of his friends and admirers, and

---

49   Sarna, *American Judaism*, 185.
50   The Pittsburgh Platform may be found in the appendix.
51   Davis, *The History of Rodeph Shalom Congregation*, 97–98.
52   It is very probable that the spice tower in the possession of Maryland Jewish Museum in Baltimore, which used to belong to Jastrow, was one element of that service. The inscription on it reads: "Gift from the guests from Warsaw, Purim 1859."
53   As noted by *Posener Zeitung* of August 26, 1884; see also AJA, SC no. 5686 [144–145], notes from January until August 1884.

speeches were made by Rabbis Sabato Morais, Joseph Krauskopf of Philadelphia, and Henry Illowizi of Cincinnati.[54] At the same time, the Board of the Congregation began to think about employing an assistant rabbi educated and brought up in America. Jastrow strongly opposed the idea, as he knew which direction the reforms were heading in. Nonetheless, a new rabbi was employed the following year. Dr. Henry Berkowitz had been a student of Wise's and a graduate of the first class of the Hebrew Union College. Jastrow was offered the following resolution and the function of Rabbi Emeritus.

> Whereas: after twenty-seven years of continued and arduous labors, devoted zealously to the welfare of Judaism and to the upbuilding and prosperity of the Congregation Rodef Shalom, the time has now come when because of weakened physical strength, it was deemed fitting to relieve our esteemed Rabbi, Rev. Dr. M. Jastrow, of the duties devolving upon him, and of placing the burdens upon younger shoulders; and
> Whereas: this Congregation desires to express its appreciation and gratitude for the work that he has done for it, and their continued confidence and adherence to the principles of our faith of which our esteemed Rabbi has been for so many years the exponent, therefore be it resolved:
> That the Rev. Dr. M. Jastrow be and is hereby made Rabbi Emeritus of the Congregation at a salary of $4000 per annum during his life.[55]

It came as a severe blow to Jastrow that he could not prevent Congregation Rodeph Shalom from going down the path of radical, rather than moderate, reform, which he preferred. On the other hand, he was falling victim to his own work, as it was he who had instilled the first fruits of Reform in the congregation—changing the language of prayer, reforming prayer books, and shortening the liturgy. Most members of the congregation believed that reforms could not be stopped halfway.

In his sorrowful farewell sermon delivered on November 27, 1892, Jastrow cautioned against rejection of the values of Judaism

---

[54] *Deborah*, November 12, 1891, 6.

[55] Davis, *The History of Rodeph Shalom Congregation*, 104. Cf. *Deborah*, October 6, 1892, 7.

and joining the radical reform camp.⁵⁶ This sermon was Jastrow's last opportunity in Rodeph Shalom to call for a compromise between various factions in the congregation. In it, he asked if it was true that the majority of the congregation were in favor of his dismissal, and concluded that his discharge was a rejection of his principles and the truth he stood by.⁵⁷ Jastrow stressed that he was not the only conservative member of the congregation, and there were certainly others more progressive. Therefore, he said, unity for the majority rather than divisions should be sought, for Judaism is a religion and mission of co-participation in the universal culture and civilization. For that reason, Congregation Rodeph Shalom should remain conservative. According to him, the advocates of reform did not want religion, but rather "so-called scientific instruction," which threatened the continuity of tradition.

> Do not forsake the banner of Israel's ancient faith, turn not aside towards those vanities of false enlightenment and upstart self-sufficiency, for vanities they are. ...I care not in what language you pray, although the truly prayerful heart is satisfied with any language even though it be one only half-understood, drawing inspiration from its very antiquity and its sacred associations.⁵⁸

Jastrow's declaration is the fullest testimony of his beliefs and his affiliation with Conservative or Positive-Historical Judaism.

Rabbi Berkowitz began his work in Congregation Rodeph Shalom on December 9, 1892.⁵⁹ The community remained divided for some time, and it was difficult for the new rabbi to work with Jastrow, who continued to have influence in the congregation and was opposed to the introduction of innovations. Jastrow expressed his views in the press as well, which resulted in the Board banning him from making

---

⁵⁶ Marcus Jastrow, A *Warning Voice. Farewell Sermon Delivered on the Occasion of his Retirement by Rev. Dr. ...*, *Rabbi Emeritus of the German Hebrew Congregation Rodef Shalom at Philadelphia* [1892]. See also *Deborah*, December 8, 1892, 7.

⁵⁷ Jastrow, *A Warning Voice*, 6.

⁵⁸ Ibid., 11.

⁵⁹ It was widely discussed in *Deborah*, December 15, 1892, 7.

any public statements about the congregation.⁶⁰ In spite of Jastrow's objections, Berkowitz replaced the *Avodat Israel* prayer book with the Union Prayer Book in 1895. This was an overt sign that the congregation was heading in the direction of Reform Judaism. Rodeph Shalom rejoined the Union of American Hebrew Congregations in the same year, while still a member of the Jewish Theological Seminary Association. Its membership in both organizations illustrates the divisions within the congregation, but Rabbi Berkowitz's arrival marked a new chapter in the history of Congregation Rodeph Shalom that is still open to this day.⁶¹

Jastrow devoted himself to academic work and was involved in many educational and social Jewish organizations during his "retirement." He died on October 13, 1903,⁶² and his funeral was a great manifestation of affection and appreciation of his work as a rabbi, preacher, teacher, academic, and religious and social activist. The most distinguished representatives of the Jewish community in America of the time took part in the funeral, and the Jewish press throughout the Diaspora reported his death.⁶³

---

60 Davis, *The History of Rodeph Shalom Congregation*, 105.

61 Ibid., 18–110; For more about Rabbi Berkowitz, see, e. g., Max E. Berkowitz, *The Beloved Rabbi: An Account of the Life and Works of Henry Berkowitz* (New York: The Macmillan Company, 1932).

62 See Philadelphia Jewish Archives Center at the Balch Institute, Rodeph Shalom Congregation Papers, BV 6, *Rabbi Berkowitz Ministerial Mortal Register 1881–1919*, 91. Davis and many authors who quote him date Jastrow's death to October 13, 1904. The commemorative plaque in the present Rodeph Shalom synagogue at Broad Street in Philadelphia also gives the wrong date of Jastrow's death. See Davis, *The History of Rodeph Shalom Congregation*, 110.

63 See, e. g., A. Berliner, "Dr Marcus Jastrow," *Israelitischer Lehrer und Cantor* 10 (1903): 37–38; "Random Thoughts," *Emanu-El. A Weekly Paper Devoted to the Interests of Jews and Judaism on the Pacific Coast* XVI, no. 26 (November 6, 1903); Solomon Schechter, *A Man of Full Stature: Address of Prof. Schechter for Memorial Services of Dr. Jasstrow* (sic!), Philadelphia, [November 5], 1903.

Chapter 6. Congregation Rodeph Shalom

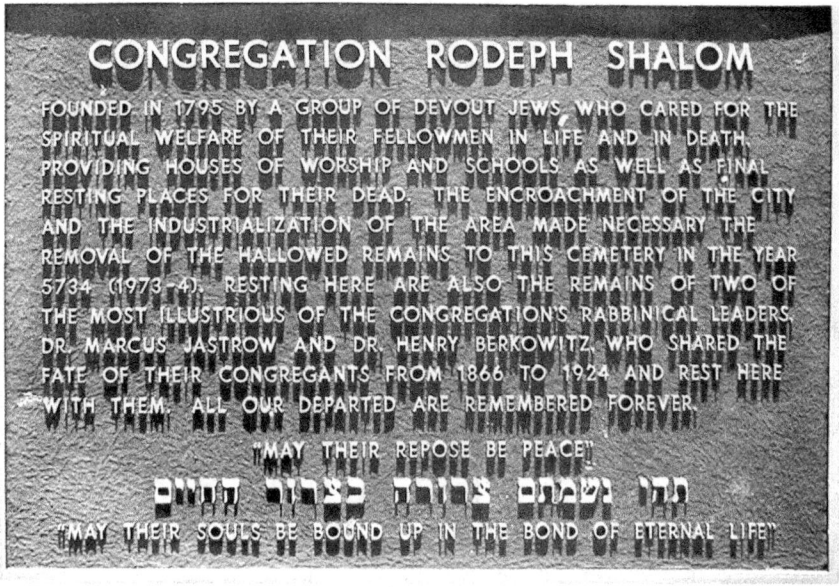

Plaque commemorating Rabbis Marcus Jastrow and Henry Berkowitz, Philadelphia.

CHAPTER 7

CONTROVERSIES

When Marcus Jastrow arrived in America, he not only began to implement reforms in Congregation Rodeph Shalom, he also actively contributed to important religious debates concerning the future of America's Jews. He understood that he was one of the best-educated rabbis in America, and he wished to share his knowledge with others, but he did not always take into consideration existing relations and ideological divisions between American communities. Therefore, in the first months of his stay in Philadelphia, Jastrow became embroiled in fierce arguments with advocates of Reform Judaism, who did not always exhibit a high level of learning and intellect.

The Conflict between Jastrow and Wise

Jastrow's conflict with Wise escalated when he encroached on Wise's area of influence. Wise purported to represent all American Jews, and often attacked his opponents in the newspapers he published— *Deborah* and *Israelite*. The main root of Jastrow's conflicts with others was in the scholarly context—he could not stop himself from sending his corrections and comments on the articles of local authors to American Jewish magazines and newspapers, above all *The Hebrew Leader*, *Deborah*, and *Israelite*. His comments, mostly relating to the articles' theological substance, were often interpreted as personal attacks because they undermined the author's authority. However, it was during these debates and conflicts that Jastrow crystallized his program, his "platform" of reform, which placed him between Wise's vision of Reform Judaism and the visions of conservative rabbis such as Isaac Leeser and Sabato Morais of Philadelphia.

The first public conflict was ignited when Jastrow criticized Isidor Kalisch[1] for his ignorance of the Bible and the Talmudic litera-

---

[1] Isidor Kalisch (1816–1886) was a rabbi in several congregations in the US..

ture. Kalisch was a close ally of Wise's, and Wise published a few articles in his defense, in which he criticized Jastrow in an unrefined manner. In response, Jastrow defended himself by publishing a pamphlet attacking both Kalisch and Wise.[2]

There was, however, another reason for the conflict between Wise and Jastrow—Wise had applied for the post of rabbi of Congregation Rodeph Shalom and had not been successful.

"You speak about integrity—" Jastrow wrote—"you, who offered your rabbinic services to Congregation Rodeph Shalom in Philadelphia when you were still in Albany, like a girl who is prepared to do any domestic work, be it reform or Orthodox, *Yekum Purkan* or David Einhorn's prayer book [*Olat Tamid*], had it existed at the time—it mattered not to you, as long as you obtained a lucrative post."[3]

Another heated exchange took place between Jastrow and Wise when the latter learned that Congregation Rodeph Shalom had plans to build a new synagogue. He wrote then:

> Congregation Rodeph Shalom in Philadelphia is considering building a new synagogue... Some members of this congregation are reform-inclined and, in addition to other improvements, they want to introduce in the new synagogue the family pews already present in many other temples, where the father, mother, and children sit together in the house of God. This new addition to our temples has done a lot of good—it introduced order, peace, and dignified decorum, put children under their mothers' supervision in the house of God, and at the same time it has put an end to waving, whispering, and looking around the house of God, contributing significantly to increased concentration.[4]

Jastrow was annoyed by Wise's article; he interpreted it as meddling in his affairs and as an attempt to manipulate and divide his congregation. He himself opposed the introduction of family pews in the

---

[2] Marcus Jastrow, *Offene Erklärung an Herrn J.M. Wise, Rabbiner und Editor des "Israelite" und der "Deborah", von ... in Philadelphia* (Philadelphia [1867]).

[3] Ibid., 28.

[4] Isaac M. Wise, "Familiensitze," *Deborah*, 1867. Cf. Jastrow, *Offene Erklärung an Herrn J.M. Wise ...*, 21–22.

synagogue as contrary to the law and spirit of Judaism.[5] According to Wise, on the other hand, family pews were the essence of reform, and if Jastrow, whom he called an "Eastern Hasid,"[6] was opposed to their introduction, then he must also have considered it immoral for men to sit next to women.[7] Wise claimed that family pews had been introduced in the most outstanding houses of God in America, both Jewish synagoguesand Christian churches. He did not deem them indecent, and continued to praise such practices.

In response, Jastrow expressed his attitude to law and tradition:

> I am not one of those people who are constantly reaching for the letter of the law, even its farthest and youngest sprouts, to artificially defend what is old and obsolete; neither am I one of those who only cite the letter of the law, interpret it, and try to be smart when it may be useful for destroying tradition, yet reject the same law as obsolete if it does not serve their purpose of winning popularity. (You know best if I had you in mind here.) ... The spirit of Judaism created a boundary of morality which endures in Israel's houses of God; I do not wish to be he who lifts his hand to Israel's structure of purity of custom, even if only by pulling out a small brick from it.[8]

As an example, Jastrow gave the practice of the Reform synagogue in Berlin, where even Samuel Holdheim—the most radical reformer, who had moved the Sabbath from Saturday to Sunday—was an opponent of family pews. Jastrow even suggested to Wise that "if you do not believe [me], you may visit the Jewish Reform synagogue at Johannisstrasse every Sunday at 10 before noon, and if you are not wearing a woman's dress, you will be directed to the section

---

[5] For more about the disputes caused by the introduction of family pews in American synagogues, see Jonathan Sarna, "The Debate over Mixed Seating in the American Synagogue," in *The American Synagogue: A Sanctuary Transformed*, ed. Jack Wertheimer (Hanover—London: Brandeis University Press, 1987), 363–394.

[6] A double allusion to Poland and Philadelphia, which was east of Cincinnati.

[7] See *Deborah*, August 23, 1867, 31; Jastrow, *Offene Erklärung an Herrn J. M. Wise*, 22.

[8] Ibid., 23.

with men's pews, which is separated from the women's gallery by a passageway… I suggested the same layout to my congregation for the synagogue extension, and it has already been accepted."[9]

The primary subject matter of this first pamphlet, though, was a critique of Kalisch's article *The Reading of the Pentateuch during Public Worship*,[10] in which, by borrowing arguments from history, Kalisch set out to prove that there were no objections to modifying the call to the Torah and limiting it to only one person. In response, Jastrow sent a review to *Hebrew Leader* in which he pointed out Kalisch's numerous mistakes and scoffed at his ignorance (for claiming that the *Mishnah* was created in Babylonia, for incorrectly giving the number of chapters of the Pentateuch as 158, and for calling the Talmudic sages a peculiar nation). But what angered Jastrow was the fact that the same article, with the same mistakes, appeared in *Israelite*[11] with Wise's approval. Jastrow held it against Wise that he did not value or try to increase the level of knowledge and education among American Jews, despite talking about it, but instead counted on cheap "false popularity," which he achieved through manipulating his tools—his newspapers. Moreover, referring to Kalisch's article, Wise wrote that "the rabbinic laws exist for us as a subject of history" and no more time should be spent on deciding whether one or more people should read the Torah. He expressed regret at having to engage in such deliberations because of "eastern Hasidim."[12]

In his next article,[13] published July 19, 1876, Wise openly attacked Jastrow by first saying that Kalisch was completely right in his dispute with him and then reproaching Jastrow for being an outsider, having no knowledge of American Judaism, and being convinced that he was the only one who knew what the Talmud, *poskim*, and *midrashim* were.

---

[9] Ibid., 24.

[10] Isidor Kalisch, "The Reading of the Pentateuch during Public Worship," *Hebrew Leader* 1, April 5, 1867; *Hebrew Leader* 2, April 12, 1867.

[11] See *Israelite*, April 12, 1867.

[12] See *Israelite*, May 31, 1867. Cf. Jastrow, *Offene Erklärung an Herrn J.M. Wise*, 10–11.

[13] *Israelite*, July 19, 1867. Cf. Jastrow, *Offene Erklärung an Herrn J.M. Wise*, 15–16.

Jastrow accused Wise of lies and pride and called him an "infallible pope" and an "anointed of the Lord" who "lies like a Jesuit."[14] This debate, initially focused on the merits of the issue, with Jastrow aiming to point out factual errors, turned into an ideological and personal conflict. Very anxious about the future of Judaism in America, Jastrow cautioned against Wise, using increasingly harsh language. His response to Wise was as follows:

> I wish to have nothing farther to do with you because I consider it a command to show, in the interests of American Judaism, on which you exert a great and harmful influence, who this bellwether setting the tone is; and I do hope that American communities, including those under your influence and equipped with *Minhag America*, have not yet lost a sense of law and truth. They require their leader above all not to be a Jesuit, a hypocrite, a sycophant, or a liar.[15]

To Jastrow, Wise's rejection of the Talmud and his critique of the nascent Maimonides College as "a Polish cheder" were symbols of departure from the values of Judaism, and placed Wise on a par with a "Karaite rabbi" or a "rabbinic Karaite."

But the conflict did not end there. After the publication of Jastrow's first brochure, Wise retaliated with a review of Jastrow's pamphlet in *Deborah*,[16] in which he accused Jastrow of calling him "a liar, a sycophant, a hypocrite, a Jesuit, a cat, and a Karaite," and of wanting to become the leader of Orthodox Judaism in Philadelphia while working on the Board of Delegates of American Israelites. Wise advised Jastrow to reject Orthodoxy and fall into the arms of the reforms, because otherwise he would not have a future in either America or Germany.[17] Without much delay, Jastrow published a second pamphlet,[18] in which he noted sarcastically that Wise under-

---

[14] Cf. ibid., 10, 19.

[15] Ibid., 21.

[16] Isaac M. Wise, "Das Pamphlet," *Deborah*, November 12, 1867.

[17] Ibid. Cf. Marcus Jastrow, "Antwort an Herrn I.M. Wise in Cincinnati, auf dessen Aufsatz betitelt, Das Pamphlet," *Deborah*, September 20, 1867, 5.

[18] Ibid.

Chapter 7. Controversies

Distinguished rabbis in America, 1868.

stood very little of what he, Jastrow, wanted to communicate to him in the first publication. He expressed his regret that Wise had completely rejected ancient Jewish history as a subject of interest and scholarly research, because if he had not he would have accepted the validity of Jastrow's arguments in his dispute with Kalisch. Jastrow also remarked that there were still rabbis in America, well-educated advocates of reform, such as Dr. David Einhorn, Dr. Samuel Adler, Dr. Samuel Hirsch, and Dr. Bernhard Felsenthal, who would concede his point.[19]

In response, Wise wrote that if Jastrow had truly supported progress in Poland and Germany and claimed that the salvation and future of Judaism were to be found only in progress, he should not join the unenlightened and long-defeated Orthodox Jews in Philadelphia.[20] Wise also called on Jastrow to "unveil his platform" and enunciate his views.[21] Jastrow tried to convince the editor of *Deborah* that he was not Orthodox but an advocate of reform, though not of a reform that consisted of adopting Wise's prayer book, *Minhag America*, and family pews. In addition, he outlined his program of reform:

> But you want my platform and I want to present it to you:
> I am for any reform that is able to influence the moral enhancement of the Jews.
> I am against any reform that issues out of a mere desire toward assimilation or grasping after innovation without its being a means toward moral elevation.
> I am for any reform that is compatible with the spirit of Judaism.
> I am against any reform that denies this spirit.
> I am for any reform which confers upon the outer appearance of Jewish thought-content beauty and dignity.
> I am against any reform that ascribes all worth to outer appearance.
> I am for any reform that links itself with the historical development of Judaism.

---

[19] Ibid., 3.

[20] Isaac M. Wise, "Das Pamphlet," *Deborah*, September 20, 1867, 46.

[21] Ibid.

I am against any reform that severs its connection with the past.

I am for any reform that makes it possible for all Jews still to find themselves in our houses of worship in spite of many changes.

I am against any reform that dissolves this link with co-religionists.

I am for any reform that arouses the consciousness and keeps it aware that outer forms are vehicles of inner thought.

I am against any reform that rejects those vehicles as unnecessary.

I am for any reform that is, without strain, consistent with the Bible and its oldest traditional interpretation, as set down in the Talmud.

I am against any reform that arbitrarily creates new interpretation, inasmuch as I know I cannot do without the traditional guide in the practical implementation of the Biblical commandments.

I am for any reform that removes the old-fashioned prayers which came into being during the Middle Ages.

I am against any reform that touches or alters the older portions of the prayers.

I am for any reform that concerns itself within the above-cited limits with the maintenance of peace with the congregation.

I am against any reform which threatens peace and promotes dissention.

This is my simplified platform. If I am on my own with it, which I think I am not, then I must and shall settle for solitude. However, I do hope that there are still many communities and instructors standing behind or in front of me.

If I am not to have a future in Germany or America with such a platform, that is—if I am left without a congregation—then I will look for other employment that will support me with God's help. I hope, though, that it will not come to that. I will certainly not join your camp because of sour grapes.

This was and is my platform in Warsaw, Mannheim, and Worms. I know that salvation is to be found only in progress; the only question is what is understood as progress.

Propagation of learning and culture—that is progress, and for that I was offered a large field in Warsaw, which I worked to the best of my abilities.

A conviction of what is fitting for man and moral in Judaism—that is progress, and on that I exerted my feeble energies in Worms and Mannheim.

Educating young people and preparing them for a truly religious, and thus truly human life—that is progress, and that has been my endeavor always and everywhere…

In short, I seek to elevate my companions in faith morally and spiritually on the path defined above and by available means, in accordance with my views. Other colleagues have other views and other means, though their goals are the same; therefore, I offer my brotherly hand, above our differences, to all who are honestly disposed, hoping that it will be accepted. But you, Mr. Wise, I cannot include among those colleagues.[22]

Jastrow's reform consisted of progress and respect for the values of Judaism. His program was implemented as far as possible in every place he came to work in. In both Europe and America he aimed his program especially at the young generation, whose American members had been neglected in terms of upbringing and religious instruction.

As might have been expected, Wise did not take long to reply. In his response he repeated almost all of his earlier arguments and invectives, but this time concentrated on Jastrow's membership in the Board of Delegates of American Israelites. To Wise, this organization consisted of representatives of Orthodox Judaism fighting progress; as such, he saw Jastrow's involvement in it as confirming his membership in "a newfangled Orthodoxy, Philadelphian-New York Polish-English party" of opponents of progress.[23] Wise was troubled by the fact that it was these people, under the auspices of the Board of Delegates, who established the first rabbinical seminary in America, Maimonides College, with "obscurantists for professors and Jastrow in the middle" (he also called Jastrow a *tsadik*).[24]

---

[22] Marcus Jastrow, *Antwort an Herrn I.M. Wise in Cincinnati, auf dessen Aufsatz betitelt "Das Pamphlet,"* 9–10.

[23] Isaac M. Wise, "Eine Erklärung," *Deborah*, November 1, 1867, 66.

[24] Ibid. This is the title for a Hasidic Rebbe, which is here used as an insulting reference to Jastrow's Polish roots.

Wise's response provoked Jastrow to write another, final pamphlet,[25] in which he justified himself, saying that had he known who he was dealing with, he would have never associated with Wise, because such conflicts were not in his nature. However, Jastrow wrote, since the conflict between the two was not only personal, he could not be silent, and his previous publications were meant to warn American Jews under Wise's influence. On the one hand, he acknowledged certain merits of his competitor for the development of Judaism in America; on the other hand, he noted that Wise was "an unworthy man who caused a lot of damage to religious life with his ruthlessness to human dignity, duplicity, changeability of character, and haughtiness,"[26] and that he identified himself with American Judaism. It was difficult for Jastrow to come to terms with the conflict between moderate reformers from Philadelphia and New York and Wise's supporters, as the conflict was not about the program of reform but in truth about personal careers. For a long time, he could not fully understand all the animosities between the two parties. The conflict between Jastrow and Wise was probably one of the bitterest that arose during the formation and shaping of the reform factions. It attracted a lot of interest—both the Jewish and non-Jewish press in America and Europe followed it until it lost its factual and substantial character. When the dispute turned personal, it was watched with distaste. The only consolation for Jastrow was the fact that his former colleagues from Germany were more objective. An article was published in *Allgemeine Zeitung des Judenthums* which depicted the dispute in the following manner:[27]

> An acute conflict broke out between Rabbi Wise of Cincinnati, the editor of *Israelite* and *Deborah*, and Rabbi Dr. Jastrow of Philadelphia (earlier Warsaw and Worms) ... Initially played out in *Israelite* and *Hebrew Leader*, the conflict has moved into separate polemic publications, such as the pamphlet *Offene*

---

[25] Marcus Jastrow, *Gegenerklärung auf die "Erklärung" des Herrn J.M. Wise in der "Deborah," Nro. 17. von ...* (Philadelphia, 1867).

[26] Ibid., 3.

[27] *AZJ* 42, October 15, 1867.

Erklärung,[28] recently published by Jastrow, which drives Wise into a corner in a very astute, convincing manner. However, the dispute has become purely personal, so it is no longer of interest. It is very important to American Jews though, as Wise has developed his position very skillfully, and he exploits that position through arrogance and insult of anything that does not suit him … so that others who are differently disposed remain silent out of fear. Neither intellect nor knowledge nor heart nor convictions are necessary to know that such a situation may last a long time in America. Therefore, Dr. Jastrow deserves gratitude for finally defying these actions. He is no longer alone. The letter to him reads as follows:

> You deserve the acknowledgement of all your well-disposed brothers in faith in this country for deprecating arrogance, usurpation, and swindle on the Jewish field with such crushing blows. Those boisterous, haughty, crude articles in *Israelite* and the like have had a morally very negative effect; they awoke a spirit of rudeness and irresponsible, shameless judgmentalism among American Israelites, or at the very least, contributed significantly to awakening such a spirit. May at least some eyes open!

Nevertheless, in time Wise proved victorious in this dispute, his vision of Judaism proving more attractive to American Jews. As he had previously in Warsaw, Worms, and Mannheim, Jastrow remained faithful to his principles and the platform of moderate reforms and respectful of tradition and history.

The conflict between Wise and Jastrow is almost absent from the historiography on Wise and the origins of Reform Judaism—barely one laconic sentence.[29] Similarly, there is very little mention of the conflict in the historiography on Jastrow.

---

[28] Jastrow, *Offene Erklärung an Herrn J.M. Wise*.

[29] See Temkin, *Creating American Reform Judaism*, 226.

Defending American Jews

Jastrow did not engage in polemics only with his "ideological opponents' from Wise's Reform camp. He also spoke out openly in defense of his friends, Jews, and Judaism. One such example is his polemical arguments with Friedrich Schünemann-Pott, the German-born co-founder of the Christian Association of Free German Congregations of North America and the chairman of this association in Philadelphia. Schünemann-Pott was also the editor of a number of periodicals which served his ideology, including *Blätter für freies religiöses Leben*. In this magazine in 1867, Schünemann-Pott published an offensive article about Rabbi Sabato Morais of Congregation Mikveh Israel, and about Jews and Judaism. Jastrow was close to Morais and felt obliged to defend both him and the honor of the Jews, who frequently came under attack in this period.[30] The reactions of Jews to the article varied, though they usually remained passive in such situations. Jastrow's overt response was thus not welcomed by all. One of those who criticized him was his neighbor, a supporter of Wise, Samuel Hirsch of Congregation Keneseth Israel.[31]

Schünemann-Pott's first article appeared in response to a sermon preached by Morais, in which he criticized the missionary work among Jews conducted by the bishop of New Jersey. Morais protested against such missions, which were quite common at the time.[32] Jastrow reacted to Schünemann-Pott's article by publishing another pamphlet.[33] In response, Schünemann-Pott wrote the article *Ein neuer*

---

[30] See e. g. Jacob Rader Marcus, *United States Jewry 1776–1985* (Detroit: Wayne State University Press, 1991), vol. II, 279–305; vol. III, 359–382.

[31] Samuel Hirsch, *Dr. Jastrow und sein Gebaren in Philadelphia. Ein ehrliches, leider abgenötigtes Wort* (Philadelphia, 1868), 13–14.

[32] Jonathan D. Sarna, "The American Jewish Response to Nineteenth-Century Christian Missions," in *Essential Papers on Jewish-Christian Relations in the United States. Imagery and Reality*, ed. Naomi W. Cohen (New York: New York University Press, 1990), 21–42.

[33] Marcus Jastrow, *Offenes Schreiben an den Bundespräsidenten Herrn Schünemann-Pott, als Erwiderung auf dessen Vortrag: Jehova versus den Dreieinigen* (Philadelphia, 1867), 8. Unfortunately, I was unable to find a copy of this text.

Ritter Jehovah's,³⁴ in which he criticized the activities of both Morais and Jews in general, and trotted out some of the accusations leveled at Jews, and unfavorable opinions of them, typical for that period, rooted in biblical interpretations of Abraham and David. He also accused Jastrow of poor knowledge of the Bible. Jastrow felt that he had to react in order to fend off attacks on religion in general, and the Jews and Judaism in particular. In a second pamphlet³⁵ he criticized Schünemann-Pott's offensive language, his ideas of evangelizing the Jews, and particularly the view that Jews were the wealthiest social group in the United States. Schünemann-Pott had accused the Jews of becoming slave owners since being granted equal rights, and Jastrow referred to statistics to prove that it was quite the opposite — Jews were one of the poorest social groups in the country.³⁶ According to Hirsch, Jastrow's reply was an abuse of the freedom of conscience and civil rights in America, and Schünemann-Pott's statements did not offend anyone.³⁷ Hirsch claimed that Jastrow's real reason for responding was his desire to make himself visible in his community, whose creed ought to be "there is no other God but Jastrow."³⁸

---

[34] Friedrich Schünemann-Pott, "Ein neuer Ritter Jehovah's," *Blätter für Freies Religiöses Leben* 3 ([Philadelphia,] 1867), 40–45.

[35] Marcus Jastrow, *Zweites und letztes offenes Schreiben an Herrn Schünemann-Pott als Erwiderung auf dessen Artikel: "Ein neuer Ritter Jehovah's'* (Siehe: *"Blätter für Freies Religiöses Leben"*, 12ter Jahrgang, No. 3), (Philadelphia, 1867), 8.

[36] Ibid., 6–7.

[37] Hirsch even wrote that "Mr. Schünemann-Pott wrote a reply which every Jew should keep framed in gold. A better, classic mockery of Christian missions among the Jews has never been written. Mr. Schüenemann-Pott said: If I was in Morais' shoes, I would have preached a completely different sermon. I would have called on my congregation — it is wealthy — to organize such missions for Christians! Thus he derides classic missionary abuses; finally, he calculates how many pounds sterling a London missionary association spent on 19 adult Jews and 1 child, and claims that 10,000 Christian souls could be converted into Jews for half that amount in 4 weeks. What can one have against this satire?" Hirsch, *Dr. Jastrow und sein Gebaren in Philadelphia*, 13.

[38] Ibid., 14.

The Controversy with Samuel Hirsch

These harsh words reveal the nature of the relationship between Jastrow and Hirsch in that period. Samuel Hirsch[39] arrived in Philadelphia in the same year as Jastrow—1866—and was a rabbi in the Reform Congregation Keneseth Israel, where he had succeeded one of the country's most radical reformers: David Einhorn. Prior to that, in Germany, he had proved himself an advocate of the radical reforms of Samuel Holdheim, from whom he had received his rabbinic ordination. Hirsch was subsequently a rabbi in Dessau and Luxembourg. He wrote many works on Jewish philosophy and theology. When he came to Philadelphia, he began competing with Jastrow for influence in the circle of Philadelphia Jews. Hirsch felt that he was a representative of a "better," modern Reform Judaism; while Jastrow had fame, erudition, and the fight for the freedom and rights of the Jews behind him. Moreover, Jastrow was offered a contract with better financial terms, and Hirsch was not happy about that.[40] These circumstances soon developed into a conflict between Hirsch and Jastrow which was both ideological and personal.

The first argument erupted when Jastrow delivered a sermon in memory of the late Isaac Leeser on February 8, 1868, in which he supposedly suggested that Hirsch was jealous when colleagues deliver better sermons or have salaries 1,000 dollars higher than his own.[41] This statement appalled Hirsch and his Cincinnati colleagues, who responded with a barrage of publications and press articles. Hirsch maintained that he did not think Jastrow a good preacher, because the sermons he delivered were on a level appropriate for twelve-year-olds, not for educated audiences. As for Jastrow's salary, he claimed Jastrow was exploiting his congregation, which was not as large as the salary

---

[39] For more about Hirsch, see, e. g., *Reform Judaism in America*, 92–94; Moshe Davis, *Emergence of Conservative Judaism*, 180–181.

[40] Hirsch wrote the following about Jastrow: "You, Reform congregations of America, you cannot have this great man cheaply. He is employed for life with an annual salary of 5,000 dollars; he has a wedding almost every week and large income from funerals... Is there no Reform congregation that would like to outbid this? You see: Jastrow reserves himself for you." Hirsch, *Dr. Jastrow und sein Gebaren in Philadelphia*, 25.

[41] Ibid., 1.

would suggest. Hirsch wanted this personal dispute to be resolved by the president of the Board of Congregation Rodeph Shalom, David Teller, but Teller was not willing to involve himself in a disagreement between two rabbis.[42]

Their theological dispute encompassed several layers and subjects. As a supporter of Reform, and of Wise, Hirsch wanted to draw Jastrow into a discussion to bring him out in support of their camp. When Jastrow refused, Hirsch described him as Orthodox and a representative of the old world, adding that America needed a new spirit—the spirit of Reform.

In January 1868, Hirsch attacked Jastrow in *Deborah*[43] for not allowing prayer with uncovered heads in the synagogue.[44] He boasted that his congregation in Keneseth Israel had been praying bareheaded for a long time. He also referred to Talmudic literature in justification of this practice, and quoted the arguments Jastrow had given when Hirsch had asked him if it was permissible to be bareheaded during a service.

According to Jastrow, taking off one's hat in the synagogue did nothing to elevate a man's decorum. He believed that "our" customs, not alien ones, should be followed, because forms of decorum themselves do not create decorum. Moving away from existing customs would be no more than an act of empty, aimless imitation. To Jastrow, reform with no benefits was an evil that engendered corruption. If one wished to introduce innovations, "one first needed to prove their positive moral aspect."[45] Thus, Jastrow allowed praying in the synagogue bareheaded, though not as a fashion and imitation but as a choice with an understanding of such an innovation. This was both in line with his platform and practical at the same time; his congregation was still Orthodox at the time, so very radical, sudden changes could have led to its destabilization.

Hirsch considered such a stance confirmation that Jastrow was closer to Orthodox, Eastern Jews. He accused Jastrow of hypocrisy,

---

[42] Ibid., 1–2, 6.
[43] Samuel Hirsch, "Hut auf oder Hut ab," *Deborah*, January 31, 1868, 118.
[44] He was referring to Jastrow's article in *Hebrew Leader*, January 17, 1868.
[45] Hirsch, "Hut auf oder Hut ab," 118.

asking if the fact that he did not cover his head during the day apart from when he prayed meant that "God was absent."

Another polemic involved the belief in the return to the Land of Israel in messianic times. The issue had already been raised in the German Reform movement, and some felt the need to remove any references to a personal Messiah and the return of the Jews to Zion, as they were contrary to the idea of full emancipation. Hirsch was one of the first to write a treatise on this topic.[46] Jastrow, who himself had agreed to the removal of some references to the rebuilding of the Temple and the cult of the Temple, nevertheless did not assent to Hirsch's treating those Jews who still believed in the return to Zion as disloyal to Judaism. Hirsch averred in one of his articles that "thoughtful Israelites," who really understood Judaism and did not want to lay it open to ridicule in the eyes of the world or to contradict themselves, rejected the political messianic idea, and hence also the idea of the Land of Israel, the Temple, sacrificial worship, and priesthood, along with all the related prayers; those who did not reject these beliefs should not live in America, which offered them full civil rights without any conditions.

> All Americans who ask God to take them to Palestine, to recreate the old Jewish state with its ancient Jewish culture, and to endow them with the messianic king, but who at the same time are American citizens with their heart and soul, and love and respect freedom above all else, contradict themselves greatly and give the lie to themselves after such prayers.[47]

Although Jastrow privately shared the view that emancipation required changes in the religious interpretations of teachings about the return to Zion,[48] he called Hirsch's publicly expressed views *Rish'us*—views that could bring down misfortune on the Jews, for they eliminated a large group of American Jews from public life and accused them of disloyalty to the state. Jastrow noted that this could lead to

---

[46] Samuel Hirsch, *Die Messias-Lehre der Juden in Kanzelvorträgen. Zur Erbauung denkender Leser* (Leipzig: Heinrich Hunger, 1843).

[47] Samuel Hirsch, "Ein Pamphlet," *Deborah*, March 13, 1868, 142. See also Hirsch, *Dr. Jastrow und sein Gebaren in Philadelphia*, 18–19.

[48] Ibid., 21.

a situation similar to that in England, where Jews who prayed for their return to Palestine could not be emancipated.[49]

The conflict in the press between Hirsch and Jastrow lasted almost half a year. Hirsch even published a 25-page pamphlet[50] in which he described his side of the controversy and painted a caricature of Jastrow over ten chapters.

According to Hirsch, Jastrow initially presented himself as an advocate of reform, giving sermons and lectures on all topics, but it soon transpired that he did not support reform. Hirsch ridiculed the school superintended by Jastrow and claimed that Jastrow was often late for classes. He recalled that Jastrow, as the guardian of morality, spoke out against family pews, while in his own opinion Rodeph Shalom was the seat of immorality:

> If women are seated inappropriately anywhere, then it is in the synagogue of Dr. Jastrow. If not for force of habit, the women would not even enter this synagogue. They are really seated as if they were arranged for an inspection. If the men did not lower their gaze to the floor, they would be able to scrutinize all the clothes of each woman, from her shoes up to her hat.[51]

Hirsch also noted that services were still held in Hebrew in Rodeph Shalom, yet the men, and more particularly the women, did not understand anything because they did not know Hebrew. It was clear to Hirsch that Jastrow did not want to introduce reforms for fear that his congregation might merge with Keneseth Israel.[52] Hirsch criticized Jastrow's activity as a person, rabbi, preacher, and activist, who did more harm than good by being too afraid to choose a side: either progress or Orthodoxy.[53]

Jastrow was defended by Benjamin Szold of Oheb Shalom Congregation in Baltimore, who had been his friend since the very

---

[49] Ibid., 5.
[50] Ibid.
[51] Ibid., 8.
[52] Ibid., 9.
[53] This conflict may also be followed in *Deborah*, January 31, 1868, 118; February 3, 1868, 155; March 13, 1868, 142; June 5, 1868, 190–191.

beginning of his time in America—indeed, they may already have met in Europe. Szold came from near Nitra, Slovakia, and first studied in a yeshiva in Bratislava. He took part in the Vienna Uprising of 1848, for which he was banished from the city. Between 1856 and 1858 he studied at the university and the Jewish Theological Seminary in Breslau. He became a rabbi in Baltimore in 1859. Jastrow and Szold were not only friends with similar views on the reform of Judaism, but they also had family ties: Jastrow's son, Joseph, married Szold's daughter, Rachel. Jastrow was also a friend and colleague of one of Szold's other daughters, Henrietta, the founder of Hadassah.[54]

In a pamphlet he wrote,[55] Szold tried to resolve the conflict, which had been going on for months, but at the same time defended Jastrow, who he believed was being slandered from many sides, mostly out of envy. Szold focused on reiterating the values Jastrow had introduced to American Jewry. He summarized Jastrow's program in three main points: the education and upbringing of youth; the inclusion of the modern Jew in a life in harmony with the culture and spirit of the time; and the struggle to acknowledge the whole of humanity as being the moral core of Judaism.

Jastrow considered Judaism to be a pure and more complete humanism, advocating freedom, brotherly love, and the autonomy of the nation.[56] He believed that Judaism should be guided by two fundamental principles—freedom and love. Szold pointed out that

---

[54] For more about Benjamin Szold and his family, see Marcus Jastrow, "Dr. Szold's 70th Birthday," *Jewish Exponent* (November 10, 1899): 8; Jastrow, "Benjamin Szold," *Jewish Exponent* (August 8, 1902): 1; William Rosenau, *In Honor of the Seventieth Birthday of Rev. Dr. Benjamin Szold* (Baltimore: Congregation Oheb Shalom, 1899); Rosenau, *Benjamin Szold* (Baltimore, 1902); Moshe Davis, *Emergence of Conservative Judaism*, 360–362; Alexandra Lee Levin, *The Szolds of Lombard Street: A Baltimore Family, 1859–1909* (Philadelphia: Jewish Publication Society of America, 1960); Lee Levin, *Henrietta Szold: Baltimorean* ([Baltimore,] 1995); Irving Fineman, *Woman of Valor: The Life of Henrietta Szold 1860–1945* (New York: Simon and Schuster, 1961); Dash Joan, *Summoned to Jerusalem: The Life of Henrietta Szold* (New York: Harper & Row, 1979); Rose Zeitlin, *Henrietta Szold: Record of a Life* (New York: Dial Press, 1966).

[55] Szold, *Auch ein Wort über Jastrow und Hirsch*. The claim was made in *Deborah* that Jastrow was the author of this pamphlet, but it did not befit him to sign it, see *Deborah*, June 5, 1868, 190.

[56] Szold, *Auch ein Wort über Jastrow und Hirsch*, 5.

Jastrow had in Warsaw already advocated freedom for black people and slaves.[57] He was called a backward Orthodox Jew in America not because he did not contribute to reform, but because he did not allow the framework of reforms to be imposed on him by local "authorities' for him to simply copy. Innovations which furthered social and spiritual development were important to Jastrow, and such development was to be achieved through education and the culture of both Judaism and the country of residence; innovations in synagogues alone could not ensure it. Szold and Jastrow held up the Vienna congregation as an example of a community that commanded respect not because of its central location and great reforms, but thanks to its excellent, intelligent rabbis, including Mannheimer and Jellinek, who skillfully perfected and ennobled the religious rituals through sermons and singing.[58]

Another issue, Szold noted, was the fact that there were no defined ideological frameworks or "dogmas' for reform in America at the time. He therefore postulated that the introduction of reforms should be left up to the rabbis of individual congregations, because they knew best what the congregations' particular expectations and needs were. An earnest and truly progressive rabbi would know how to perform his task in compliance with the spirit of the times.[59] According to Szold, Jastrow had such a program, which he had implemented in Warsaw, Mannheim, and Worms. The program had made him famous in Europe, because in it Jastrow had followed such ideals as freedom, democracy, and care for the welfare of his fellow men.[60] He also implemented this program in his congregation in Philadelphia.

This was how Szold and Jastrow opposed the idea put forward by Wise, Hirsch, and Lilienthal to unite all synagogues, or at least all Reform synagogues, and introduce uniform rituals and prayer books, ideally Wise's *Minhag America*. Instead, Szold and Jastrow proposed a common platform of rabbis who would supervise the introduction of reforms as religious leaders, but above all prevent disintegration of the unity of the followers of Judaism.

---

[57] Jastrow, *Israels Auserwählung*, 19.

[58] Szold, *Auch ein Wort über Jastrow und Hirsch*, 7.

[59] Ibid., 8.

[60] Ibid., 9.

Szold wrote that Hirsch should not call himself a defender of American democracy, because back in Europe he had lauded the monarchial system and called the nation an "ill-mannered boy." Hirsch, an "absolutist and servile toady," had been dismissed from his congregation in Dessau for having such views. In his works from his German period there are fragments in which he demanded that the state exercise religious supervision over the Jews, as emancipation was harmful and dangerous to Jewish religious life.[61] Szold wrote that such views resembled the views of ultra-Orthodox, not reform-minded, Jews. He also pointed out that in the introduction to one of his books, Hirsch had written that the principle that "outside the church there is no salvation" should also apply to the Jews and could cancel out the principle of the freedom and autonomy of individuals and congregations in Judaism.[62] Szold also demonstrated how Hirsch's views on the Messiah had changed over time (Hirsch had in Europe linked the Messiah with the idea of a monarchy in Israel, but then changed his views in America). Szold explained this discrepancy in Hirsch's opinions by referring to a Talmudic legend:

> A man, as an embryo in his mother's womb, has all possible knowledge. As he is coming into the world, though, an angel comes and hits him on the mouth, which causes him to forget everything. This was the case with Dr. Hirsch as well. As he was coming to the new world, where majesty belongs to the people—that ill-mannered boy—an angel came, but not a good one; it was an evil demon, a demon of the pursuit of fame and greed, and it hit him on the mouth; he [Hirsch] then forgot what he had previously written and advocated.[63]

---

[61] Ibid., 15.

[62] Ibid., 17–18. Hirsch wrote, "As a result of our research and work we may say: Jews are forced, it is required by the very truth of the cause, to accept fully and completely the principle that *extra ecclesia nulla salus*; but the church, on the basis of the same truth, is forced to accept the clause *nisi Judaeis in religion eorum*, and it will need to announce this before long. When it is mutually accepted, a higher peace will be achieved and one may side with political emancipation, being able to accept responsibility before God."

[63] Ibid., 20.

Szold's dispute with Hirsch is very revealing to us, because in the course of his polemic Szold presented in detail his and Jastrow's interpretation of reform. It reveals that the starting point for both Jastrow and Szold was to elevate the spirit of true Judaism, open to the world and full of humanitarian values, among its congregants. Both men considered reform a means to an end, rather than the end in itself, and therefore they thought that it should follow the progress of the people instead of anticipating their readiness to understand the symbolism and meanings of any changes.

This exposé of Hirsch's views should also turn our attention to how these evolved between the European and American periods. We do not know to what extent Hirsch took to heart Szold's remarks about a lack of "doctrine," theological interpretation of reform, but a year later it was Hirsch who hosted the first conference of reformers in Philadelphia. Hirsch's views are apparent in the first American platform proclaimed during this conference. The platform did not differ much from the program of the German moderate Reform movement, as there was still hope that all Jewish communities could be united under the Reform camp of Wise, Hirsch, and Lilienthal.[64]

Jastrow's conflicts with Wise, Kalisch, and Hirsch were not the only controversies in which he was involved during his time in America. He always defended himself when he saw a threat to the values of Judaism he believed in, or reprehensible treatment of the history of Judaism and the Jews by American authors. Jastrow was one of the most vehement opponents of Wise—the father of Reform Judaism in America, but his intransigence in religious matters forced him to lay aside dreams of leadership and rivalry after his first turbulent years in the United States. In later periods he focused more on education and academic work. Nonetheless, in his rivalry with Wise and his supporters Jastrow failed as a rabbi and preacher, because his own congregation, where he had sown the first ideas of reform, did not wish to remain in the middle—between Orthodox and Reform Judaism. He lost not only then, but later too: His name is very rarely present in the historiography of Reform Judaism in America, perhaps due to the controversies presented in this book. Were it not for "Jastrow's Dictionary," his name would have probably been completely forgotten in the United States.

---

[64] See *Philadelphia Platform* in Michael A. Meyer and W. Gunther Plaut, *The Reform Judaism Reader*, 196–7.

Chapter 7. Controversies

Jastrow on the steps of the Rodeph Shalom synagogue.

Chapter 8

Liturgy: The Minhag Jastrow

The bond between Jastrow and Szold is most clearly visible in their liturgical work—the editing and revision of prayer books to serve their communities.

The Jewish immigrants from European countries who arrived in America at the beginning of the nineteenth century needed to adjust to the conditions they found, such as the different rituals in local American synagogues. Most of these used the Sephardi rite—*Minhag Sefarad*—which did not always suit the Ashkenazi congregants. New congregations were established, or existing ones taken over, with the influx of Ashkenazi Jews, who wished to implement their own rituals and customs, such as *Minhag Polin* or *Minhag Ashkenaz*, which were often modified in the nineteenth century in the spirit of Reform.[1] With progressive acculturation and the gradual move away from the study of Hebrew, an increasing number of prayer books needed to be translated into German and, later, English. Such pluralism led to the decentralization of religious life and the loss of its unity. By 1873, there had been over two hundred print runs of various prayer books for the few congregations existing in the United States at the time.[2]

Prayer books—*siddurim* and *mahzorim*—have for centuries been not only tools for prayer and rituals, but also a reflection of the religious, theological, and social views of Jewish communities in various countries during different periods. Hence, differences in customs and liturgies arose.[3] It should not come as a surprise that there were also drives in America to edit and re-print prayer books to reflect new cir-

---

[1] See the classic work of Jakob J. Petuchowski, *Prayerbook Reform in Europe: The Liturgy of European Liberal and Reform Judaism.*

[2] See Sharona R. Wachs, *American Jewish Liturgies: A Bibliography of American Jewish Liturgy from the Establishment of the Press in the Colonies through 1925* (Cincinnati: HUC Press, 1997).

[3] Abraham E. Millgram, *Jewish Worship* (Philadelphia: Jewish Publication Society of America, 1971), 391 ff.

cumstances and religious needs. From the mid-nineteenth century, most progressive prayer books were published in bilingual versions, German-Hebrew or English-Hebrew. Orthodox congregations, however, preserved the customs and liturgy from their countries of origin.

During the first rabbinical conference in Cleveland, organized on Wise's initiative in 1855, the decision was taken to draft a common prayer book which would be the standard for all American congregations. In addition to Wise, Isidor Kalisch, Leo Merzbacher, and others worked on the new prayer book. The fruit of their work was *Tefilot Bnai Yeshurun: Minhag Amerika*, published in 1857.[4] Even though *Minhag Amerika* later became the symbol of Reform, it is actually quite conservative, due to the compromise that Wise wished to achieve in order to avoid disaffecting the traditional Jews.[5] The first Reform prayer book formulated in the spirit of Samuel Holdheim's radical Reform was *Olat Tamid*, prepared by David Einhorn,[6] the leader of radical Reform in America.[7]

When Benjamin Szold arrived in the United States in 1859, he could not find an appropriate prayer book for his congregation, Oheb Shalom, which would suit his vision of reform. Neither the *Olat Tamid* compiled by his neighbor from Baltimore, which he considered too radical, nor *Minhag Amerika*, which he thought was not precise or coherent enough, suited him. Therefore, Szold decided to compile his own version of the prayer book for his congregation. *Avodat Israel* was first published in 1864[8] and was subsequently reprinted several times. In addition, Szold published many other collections of prayers for

---

[4] *Tefilot Bnai Yeshurun: Minhag Amerika: The Daily Prayers of American Israelites* (Cincinnati, 1857).

[5] See Joseph Hirsch, *Avodat Yisrael and Minhag Amerika*, AJA SC no. 5045 [19]. For more about the influence of *Minhag Amerika*, see Eric Friedland, "Isaac Mayer Wise and Minhag Amerika," in his *"Were Our Mouths Filled with Song"*, 50–54.

[6] David Einhorn, ed., *Olath Tamid. Gebetbuch für israelitische Reform-Gemeinden* (Baltimore, 1856). See also Eric Friedland, "David Einhorn and Olath Tamid," in *"Were Our Mouths Filled with Song,"* 17–49.

[7] For more about individual prayer books in America, see Wachs, *American Jewish Liturgies*.

[8] *Awodat Israel. Israelitisches Gebetbuch für den öffentlichen Gottesdienst im ganzen Jahre*, geordnet und übersetzt von Benjamin Szold, Rabbiner der Oheb Schalom-Gemeinde in Baltimore (Baltimore, 1864).

various occasions.⁹ However, the reason he set out to prepare prayer books for his congregation in the first place was the fact that when he arrived in Baltimore, congregation Oheb Shalom used a Reform prayer book during the week and an Orthodox one for Sabbath. There was, clearly, an acute need to regulate this issue.

When Jastrow steered Congregation Rodeph Shalom onto the path of "progress' by introducing religious reforms and sermons in German and English, he also began the search for a prayer book appropriate for his congregation. In 1870 he proposed Szold's *Awodat Israel* as the official prayer book, which he would edit. The first Hebrew-German edition of the prayer book with Jastrow's name on it appeared in 1871.¹⁰ It immediately attracted much attention, but only became widely acknowledged across the United States after it was translated into English in 1873.¹¹ The prayer book has since then been known as "Minhag Jastrow,"¹² despite the fact that Szold's name was still featured in subsequent editions.

What made *Awodat Israel* so popular, and what distinguished it from other prayer books? *Awodat Israel* has always been classified as a Reform prayer book¹³ due to the elimination of all references to the Temple in Jerusalem, the restoration of the cult of the Temple, a per-

---

[9] See, e. g., *Kodesh Hillulim: Pijutim, Gebete und Gesänge* (Baltimore, 1862); *Sefer ha-Chajjim. Andachtsbuch zum Gebrauche bei Krankheiten und Sterbefallen, und auf dem Friedhofe* (Baltimore, 1866); *Hagjon-Lew. Israelitisches Gebetbuch für häusliche Andacht* (Baltimore, 1867).

[10] *Awodat Israel. Israelitisches Gebetbuch für den öffentlichen Gottesdienst im ganzen Jahre*, geordnet und übersetzt von Benjamin Szold, Rabbiner der Oheb Schalom-Gemeinde in Baltimore. 3. Aufl., revidiert von M. Jastrow, Rabbiner der Rodef-Schalom Gemeinde zu Philadelphia und H. Hochheimer, Rabbiner der Oheb Israel-Gemeinde zu Baltimore (Baltimore, 1871).

[11] *Avodat Israel: Israelitish Prayer Book, for all the Public Services of the Year.* Originally Arranged by Rev. Dr. Benjamin Szold of Baltimore. Second Edition (Hebrew and German), revised by Rev. Drs. M. Jastrow of Philadelphia, and H. Hochheimer of Baltimore. Hebrew and English Edition, in Text and Typographical arrangement fully corresponding with the Revised Hebrew-German Edition, by M. Jastrow Rabbi of the Congregation Rodef-Shalom (Philadelphia, 1873).

[12] See Eric Friedland, "Marcus Jastrow and Abodath Israel," in *Texts and Responses*, 191. Cf. Davis, *Emergence of Judaism…*, 143.

[13] See, for instance, the catalogues of the libraries in the Hebrew Union College and Jewish Theological Seminary of America.

sonal Messiah, and the resurrection of the dead. These were the main difference between *Awodat Israel* and traditional prayer books; modifications to the rest of the prayer book were minor. Jastrow believed in the revelation at Mount Sinai and the divine origin of the Torah, and he and Szold were among the few Reformers who did not dissociate themselves from Zionism. On the contrary, Jastrow would later be one of the most important activists in Zionist organizations. Jastrow and Szold wanted their prayer book to be practical and of educational value, as compared to other Reform *siddurim*, rather than to be distinguished by theological innovations. Jastrow was aware that few of his congregants would be able to read and understand prayers in Hebrew; that is why he prepared a bilingual version for all of the prayers. The English version was expanded and does not fully correspond with the Hebrew. Jastrow was probably influenced in this matter by the resolution of the Leipzig Synod of Reform rabbis, who agreed in 1869 that the introduction of additional prayers and meditations in the vernacular was permissible even on Yom Kippur.[14]

Eric Friedland, a leading expert on Jewish liturgy, praised Jastrow for his ability to combine new and conventional prayers, and asserted that "the technical apparatus of the prayerbook is faultless."[15] Jastrow's predilection for Spanish-Jewish culture was evident in the fact that he replaced some of the Ashkenazi *piyyutim* in Szold's *Awodat Israel* with Sephardi ones,[16] which he considered more poetic.[17] He was probably influenced by Michael Sachs, who was also fascinated by medieval Sephardic poetry. He also believed that David was not the author of the Psalms; hence, all mentions of David's authorship of the Psalms were also removed. Moreover, fragments about sacrifices made in the Temple were omitted from the Musaf.[18] Jastrow shortened certain prayers, such as *Lecha Dodi*, which was necessary because the duration of services had been shortened in Congregation Rodeph

---

[14] David Philipson, *The Reform Movement in Judaism* (New York: Ktav, 1967), 284–328.

[15] See Friedland, *Marcus Jastrow and Abodath Israel*, 192.

[16] For instance, *Melekh elyon, Imeru lelohim, Enosh eykh yitzdaq, Omnam ken*. See Friedland, *Marcus Jastrow and Abodath Israel*, 194–195, for more examples.

[17] Ibid., 194–195.

[18] Wolf? Willner, *Marcus Mordecai Jastrow: Read before the South Rabbinical Association*, March 10, 1904, AJA SC no. 13012, 11–12 (typescript).

Shalom. Eventually, an triennial cycle of Torah reading was implemented, and the Sabbath service was moved to a set time on Friday evening so that all congregants would be able to attend it after work. Thus, the practical aspect of the new prayer book must have been of great importance.

Although the prayer book was replaced with the *Union Prayer Book* at the beginning of Rabbi Berkowitz's era in Congregation Rodeph Shalom, *Minhag Jastrow* continued to be used in other congregations, including some Conservative congregations,[19] and was frequently reprinted.[20] It was in use for the longest period in Temple Ohabei Shalom — the oldest Boston Reform congregation.

Jastrow's work in the field of liturgy was not limited to the co-revision of *Avodat Israel*. He edited a few other collections of prayers, some of them together with Szold. One of his best-known collections is called *Songs and Prayers and Meditations*, and it was often distributed alongside *Minhag Jastrow*. It was published only in English.[21]

Szold and Jastrow revised a number of collections of prayers for home use[22] as well as for use in schools and during services for chil-

---

[19] See Friedland, *Marcus Jastrow and Abodath Israel*, 199. Detailed information about *Avodat Israel* may be found in Joseph Hirsch, *Avodat Yisrael and Minhag Amerika*, AJA SC no. 5045; Eric Friedland, "Were Our Mouths Filled With Song," chapter 3 and passim; Eric Friedland, "The Historical and Theological Development of the Non-Orthodox Prayerbooks in the United States' (PhD diss., Brandeis University, 1967); and Eric Friedland, "Hebrew Liturgical Creativity in Nineteenth-Century America," *Modern Judaism* 1, no. 3 (1981): 323–336.

[20] *Avodat Israel* was published in the following years: 1907, 1910, 1912, 1916, 1921, 1922, 1924, 1925, 1927, 1930, 1944, 1946, and 1948. See Wachs, *American Jewish Liturgies…*, index.

[21] *Songs and Prayers and Meditations for Divine Service of Israelites*, compiled by B. Szold Rabbi of the Congregation Oheb-Shalom, Baltimore. Translated from German by M. Jastrow, Rabbi of the Congregation Rodef-Shalom (Philadelphia, 1873). See also *Hymns and Responses from Jastrow's Prayer Book*, Especially Adopted for Congregational Singing in Congregation Rodeph Shalom ([Philadelphia,] 1894).

[22] *Hegjon Lew. Israelitisches Gebetbuch für die häusliche Andacht*, geordnet von Benjamin Szold. Zweite gänzlich umgearbeitete Auflage, herausgegeben von M. Jastrow (Philadelphia, 1875); *Kicur hagada le-Lew: Family Service for the Eve of Passover*, Hebrew and English, by M. Jastrow Rabbi of the Congregation "Rodef Shalom" (Philadelphia, 1878).

dren, which were largely based on *Avodat Israel*.²³ Through his subsequent revisions, Jastrow surpassed the initiator of the abovementioned publications, Benjamin Szold. His place in the history of Jewish liturgy in the United States is therefore unquestionable. *Minhag Jastrow* was well known throughout the American Diaspora, but unfortunately no research has been undertaken to examine the impact it might have had in the nineteenth and at the beginning of the twentieth century.

Jastrow strove to raise the level of religiosity in his congregation not only by reforming the liturgy and educating people about its importance, but also by giving popular lectures to his congregation and associations on various aspects of the history and religion of the Jews, which were later published or extensively discussed in the Jewish press (mainly the *Hebrew Leader, Jewish Exponent, American Hebrew, Deborah,* and *Israelite*).²⁴ He also expressed his opinions on topics relating to the situation of the Jews in America and other countries, mainly Russia and Romania, where the situation was particularly difficult due to repression and persecution.²⁵

In order to summarize this area of Jastrow's activity, let us take note of his statement about the reforms in his congregation. He said

---

23   *Gebete für Kinder für Haus und Schule*, Antworten von Benjamin Szold, revidiert von M. Jastrow (Philadelphia [1875]); *The Hebrew Reader, For Schools*, from the Prayer Book of Rev. Dr. B. Szold, revised by Rev. Drs. Jastrow and Hochheimer (Philadelphia, 1884).

24   Listing all of them would take up many pages, but a few examples are: Marcus Jastrow, "Leopold Zunz: Delivered before the Hebrew Literary Society of Philadelphia, April 11, 1886," *American Hebrew,* April 24, 1886; Marcus Jastrow, "Geschichtliches Verhältnis der Juden zur Zivilisation der Völker (Ein Vortrag gehalten in der Halle der Deutschen Gesellschaft zu Philadelphia)," *Hebrew Leader* 14, no. 8, 10, 11, 12, 13, 14, 16, 19 (1869); Marcus Jastrow, "Der Prophet Samuel, der letzte israelitische Republikaner. Ein Vortrag gehalten in der Harmeshalle zu Philadelphia zu Gunsten der United Relief Assoc.," *Hebrew Leader*, May 17 and May 26, 1867; Marcus Jastrow, "The Zionist Movement," *Public Ledger*, April 9, 1903.

25   Marcus Jastrow, *The Causes of the Revived Disaffection against the Jews, by Rev. Dr. …Address delivered before the Conference of the Jewish Ministers' Association in New York, Tuesday, May 27th, 1890* (New York, 1890), 3–15; Marcus Jastrow, "The Causes of Disaffection towards us Jews," *Jewish Exponent*, October 4, 1900; Marcus Jastrow, "Die Juden in Russland und ihre Auswällen," *Hebrew Leader*, February 22, 1870. Die Juden in Russland und ihre Auswällen

that his congregants did not have an ideal to fight for; "their reform is easy, they need not sacrifice anything to become reformers, and they are attracted to a religion which requires few, if any, sacrifices."[26] When he was asked if more attention should be paid to the next generation, which would live in prosperity without having to worry about everyday life, given that the generation of his contemporaries saw America as a country of the dollar, Jastrow responded:

> But those people who came to the "golden" America do have ideals! You see, they are not as attached to earning money because they often close their businesses even for two subsequent days; the next generation will not do so anymore. Rosh Hashanah and Yom Kippur will be the only days they will celebrate without business, and soon even these two days will be too many for them! The older generation, your money earners, sacrifice their comfort to follow kashrut; your generation knows no prohibitions on its appetite. You are mistaken—people who do not sacrifice anything do not have religion.[27]

Jastrow's fears were fulfilled: in successive generations: many of those who chose the path of easy reform—reform by imitation rather than change—often moved away from Judaism. It is worth adding that present-day Reform Judaism is returning to its roots: to halakhah and respect for the Hebrew language and the history of the Jews; it supports Zionism. To these people, Jastrow may be a role model today.

---

[26] Willner, *Marcus Mordecai Jastrow*, 12.
[27] Ibid., 12.

Chapter 8. Liturgy: The *Minhag Jastrow*

Jastrow with his dog, Knell.

Chapter 9

Jastrow and the "Historical School"

In his 1963 book *Emergence of Conservative Judaism: The Historical School in 19th-Century America*,[1] Moshe Davis profiled a group of rabbis, *hazanim* and laymen who reportedly shared the idea of respect for law and education combined with the goal of the full participation of Jews in American society. Davis named the group "the Historical School." There are grounds for certain objections regarding whether such a "school" really existed, or at least whether it existed in the minds of those who were supposedly its members from 1820 until 1902—that is, until the formation of Conservative Judaism. The people who are said to have comprised this "school" and, consequently, Conservative Judaism, including Isaac Leeser, Sabato Morais, Marcus Jastrow, Benjamin Szold, Alexander Kohut, Samuel Mayer Isaacs, Aaron Bettelheim, Joseph Blumenthal, Jonas Bondi, Lewis N. Dembitz, Bernard Drachman, Moses Aaron Dropsie, Henry Hochheimer, Frederick de Sola Mendes, Henry Pereira Mendes, Morris Raphall, Solomon Solis-Cohen, Mayer Sulzberger, and Aaron Wise, to name only those whose brief biographies Davies included in his book, held views too varied and different, and worked in conditions too dissimilar, to form one "school."[2] Perhaps it would be more accurate to refer to them as belonging to the "Historico-Critical" or "Positive-Historical" schools of Jewish thought.[3] According to Davis, what connects the representatives of this "school" is the shared view

---

[1] Davis, *Emergence of Conservative Judaism*.

[2] For more about the problems with the definition of the "Historical School," see Bernard H. Pucker, [review] *"Emergence of Conservative Judaism: The Historical School in 19th-Century America* by Moshe Davis, Jewish Publication Society of America," *American Jewish Historical Quarterly* 54, no. 4 (1965): 481–483.

[3] Such was the term for the followers of Judaism close to Frankel and the Seminary in Breslau. Cf. Nathan Stern, *The Jewish Historico-Critical School of the Nineteenth Century* (New York [1901]).

that the Bible and Talmud constitute the basis of Judaism, though they differ in their attitudes toward the *Shulhan arukh*.[4] Nonetheless, there are many points of concordance between the abovementioned names—most of them lived on the East Coast, mainly in Philadelphia and New York; many were educated in Europe prior to their arrival in America; they had a traditional attitude to the fundamental values of Judaism; and they advocated affirmation of Jewish and secular education. This stance often placed them between the radical Reformers and Orthodox Jews. Even if some of them worked alongside the Reformers from Cincinnati, they were motivated by a desire to maintain the unity of the Jews and Judaism in America. The unquestionable leader and first ideologist of the group was Isaac Leeser, who was succeeded by Sabato Morais. They were both from Philadelphia—the center of conservative Judaism until the late eighties. The center later shifted to New York, which had the largest Jewish community in America.

When Szold and Jastrow arrived in America, they were considered Orthodox Jews by the radical Reformers (for instance Einhorn), and Reformers by people like Morais and Isaacs.[5] Indeed, Jastrow, Szold, and Hochheimer did initially join Wise's Reform camp, and supported limited reform efforts in their congregations. Later, they were unable to halt this process, and Jastrow paid for it with his early retirement.

What connected the abovementioned characters, which transcended what differentiated them, was their work toward the advancement of Judaism in America, in particular as regards the education of youth, future rabbis, and preachers.

Maimonides College

From the very beginning of his time in Philadelphia, Jastrow did not limit his activity to his congregation, Rodeph Shalom, but eagerly joined in any initiatives promoting the education and progress of American Jews, in accordance with his ideals and the spirit of reform. When in 1867 he was offered the chance to take part in the nascent

---

[4] Davis, *Emergence of Conservative Judaism*, 231.
[5] Ibid., 138–139.

Jastrow in the 1880s.

project of establishing Maimonides College—a Jewish school of higher education—he eagerly agreed to join.

It was not the first such idea—Isaac Leeser had proposed the founding of such a national school as early as 1841, but his idea had failed due to lack of interest and support from other congregations.[6] Another project was launched in 1852 by Sampson Simson of New York, who wished to establish a Jewish Theological Seminary and Scientific Institute, but his idea also failed at an early stage.[7] Three years later, in 1855, Isaac M. Wise announced the opening of Zion College in Cincinnati, which was to offer both religious and secular

---

[6] Bertram Wallace Korn, *Eventful Years and Experiences: Studies in Nineteenth Century American Jewish History* (Cincinnati: American Jewish Archives, 1954), 154.

[7] Ibid., 155.

education.⁸ Fourteen students, including two Christians, registered for the first year, but unfortunately the college could not fulfill its curriculum, particularly with regard to secular courses, and many students left for regular schools in Cincinnati. Zion College was closed down in 1856, with Wise's character played a role in its failure, as he could not find partners for his enterprise.⁹

Leeser, who initiated the establishment of Maimonides College, knew that he needed to win the support of many congregations and sponsors for the school to open and fulfill its role. Therefore, he turned to the only all-American Jewish organization at the time—the Board of Delegates of American Israelites, founded in 1859 and comprising twenty-five congregations, mostly Orthodox or Conservative.¹⁰

In 1864, Leeser and a group of people from Philadelphia decided to officially submit a proposal to open a school that would educate youth and ministers in that city.¹¹ The Hebrew Educational Society of Philadelphia supported them in their efforts. The program and plan of action were agreed upon during the founding meeting on May 27, 1867, which drew together rabbis and representatives of the two organizations from New York and Philadelphia. Maimonides College was to educate Jewish ministers who would speak English, so that there would be no need for rabbis from Germany. This appalled Jastrow, who had just arrived from Germany and who felt that the presence of rabbis educated in Europe had a positive influence on the standard of education in America.¹² The opening of Maimonides College, as well as its structure and by-laws, were officially announced after the meeting.¹³

---

8   See the curriculum of Zion College in Korn, *Eventful Years and Experiences*, 157–158.

9   For more, see Davis, *Emergence of Conservative Judaism*, 56–57, and Korn, *Eventful Years and Experiences*, 159.

10 For more about the circumstances surrounding the establishment and operation of the Board of Delegates of American Israelites, see Allan Tarshish, *Board of Delegates of American Israelites (1859–1878)*, AJA SC no. 14240; Kohler, *The Board of Delegates of American Israelites*; and Davis, *Emergence of Conservative Judaism*, 101–108, 197–199.

11 Sussman, *Isaac Leeser and the Making of American Judaism*, 238–239.

12 Korn, *Eventful Years and Experiences*, 165.

13 The statute of Maimonides College can be found in Korn, *Eventful Years and Experiences*, 206–209, and Davis, *Emergence of Conservative Judaism*, 378–380.

Leeser was appointed provost and professor of homiletics and comparative theology, and Jastrow became professor of Talmud, Hebrew philosophy, and Jewish history and literature.[14] Other lecturers were Sabato Morais, who taught the Bible and biblical literature; Aaron S. Bettelheim, professor of *Mishnah* with commentaries, *Shulhan arukh*, and *Mishneh Torah*; and Laemmlein Buttenwiesser, who taught Hebrew and Aramaic. Other members of the faculty included George Jacobs, Hyman Polano, and William H. Williams, head of the department of English language and literature and the only non-Jew among the professors at the college. The course of study was to last five years, and the students would receive the title of doctor of theology upon graduation. Candidates were required to demonstrate their ability to translate fragments of the Hebrew Bible relating to the history of Israel.[15]

The college began operating in October 1867. Its professors, with the exception of Williams, worked for small salaries or even without payment, but they treated their work as a mission for the future of the Jews in America. Lectures took place in the building of the Hebrew Educational Society or at the school alongside Congregation Rodeph Shalom. Eight students were admitted to the first year, but only four started the course. Three further students joined over the course of the first year.

In the summarizing report for the first year of operation, in the column for what Jastrow wished to achieve with his students, he wrote that the students should have general knowledge of the Bible—they should know the number of the books and their structure, and the most important historical events and their significance for Judaism. He had also begun to read Maimonides' *Yad Hachazakah* with his students.[16] However, the report on the assessment of his teaching suggests that instead of giving lectures on the history of Israel, [he] read historical fragments of the Bible and made comments about them for which the students had not been sufficiently prepared.[17] Jastrow taught and

---

[14] *Minutes of Maimonides College*, AJA, SC no. 9585, 3.

[15] Korn, *Eventful Years and Experiences*, 168–171; Davis, *Emergence of Conservative Judaism*, 61.

[16] *Messenger*, August 7, 1868, 2–3.

[17] *Minutes of Maimonides College*, AJA, SC no. 9585, 18. Cf. Korn, *Eventful Years and Experiences*, 179.

Chapter 9. Jastrow and the "Historical School"

Editorial board of *The Jewish Encyclopedia*.

read *The First Book of Samuel* and fragments of *Mishneh Torah* with the students in the next year.

Of this small number of students, only three continued their education after the summer break. The size of the student body was considered a failure for the college and its lecturers, who even gave private lessons in order not to lose anyone. Neither did the situation improve in subsequent years. After Leeser's death in 1868, Jastrow became the provost of Maimonides College, and some impute its failure to him[18]—not to any incompetence or lack of good will, but rather to his lack of knowledge about the overall situation of American Jews and existing relations.[19] During this period, Jastrow was also involved in many conflicts with opinion-makers such as Isaac Wise, Isidor Kalisch, and Samuel Hirsch, who used the press to criticize him and, at the same time, Maimonides College. Wise in particular criticized the Philadelphia college loudly for being Orthodox and for not taking the right attitude to reform. Despite all of the difficulties, in 1871 the Maimonides College authorities managed to secure the consent of the University of Pennsylvania to enroll its students there, which gave them additional opportunities.[20]

With the College experiencing difficulties, Wise achieved his goal: in 1873 he founded the Union of American Hebrew Congregations, an all-American organization uniting mostly progressive congregations. The Hebrew Union College in Cincinnati was established two years later, thanks to the support of the UAHC. Wise wished to make use of the existing structure and turn Maimonides College into a branch of the Hebrew Union College to serve the eastern states, but his proposal was not accepted in Philadelphia.[21]

Unfortunately, due to the lack of interest in Maimonides College and the criticism of it, it evolved into a college with private teachers preparing students for preachers' posts in American congregations. The college was closed in 1875, and its formal end was marked by the merger of the Board of Delegates of American Israelites with the Union of American Hebrew Congregations in 1878.

---

[18] Korn, *Eventful Years and Experiences*, 191.

[19] Davis, *Emergence of Conservative Judaism*, 62.

[20] Korn, *Eventful Years and Experiences*, 181.

[21] Ibid., 189.

Toward a New Seminary

The collaboration of Wise's Reform camp with new institutions gradually united rabbis and congregation leaders with conservative views. Most of the followers of Positive-Historical Judaism did not support the establishment of the Union of American Hebrew Congregations in 1873 and the Hebrew Union College in 1875. Jastrow and Szold initially did, later claiming they supported it in the name of the unity of Judaism. However, they soon became disaffected with both institutions.

A number of events contributed to the split between the advocates of the reform of Judaism and moderate and conservative Reformers. The first was the conference of Reform rabbis in Philadelphia in 1869, during which a common platform was adopted which did not go beyond moderate reform. However, the conference rejected the *ketubah*, which some people found very difficult to accept.[22] It was decided at the subsequent two conferences in Cleveland in 1870 and in Cincinnati in 1871 that Wise's prayer book, *Minhag Amerika*, would be used in the Union. The idea of a personal God was also rejected, which caused a wave of protest in the Jewish press.[23]

Further events made permanent the rift in Progressive Judaism represented by the followers of Reform and Positive-Historical Judaism. The first of these was the merger of the Union of American Hebrew Congregations and the Board of Delegates of American Israelites, which was the only organization in which traditionalists and followers of Positive-Historical Judaism still had some influence. The next event was the so-called "Trefa Banquet" and the subsequent reactions to it, which demonstrated a negative attitude to the law and *mitzvot*. Ultimately, it was the announcement of the Pittsburgh Platform[24] in 1855 which overtly broke ties with the Oral Torah and tradition. The abovementioned events led to the emergence of Reform Judaism as a separate denomination in Judaism, with its own organizational structure, ideological platform, and modified liturgy.

The unification of the Reform camp also contributed to the consolidation of the followers of Positive-Historical Judaism, who

---

[22] Davis, *Emergence of Conservative Judaism*, 222.
[23] Ibid., 156–159, 166.
[24] See the full text of the *Pittsburgh Platform* in Michael A. Meyer and W. Gunther Plaut, *The Reform Judaism Reader*, 197–199.

established the Jewish Theological Seminary Association in 1886 on the initiative of Sabato Morais. Its main goal was to create an institution educating rabbis in the spirit of respect for Jewish history and tradition. The board of the seminary comprised Marcus Jastrow, Sabato Morais, Alexander Kohut, Bernard Drachman, Frederick de Sola Mendes, Henry Pereira Mendes, Aaron Wise, Abraham Pereira Mendes, Henry S. Jacobs, and H. Schneeberger.[25]

Before the seminary opened, its founders needed to discuss its future form. Ideological confrontations between moderate reformers and traditionalists proved unavoidable. Morais suggested that a common prayer book, like that in the Reform camp, should be prepared on the basis of the Sephardi Siddur. The Ashkenazi rabbis, who already were in the majority, did not agree to this. Morais also spoke out against installing organs in synagogues. In order to convince Morais, other members discreetly approached Rabbi Adolf Jellinek of Vienna about this and asked whether installing organs in synagogues was compatible with the law. Jellinek answered that he saw no conflict.[26]

Morais, who considered the seminary his achievement, suggested that it should be called "The Orthodox Seminary," but Alexander Kohut, its real organizer, proposed the name "Jewish Theological Seminary". He did so for two reasons: firstly, he wanted the seminary to be an open, universal institution for all branches of American Judaism; secondly, as a graduate of the Seminary of Breslau, Kohut considered that institution the ideal, and a model that was later followed in the organizational, didactic, and academic respects. There were other former students of the Seminary of Breslau among the founders of the Jewish Theological Seminary, including Benjamin Szold, Frederick de Sola Mendes, and Bernard Drachman. Jastrow did not study there, but he was friendly with many of the members of its faculty and maintained contact with them.[27]

---

[25] Israel Davidson, "The Academic Aspect and Growth of the Rabbinical Department: The Seminary Proper," in *The Jewish Theological Seminary of America: Semi-Centennial Volume*, ed. Cyrus Adler (New York: The Jewish Theological Seminary of America, 1939), 73–74.

[26] Davis, *Emergence of Conservative Judaism*, 212.

[27] Ibid., 235. This connection between the JTS and the Seminary of Breslau is not prominent in Davis' book.

There were also other issues on which the founders had differing opinions. For example, they all believed in the divine revelation on Mount Sinai, but they disagreed on the questions of immortality and reward and punishment after death. Some, including Jastrow, did not believe in a personal Messiah, the rebuilding of the Temple, or a return to the sacrificial system.[28] As Jastrow, Szold, Kohut, and Solis-Cohen took a critical approach to studying the Bible, it was difficult for them to accept all of Maimonides' *Principles of Faith*, particularly the belief in all of the prophets' words. Nonetheless, more connected the founders than divided them, and their differences became smaller and less significant with time.

The official opening of the seminary took place on January 2, 1887. Classes began a month later, held in the building of Congregation Shearith Israel in New York since the seminary did not yet have a separate building at its disposal.[29] The first president of the seminary was Sabato Morais,[30] and ten students enrolled for the first year.[31] Jastrow and Kohut were among the best-educated of the teachers, but both had prior commitments and duties which prevented them from giving regular lectures. In addition, Jastrow was experiencing health problems, so he only delivered occasional open lectures. He gave a lecture on *Psalms*[32] on June 29, 1880, and on April 26, 1891, delivered a lecture entitled "The Rabbi in Public Life," which was later published under the title *The Minister and Public Movement*.[33]

---

[28] It is evident in his prayer book, *Awodat Israel*.

[29] The Jewish Theological Seminary was moved to its current location in 1902.

[30] The most comprehensive study on Morais is Arthur Kiron, "'Golden Ages, Promised Land': The Victorian Rabbinic Humanism of Sabato Morais' (PhD diss., Columbia University, 1999).

[31] Davidson, *The Academic Aspect and Growth of the Rabbinical Department*, 74. This contains the curriculum and a description of classes, 74–78. See also the unpublished extended version of Davidson's article in the Jewish Theological Seminary Archives, Solomon Schechter Papers.

[32] According to Davidson, *The Academic Aspect and Growth of the Rabbinical Department* (typescript), Jewish Theological Seminary Archives, Solomon Schechter Papers. Unfortunately, I was unable to locate the text of the lecture.

[33] Marcus Jastrow, "The Minister and Public Movement," in *The Activities of the Rabbi: A Course of Lectures Delivered under the Auspices of the Jewish*

In this lecture, intended for younger students, Jastrow discussed the experience of maintaining his uncompromising attitude in his preaching work. He cautioned them that if they knew who to reprimand or call to order, they should do so, rather than avoiding public discussion when something negative was happening. He said that a preacher must react to the corruption and mistakes of his wards. Jastrow gave Einhorn, Szold, and Morais as examples of people who had differing religious views, but "the words of the freedom of justice flowed out of their mouths causing hindrance to many who were releasing venom."[34]

What is most surprising, though, is that even after so many years in America Jastrow listed the men who had taught him to preach as examples to emulate. These were Michael Sachs of Berlin, Isaac Noah Mannheimer of Vienna, and the "long-bearded" Orthodox Rabbi Baer Meisels of Krakow and Warsaw, who had spent a few months at the Citadel with Jastrow for his part in the freedom struggles.[35] Jastrow remained faithful to his ideals and teachers for many years, and it does not seem that his views changed much in that time.

Jastrow was in permanent contact with the seminary and its subsequent presidents. After Morais'[36] death in 1897, Solomon Schechter—an eminent scholar and professor at the University of Cambridge, who spoke highly of Jastrow—became its new president.[37] During Schechter's time there were plans to bring to the seminary Rabbi Samuel A. Poznański, in a sense Jastrow's successor in Warsaw, who was offered the post of Bible lecturer. However, his duties as preacher at the Great Synagogue on Tłomackie Street and his state of health did not permit him to accept the offer.[38] Cyrus Adler, president of the sem-

---

Theological Seminary, February- May, 5652 (New York: Jewish Theological Seminary Association, 1892), 65–72.

[34] Ibid., 72.

[35] Ibid.

[36] See "Dr. Jastrow's Address," in *Seminary Convention: Biennial Meeting of the Jewish Theological Seminary Association. Business Session Followed by Addresses by Well Known Speakers. Tributes to the Late Dr. Morais, The Jewish Exponent* (March 25, 1898): 2–3.

[37] "Dr. Jastrow Pleads for Seminary," in *Philadelphia Branch of Jewish Theological Seminary, The Jewish Exponent* (April 10, 1903): 2.

[38] Davidson, *The Academic Aspect and Growth*, 79. Another connection between the Jewish Theological Seminary and Poland was Moses Schorr's receipt of

inary between 1915 and 1940 and previously an acolyte of Jastrow's, wrote of him as a great scholar, rabbi, and man.

> Dr. Jastrow ... was an intellectual aristocrat of the first order. If anyone were needed to impress upon my mind the lesson, which I learned in my own home, of the lack of importance of money, he did it. It was his constant theme that the only thing worth while in this world was what you had in your head, and he used to say: "Unless you become insane ... you will never lose what is in your head ... and those who have money ... take away their money and what are they?"[39]

The establishment of the seminary, in which Jastrow played an active role, was only the beginning of the process of the formation of Conservative Judaism, which was an answer to Reform Judaism. The theological and organizational framework of this denomination was shaped over time. Conservative Judaism, along with the Orthodox and Reform branches of Judaism, shaped the image of American Judaism for many years. Unfortunately, Jastrow's name appears increasingly rarely in contemporary studies on the history of the Jewish Theological Seminary and Conservative Judaism.[40]

---

an honorary degree from JTS in 1937.

[39] Cyrus Adler, *I Have Considered the Days* (Philadelphia: Jewish Publication Society of America, 1945), 40–41.

[40] For more on the beginnings of the Jewish Theological Seminary and Conservative Judaism, see Hasia Diner, "Like the Antelope and the Badger. The Founding and Early Years of the Jewish Theological Seminary, 1886–1902," in *Tradition Renewed: A History of the Jewish Theological Seminary*, vol. I: *The Making of an Institution of Jewish Higher Learning*, ed. Jack Wertheimer (New York: Jewish Theological Seminary, 1997), 3–42; Robert Fierstien, *A Different Spirit: The Jewish Theological Seminary of America, 1886–1902* (New York: Jewish Theological Seminary of America, 1990); Cyrus Adler, ed., *The Jewish Theological Seminary of America: Semi-Centennial Volume* (New York: The Jewish Theological Seminary of America, 1939); *The Jewish Theological Seminary of America: Documents, Charters and By-laws* (New York: The Jewish Theological Seminary of America, 1903); Robert Fierstien, "A Noble Beginning. The Seminary Alumni Association: 1901–1918," in *A Century of Commitment: One Hundred Years of the Rabbinical Assembly*, ed. Robert Fierstien (New York: Rabbinical Assembly, 2000), 1–20.

THE MARCUS JASTROW
MEMORIAL LIBRARY

Ex libris from the library of the University of Pennsylvania.

CHAPTER 10

WISSENSCHAFT DES JUDENTUMS

"Jastrow's Dictionary"

The early part of Jastrow's time in Rodeph Shalom was a period of active involvement in the work of the Jewish community in Philadelphia and throughout the United States, which resulted in the numerous conflicts and controversies discussed earlier. However, one of the fruits of these controversies was Jastrow's friendship with Benjamin Szold and his close relationships with other representatives of the so-called Historical School—Isaac Leeser, Sabato Morais, Henry Hochheimer, and others who, in addition to their attachment to tradition, had a positive attitude toward Wissenschaft des Judentums. It was with these people that Jastrow established and worked in Maimonides College, the first rabbinical college in America. His experiences in performing this work—which was undoubtedly unsatisfactory for him—led to his taking up other research and academic work. During his time in Philadelphia, he delivered many lectures in various places and published numerous articles in American, German, and French academic journals. Unfortunately, they have not all survived, but those that have, scattered across a number of libraries, may be divided into a few categories reflecting Jastrow's interests.

The first and largest category comprises studies on the ancient history of the Jews, as well as linguistics and the etymology of Jewish languages in biblical and talmudic times.[1] They were a preparation for

---

[1] Marcus Jastrow, *Transposed Stems in Talmudic Hebrew and Chaldaic, Dedicated in Reverence and Admiration to M. Joseph Derenburg in Commemoration of His Eightieth Birthday* (Leipzig, 1891); Marcus Jastrow, *The History and the Future of the Talmudic Text: A Lecture Delivered before the Gratz College of Philadelphia December 9, 1895 by Marcus Jastrow, Ph.D. Rabbi Emeritus of the Congregation Rodef Shalom* (Reprinted from Gratz College Publication, No. 1), (Philadelphia, 1897), 75–103; Marcus Jastrow, "Light Thrown on Some Biblical Passages by Talmudic Usage," *Journal of Biblical Literature* 11, no. 1 (1892): 126–130; Marcus Jastrow, "On Transposed Stems in

Jastrow's *magnum opus*—*A Dictionary of the Targumim, The Talmud Babli and Yerushalmi, and the Midrashic Literature*[2]—a work which contributed to the development of Jewish Studies in America and ensured that Jastrow's name has not been completely forgotten.

Work on the dictionary was completed in 1903, shortly before Jastrow's death. The idea was probably born when he was a professor and provost of Maimonides College, whose aim was to educate rabbis in the spirit of moderate Reform and respect for tradition. The language of instruction of most classes was English, but there were no texts or academic resources in this language, so the professors were forced to use studies and texts in German, which was spoken by very few Jews born in America. Was this the reason why Maimonides College never enjoyed popularity, and ultimately closed down? It might have played a part, though it probably was not the main reason. Jastrow was often ill in the 1870s and 1880s and, in the interest of future generations of American Jews, decided to compile a dictionary that would be a tool for the study of the Talmud and Midrashic literature. He began working on the dictionary in 1876.[3] He initially thought of drafting

---

the Talmudic, Hebrew and Chaldaic," *Journal of the American Oriental Society* 14 (1888): 40–42; Marcus Jastrow, "Eine eigenthumlich corumpirte Midraschstelle," *Magazin für die Wissenschaft des Judentums* 12 (1885): 143–145; Marcus Jastrow, "Hebräische und Chaldäische Wortbildungen in der Talmudischen Zeitperiode," *Magazin für die Wissenschaft des Judentums* 14 (1887): 18–28; idem, "Biblische Analekten," *MGWJ* 20 (1871): 241–248, and 21 (1872): 1–7, 145–150; Marcus Jastrow, "Einiges über den Hohepriester Onias IV in Ägypten und die Gründung des Tempels zu Heliopolis," *MGWJ* 21 (1872): 150–155; Marcus Jastrow, "Eine angebliche griechische Stelle im Midrasch," *MGWJ* 30 (1881): 176–178; Marcus Jastrow, "Einiges zur talmudischen Etymologie," *MGWJ* 31 (1882): 183–187; Marcus Jastrow, "Traditions mal comprises par le Talmud de Babylone," REJ 8 (1883): 149–152; Marcus Jastrow, "Note ser les mots "qwaqi u-dimoniki"," *REJ* 14 (1887): 277–279; Marcus Jastrow, "'Alima" et "eluli, ilmale"," *REJ* 7 (1883): 157–158; Marcus Jastrow, "Scenes de chasse dans le Talmud," *REJ* 23 (1896): 147–149; Marcus Jastrow, "Les Ludim ou Ludaï," *REJ* 23 (1896): 308–310; and Marcus Jastrow, "Les Juifs et les jeux olympiques," *REJ* 10 (1885): 124–126.

2 *A Dictionary of the Targumim, The Talmud Babli and Yerushalmi, and the Midrashic Literature*, compiled by Marcus Jastrow, Ph.D. Litt. D. with an Index of Scriptural Quotations, Volume I–II (London: W.C. Luzac & Co.; New York: G.P. Putnam's Sons, 1903).

3 Menachem Butler, *The History and Future of the Jastrow Dictionary* ([New York,] 2003), 1.

an English version of the dictionary based on two dictionaries by Jacob Levy—*Neuhebräisches und chaldäisches Wörterbuch über die Talmudim und Midraschim*[4] and *Chaldäisches Wörterbuch über die Targumim: und einen grossen Theil des rabbinischen Schriftthums*,[5] which were considered the latest achievements in the field—and later added entries from his own knowledge.[6] "Jastrow's Dictionary," as it is commonly referred to, was first published in sixteen fascicles starting in 1886.[7]

The introduction to the full edition of the dictionary included references to works by Leopold Zunz, Samuel Loeb Rapaport, Heinrich Graetz, Zacharias Frankel, Michael Sachs, Salomon David Luzzatto, Abraham Geiger, Manuel Joël, Joseph Perles, and Alexander Kohut, along with the relevant acknowledgments. Most of the names listed are those of Jastrow's teachers and the friends he had met in Germany, who were actively involved in the Wissenschaft des Judentums movement and the "Positive-Historical" school.[8]

The dictionary attracted a lot of interest, demonstrated by the fact that the first opinions and reviews appeared right after the publication of the first volumes in Europe and America. It should not come as a surprise that the first reviews were published in

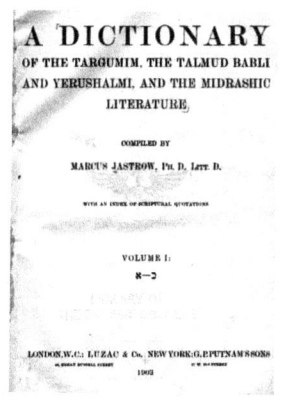

The front page of *A Dictionary of the Targumim, The Talmud Babli and Yerushalmi, and the Midrashic Literature*, compiled by Marcus Jastrow, Ph.D. Litt. D. with an Index of Scriptural Quotations, Volume I-II (London: W.C. Luzac & Co., New York: G.P. Putnam's Sons, 1903).

---

[4] Jacob Levy, *Neuhebräisches und chaldäisches Wörterbuch über die Talmudim und Midraschim* (Leipzig: F. A. Brockhaus, 1876–1889).

[5] Jacob Levy, *Chaldäisches Wörterbuch über die Targumim: und einen grossen Theil des rabbinischen Schriftthums* (Leipzig: Baumgärtner, 1867–1868).

[6] Jastrow also referred to two other works, by Alexander Kohut, *Aruch completum* (Vienna, 1878–1892) and Johannis Buxdorf, *Florilegium Hebraicum Continens Elegantes Sentencias, Proverbia, Apophthegmata* (Basel, 1648).

[7] These volumes were published by two publishing houses—Truebner and Luzac in London, and Putnam in New York.

[8] For more about the place of Jastrow's Dictionary in Jewish lexicography, see Brisman Shimeon, *History and Guide to Judaic Dictionaries and Concordances*, vol. 3, *Part One of Jewish Research Literature* (Haboken NJ: KTAV, 2000), 105–106.

Europe. They were critical and full of objections than the later American ones, with some authors wondering how anyone could have dared to publish a new dictionary after Jacob Levy's.

Immanuel Loew of Szeged, Hungary, wrote in his review of the first part of Jastrow's dictionary in 1888 that any new attempt to compile a dictionary similar to Levy's work—so significant for Jewish lexicography—should be approached with caution.

> New material may be collected, numerous manuscripts hitherto insufficiently consulted may be exploited, Talmudic lexicography developed, and Levy's work supplemented or corrected with more detailed works; but undertaking comprehensive tasks in this field would be risky. For all these reasons, I opened M. Jastrow's work with some apprehension and, having studied it carefully, I arrived at the conclusion that indeed this work cannot be considered successful. If truth be told, it is merely a compilation made using Levy's dictionaries. …Levy's diligence in collecting the material may only be appreciated when one studies the works of his imitators, one of whom is M. Jastrow.[9]

According to Loew, there were few detailed explanations of the author's personal views in Jastrow's work, which one would perhaps read with pleasure if they were published in an article. However, Loew did not believe that these were sufficient justification for the publication of a thick, two-thousand-page dictionary. He admitted, though, that Jastrow noticed and corrected some of Levy's mistakes, particularly in quotations; he also praised some of Jastrow's explanations and conclusions.[10]

A similar review of the fifth and sixth parts of the dictionary was written by Samuel Krauss of Budapest in 1895, after they were published.[11] This is a detailed analysis of a small number of selected entries from the dictionary, but Krauss's general views may be derived from it. He shared Loew's opinion of the strengths and weaknesses of the previous volumes of Jastrow's dictionary. He noted that the arrangement

---

9   Immanuel Loew, [Review], *REJ* 16 (1888): 154.
10   Ibid., 155.
11   Samuel Krauss, "Besprechung," *MGWJ* 39 (1895): 282–285.

of the material was scrupulously alphabetical and more consistent than that of the dictionaries of Levy and Kohut. He praised Jastrow for often giving more grammatical forms than his predecessors. Krauss also believed that "accuracy, conciseness, and thematic arrangement of material [were] as important in dictionaries as the explanation of a term itself. Jastrow tries to meet these requirements to the best of his ability, though it is a pity that the drive for conciseness overrides other considerations too much, at the expense of both the accuracy and at times comprehensibility of the dictionary."[12] Krauss ended his review with a conclusion that a more general assessment of the work would be in order after all of the volumes were published — which occurred in 1903.

The reviews in America, much like those in Europe, compared Jastrow's dictionary to the achievements of his predecessors, though they concentrated more on demonstrating the uniqueness of the dictionary and its utility rather than pointing out its errors and shortcomings. For instance, Emil G. Hirsch, a professor at the University of Chicago, declared prophetically in 1901 that this dictionary was an example of the best scholarly work and the author's competence, and evidence of the high standard of Jewish Studies in America. He also predicted that it would be the most-cited work in this field.[13] Although Hirsch found mistakes and shortcomings in Jastrow's dictionary, he contrasted them with the significance of the publication for the development not only of Jewish Studies, but also of American scholarship in general. In his view, Jastrow enabled American researchers and the public to access a vast swathe of Jewish literature, which constitutes a part of world cultural heritage. "Dr. Jastrow has opened to the American student a part of Jewish literature that has a determinative influence in the shaping of religions of the civilized portion of the human race."[14]

Solomon Schechter, president of the Jewish Theological Seminary in New York and the leading authority in the field of Jewish studies at the beginning of the twentieth century, also expressed his opinion of Jastrow's dictionary. His reaction was published in an article under the title "Dr. Jastrow's Great Work: A Review of the Famous Jewish Scholar's

---

[12] Ibid., 283.

[13] Emil Hirsch, *The Alumni Register* (Philadelphia: Penn State University, 1901), 497–503.

[14] Ibid., 502.

Dictionary of Talmud"[15] shortly after Jastrow's death. Schechter called the dictionary Jastrow's *magnum opus* and stressed the author's thorough preparation, which could not have failed to bear fruit. Jastrow was a first-class expert on rabbinic literature, educated and influenced by his European teachers. His traditional education in Rogoźno; his university studies, which included Greek and Latin, in Berlin; and his studies under many distinguished rabbis in Berlin and Breslau all contributed to the end result—"Jastrow's Dictionary." However, the main goal of his work was practical—to help expound the Talmud and midrashic literature. There had not been a work that would facilitate English-speaking students' and researchers' access to the extensive rabbinic literature before Jastrow's groundbreaking work.[16]

"Jastrow's Dictionary" was very popular, and successive reprints appeared one after another. In the 1920s, Jastrow's children were close to bringing an action against a publisher in Germany for publishing an edition of the dictionary without their permission.[17]

When Jastrow's dictionary is criticized today, the main weaknesses mentioned are the juxtaposition of several languages (Hebrew, Aramaic, and others), erroneous vocalization in a few instances, and departure from the European methodology of Jewish lexicography. Its strengths, on the other hand, are its ability to refer to earlier lexicons, the alphabetical division of the material, the use of newer material than than in other dictionaries, and unprecedented attention to Akkadian influences. The ideology of the Reform movement in Judaism is evident in the dictionary. In accordance with the spirit of his time, Jastrow made reference to the achievements of Christian scholars and biblicists. He himself also saw their influences in his mapping of the word "dominica" in the talmudic and midrashic literature.[18]

---

[15] Solomon Schechter, "Dr. Jastrow's Great Work. A Review of the Famous Jewish Scholar's Dictionary of Talmud" *The New York Times*, January 30, 1904, 65–66.

[16] For more about the reception of Jastrow's Dictionary, see also Kaufmann Kohler, "Jastrow's Talmudic Dictionary," *Hebraica* 5, no. 1 (1888): 1–6; Max L. Margolis, "Jastrow's Targumic-Talmudic-Midrashic Dictionary," *The American Journal of Semitic Languages and Literatures* 18 (October 1901-July 1902): 56–58.

[17] Correspondence relating to this matter may be found in AJA, SC no. 5687.

[18] See, e. g., Marcus Jastrow, "Alima" et "eluli, ilmale," *REJ* 7 (1883): 157–158.

Although Jastrow's work was published over a hundred years ago, reprints and new editions continue to be published today, and it is still used in yeshivot and universities worldwide. This is not because there are no more recent lexicons available[19] — many have been published since, such as the recent works by Michael Sokoloff,[20] which are more extensive and academic than Jastrow's dictionary — but Jastrow's work outclasses others in its practicality and usefulness, although it has been in use for over a hundred years now. If dictionaries were listed in bibliographies of works in the field of Jewish Studies, Jastrow would probably be the most-cited author.[21]

The Jewish Encyclopedia

Jastrow undertook a number of academic projects on his own, but he also took an active part in new initiatives, helping shape Jewish studies in America from the beginning. When an opportunity arose to compile the first Jewish encyclopedia, he eagerly accepted the invitation to work on editing it.

The idea of compiling *The Jewish Encyclopedia* came from Isidor Singer, a writer and journalist from Moravia. Singer was a secretary of

---

[19] Some of the more modern dictionaries are Chaim and Biniamin Kasowsky, *Otsar ha-shemot le-Talmud bavli*. *[Thesaurus nominus, quae in Talmude Babylonico reperiuntur]* (Jerusalem: The Ministry of Education and Culture, Government of Israel/New York: The Jewish Theological Seminary of America, 1976); Daniel Sperber, *A Dictionary of Greek and Latin Legal Terms in Rabbinic Literature* (Ramat-Gan: Bar-Ilan University Press, 1984); Frank Yitshak, *The Practical Talmud Dictionary* (Jerusalem–Spring Valley, NY: Feldheim Publishers, 1991).

[20] Michael Sokoloff, *A Dictionary of Jewish Palestinian Aramaic of the Byzantine Period* (Ramat-Gan: Bar Ilan University Press; Baltimore: Johns Hopkins University Press, 2002); Michael Sokoloff, *A Dictionary of Jewish Babylonian Aramaic of the Talmudic and Geonic Periods* (Ramat-Gan: Bar Ilan University Press; Baltimore: Johns Hopkins University Press, 2002); Michael Sokoloff, *A Dictionary of Judean Aramaic* (Ramat-Gan: Bar-Ilan University Press, 2003).

[21] For more about Jastrow and the history of Jewish lexicography, see "The Meaning of Words: Marcus Jastrow and the Making of Rabbinic Dictionaries," Penn Libraries, http://www.library.upenn.edu/exhibits/cajs/jastrow/ (accessed 28.04.2013). This exhibition is a product of a conference which took place in 2003 at the University of Pennsylvania.

the French ambassador in Vienna between 1884 and 1885, and in 1887 he moved to Paris, where he was actively involved in the work of Jewish organizations, particularly in matters concerning the Alfred Dreyfus case. It was in Paris that, with a view to protesting against anti-Jewish prejudice and antisemitism, he undertook the task of preparing a monumental work that would portray the Jews through their history, religion, and literature, particularly demonstrating their contribution to world civilization. The book was originally meant to be called *The Encyclopedia of the History and Mental Evolution of the Jewish Race*.[22] Unfortunately, no one in Europe seemed to be interested in the project, so in 1895 Singer traveled to New York. He believed that his idea could only be implemented in America because of the religious freedom and financial resources there, and he indeed managed to find a publisher—Isaac Kauffman Funk—who agreed to invest in the project. The decision to entitle the book *The Jewish Encyclopedia* was taken in 1899, and it was agreed upon that it would be published in twelve volumes, comprising 6,000 pages. The editorial board was chosen that year too, as were the editors responsible for the various sections—leading experts in their particular fields in Jewish studies in America. These editors were:

> Cyrus Adler—post-Talmudic archeology; customs, literature, and history of the Jews in America;
> Gotthard Deutsch—Jewish history between 1492 and 1901;
> R. Gottheil—post-talmudic literature and Jewish history from post-Biblical times until 1500;
> Marcus Jastrow—the Talmud and talmudic literature;
> Morris Jastrow—biblical literature and the history of Israel;
> Kaufmann Kohler—Jewish theology, philosophy, and ethics;
> Geo F. Moore—biblical archeology, the history of biblical exegesis, Hebrew philology, Hellenic and biblical literature, and the history of Israel.

The editorial board changed during the publication of the encyclopedia, and after Jastrow's death his place was taken by Louis

---

[22] Shimeon Brisman, *A History and Guide to Judaic Encyclopedias and Lexicons, Vol. Two of Jewish Research Literature* (Cincinnati: Hebrew Union College Press, 1987), 27.

Ginzberg.²³ Jastrow played an important role in the compilation, as he was one of the most experienced members of the editorial board in terms of scholarly work. Because of his moderate views, he was often the catalyst of conflicts between the Reformers and traditionalists concerning the edition and assessment of texts. He sometimes also successfully prevented his son, who was at the time already a professor of Semitic languages and a librarian at the University of Pennsylvania, from expressing excessively radical opinions in his biblical exegesis.²⁴ However, Morris Jastrow played a significant part in suggesting an approach for the material being prepared. He pointed out that the encyclopedia should be written in a manner comprehensible to ordinary readers, who were not necessarily of Jewish origin. His view was not shared by all of the editors, which caused further friction.²⁵

Marcus Jastrow followed this direction too, suggesting entries relating to the Talmud. Apart from a general entry about the Talmud, all entries relating to specific Talmudic tractates were prepared separately and included in the work as individual entries, in alphabetical order. He explained the reason for this decision by saying that the encyclopedia would not be "an academic textbook, but rather should serve educated laymen as a convenient source of information."²⁶ Jastrow also kept on the lookout for talented authors—it was thanks to him that the little-known Louis Ginzberg became part of the editorial team.²⁷ Jastrow was only involved in the work on the first three volumes of the encyclopedia, which were published before his death.

The *Jewish Encyclopedia* was published gradually between 1901 and 1906, with the involvement of 605 authors from Europe and America. When the first volume was published, Jewish scholars from Europe were amazed that work of such a high standard could have been produced in America. It may be said that the publication of the *Jewish Encyclopedia* was a crucial moment in the development of Jewish

---

23   Ibid., 31–32; Shuly Rubin Schwartz, *The Emergence of Jewish Scholarship in America: The Publication of the Jewish Encyclopedia* (Cincinnati: HUC Press, 1991), 45.

24   Schwartz, *The Emergence of Jewish Scholarship in America*, 48.

25   Ibid., 57.

26   Ibid.

27   Eli Ginzberg, *Keeper of the Law: Louis Ginzberg* (Philadelphia: Jewish Publication Society of America, 1966), 63–82.

studies in the United States. From that time onward, Jewish scholars collaborated with their European colleagues without any feeling of inferiority. Jastrow's contribution to the fact that America soon became the center of Jewish scholarship was significant.[28]

The Jewish Publication Society

Jastrow's scholarly work in America cannot be discussed without a mention of another institution with which he was associated between 1888 and 1903—the Jewish Publication Society. The establishment of the first institution with this name cannot be dated precisely, but it may have been as early as 1845. It was founded by Isaac Leeser, whose two goals were defense against Christian proselytism and the promotion of Jewish literature in English. Few books were published under the auspices of the Jewish Publication Society at the time, and those that were, were mostly anthologies of foreign works or books written by Leeser. The first Jewish Publication Society was dissolved in 1851, largely for financial reasons.[29]

Another attempt was made under the aegis of the Board of Delegates of American Israelites. In 1867 a special committee was appointed to establish the Hebrew Publication Society. Its members—Isaac Leeser, Marcus Jastrow, and Samuel M. Isaacs—decided on a plan of action and methods for obtaining publishing funds, but when Leeser fell ill, the work of the committee lost its impetus.[30] The idea remained very much alive, though, so when the American Jewish Publication Society was established in 1871, Jastrow persuaded its members to return to the earlier projects. During the rabbinical conference in Cincinnati, Max Lilienthal set forth the objectives of the new society in the following words:

---

[28] For more about the history of the *Jewish Encyclopedia*, see Schwartz, *The Emergence of Jewish Scholarship in America*; Brisman, *A History and Guide to Judaic Encyclopedias and Lexicons*, 27–34; Nancy L. Barth, "History of the Publication of the Jewish Encyclopedia" (MA diss., University of Chicago, 1969).

[29] Jonathan D. Sarna, *JPS: The Americanization of Jewish Culture 1888–1988* (Philadelphia: Jewish Publication Society of America, 1989), 2–3.

[30] Ibid., 7.

(1) Jewish literature in English "is almost a blank"; (2) suitable books in German are "closed to our American Jewish youth, who prefer to read books written in their vernacular"; (3) "our Christian brethren … wish to be instructed on religious topics of the Israelite," but we have no books to guide them; and (4) the books published "will be of the highest use and value to the pupils of our future rabbinical seminaries."[31]

This appeal sounds very similar to Jastrow's appeal in Warsaw to publish books on Jewish topics in Polish. Jastrow, too, became a member of the committee of the new American Jewish Publication Society, this one based in New York. Again most of the publications were translations. It seems that it was on Jastrow's initiative that the translation of the fourth volume of Heinrich Graetz's *History of the Jews* (the very same volume that Jastrow had promised to publish in Warsaw in 1864) began. Why was the fourth volume chosen? It covers the period from the downfall of the Jewish state until the completion of the Talmud—a period very important for the formation of rabbinic Judaism. Other works by great German historians—Abraham Geiger, Leopold Zunz, Joseph Perles, and many others—were announced, but again, the plans were not fulfilled due to lack of interest. The American Jewish Publication Society was dissolved in 1876.[32]

Only the Jewish Publication Society, founded in Philadelphia with the involvement of prominent representatives of various Jewish groups, was able to boast significant achievements and continuous operation until today. Jastrow was involved in the establishment of this society as well, and played an important role in its history. He immediately became a member of the Publication Committee, which also comprised Joseph Krauskopf, Simon Stern, and Mayer Sulzberger of Philadelphia; Cyrus Adler and Henrietta Szold of Baltimore; Bernhard Felsenthal of Chicago; Charles Gross of Cambridge; and Abram S. Isaacs of New York.[33] These people set out the organization's program and goal, which was to turn America into a publishing center of Jewish academic literature, as the Jews of Spain, Poland, and Germany had done in their

---

31 Ibid., 9.
32 Ibid., 10–11.
33 Ibid., 23–24.

countries. Henrietta Szold of Baltimore, the secretary of the publishing committee between 1893 and 1916, also played an important role in the functioning of the new Jewish Publication Society. She lived with the Jastrow family for some time after moving to Philadelphia, so she had a close relationship with the whole family.[34]

Jastrow played a crucial role during the early period of the Jewish Publication Society. It was on his recommendation and through his persistence that the translation of Graetz's complete *History of the Jews* was undertaken.[35]

The project for which Jastrow was personally responsible in the Jewish Publication Society was that of publishing the Bible in English "for Jews and by Jews." Jastrow was valued for his translation skills, which he used in his revisions and editing of successive versions of prayer books; he also published many translations and interpretations of fragments of biblical texts, including quite a number of the Psalms.[36] A "committee of three" (Jastrow, Adler, and Krauskopf) was appointed on November 27, 1892, to prepare a plan of action. A meeting was organized in Atlantic City the following year, on July 30 and 31, to which Adler, Mayer Sulzberger, Benjamin Szold, Kaufmann Kohler, Sabato Morais, Franz Lansberger, Isaac Wise, Gustav Gottheil, and Jastrow were invited.[37] Some of these people were unable to attend (among them Landsberger, Wise, and Morais), so they sent their comments.

---

[34] Ibid., 48; the correspondence between Henrietta Szold and Jastrow indicates their great familiarity: Henrietta Szold Papers, AJA (microfilm).

[35] [Henrietta Szold], "Marcus Jastrow," *The American Jewish Year Book* 5665, 403–404.

[36] Marcus Jastrow, *Der Neunzigste Psalm*, übersetzt und erläutert von Dr. M. Jastrow (Leipzig 1893); Marcus Jastrow, "An Interpretation of Two Psalms. Psalm LXXIII and Psalm XC," in *Oriental Studies: A Selection of the Papers Read before the Oriental Club of Philadelphia 1888–1894* (Boston, 1894), 35–51; Marcus Jastrow, "An Analysis of Psalms LXXXIV and CI," in *Semitic Studies in Memory of Rev. Dr. Alexander Kohut* (Berlin, 1897), 254–263.

[37] According to various sources, Morais, Gottheil, and Wise did not take part in the meeting, instead sending their comments by mail. See Philadelphia Jewish Archives Center at the Balch Institute, JPS Papers, acc. 1765, box 87, The Bible Translation of the JPSA, 1. Cf. Philadelphia Jewish Archives Center at the Balch Institute, JPS Papers, Mss 50, Serio III, box 1, Minutes of the Publication Committee of the Jewish Publication Society of America 1888–1905, 27.

The Bible Translation Committee was appointed in 1893.[38] The Committee initially planned that the new edition would be based on the first Jewish translation of the Bible into English by Isaac Leeser,[39] but it was later decided, under Jastrow's influence, that the new edition would be a new critical translation.[40] Thirty-two of the most distinguished rabbis and scholars in the United States were invited to take part in the project, and they were each allocated specific books of the Bible to work on.[41] Jastrow, who was text editor and editor-in-chief[42] from 1896, reserved the main editing of both individual books and the whole Bible for himself. He was helped by his daughter, Annie M. Jastrow.[43] Unfortunately, the work advanced very slowly: not all of the translators set to work as eagerly as others, and when Szold fell ill in 1901, Jastrow needed to find someone to assist with the translation of the *Book of Job*. Interestingly, he approached Solomon Schechter, who was then still a professor at the University of Cambridge. Jastrow possibly turned to him because Schechter was very positive about Jastrow's project in *The Jewish Chronicle*.[44] It seems that Schechter's reply was negative, and Jastrow made efforts to complete the translation of this book himself.[45] His son, Morris, later made use of his father's work when he published the *Book of Job*.[46]

---

[38] Sarna, *JPS: The Americanization of Jewish Culture*, 48.

[39] *Biblia Hebraica* (Philadephia, 1848).

[40] The aims and objectives of this project were set forth in a list of 15 points at the meeting in Atlantic City. Philadelphia Jewish Archives Center at the Balch Institute, JPS Papers, acc. 1765, box 87, The Bible Translation of the JPSA, 1.

[41] See the list of names in Philadelphia Jewish Archives Center at the Balch Institute, JPS Papers, acc. 1765, box 87, The Bible Translation of the JPSA, 3.

[42] Philadelphia Jewish Archives Center at the Balch Institute, JPS Papers, acc. 1765, box 87, The Bible Translation of the JPSA, 2, 4.

[43] Her name features in the correspondence as "Annie M. Jastrow Secretary of the Editor in Chief"; Philadelphia Jewish Archives Center at the Balch Institute, JPS Papers, OS –1, Letter Copy Book of Marcus Jastrow.

[44] Jastrow's letter to Schechter of April 25, 1901, Jewish Theological Seminary Archives, Schechter Collection.

[45] See his translation with commentary in Philadelphia Jewish Archives Center at the Balch Institute, JPS Papers, Mss 50, Series IV, The JPS Bible, box 3, folder 3.

[46] *The Book of Job: Its Origin, Growth and Interpretation*; together with a New Translation Based on a Revised Text (Philadelphia: Jewish Publication Society of America, 1920).

Before long Jastrow, too, fell ill, and when he died in 1903 only one book was ready for publication—the *Book of Psalms*, translated by Kaufmann Kohler. It was published after Jastrow's death.[47] Solomon Schechter, who was already president of the Jewish Theological Seminary in New York, took charge of the project after Jastrow's death.

Jastrow's work and achievements in promoting Jewish Studies were noted not only in the Jewish world but also in Philadelphia academic circles. In 1900 the University of Pennsylvania awarded him an honorary degree for this contribution. As an act of gratitude, Jastrow bequeathed his collection of books to the university library, which still holds volumes with his ex libris in them.

The Tombstone at the Cemetery in Philadelphia

---

[47] *The Psalms* were ready for printing in 1901, but their translator, Kohler, refused to implement Jastrow's amendments. Philadelphia Jewish Archives Center at the Balch Institute, JPS Papers, acc. 1765, box 87, The Bible Translation of the JPSA, 6–8. The report on the work completed by April 1903 can be found in Philadelphia Jewish Archives Center at the Balch Institute, JPS Papers, acc. 1765, box 87, The Bible Translation of the JPSA, 9. See also Sarna, *JPS: The Americanization of Jewish Culture*, 102. For more about the reception of this translation of the Bible, see also Jonathan D. Sarna, Nahum M. Sarna, "Jewish Bible scholarship and Translations in the United States," in *The Bible and Bibles in America*, ed. E.S. Frerichs (Atlanta: Scholars Press, 1988), 83–116.

Conclusion

Marcus Jastrow was an exceptionally colorful figure with an eventful life full of unexpected turns. Wherever he worked, he found himself embroiled in numerous conflicts and disputes, most of which concerned his vision of the reform of Judaism.

The answer to the question of whether Jastrow was an advocate of reforming Judaism is that he most certainly was. Although he never laid out a synthetic program for the reform of Judaism, his many activities and publications—the sermons, pamphlets, and press articles referred to in this book—combine to produce a coherent vision that he consistently implemented throughout his life. Jastrow's specific vision of the reform of Judaism was undoubtedly affected by his life experiences, as well as the values in which he believed and to which he stayed true.

It appears that he took from his upbringing in Rogoźno a certain openness to the world, a respect for followers of other religions, and general humanistic values. This is confirmed by the fact that he graduated from a state gymnasium in Posen, where his elective subject was Polish, as well as by his careful observation of the changes taking place in 1848.

In Berlin, Jastrow explored Jewish studies and continued on his path to ordination as a rabbi, but did not neglect his general development, studying philosophy, medieval history, and Greek literature. Nevertheless, it was the teachers from his youth—Rabbi Moses Feilchenfeld of Rogoźno, as well as Michael Sachs, David Rosin, Heinrich Graetz, Manuel Joël, and the teachers of the Jewish Theological Seminary of Breslau—who had the greatest influence on his future career and who shaped the young Jastrow's views the most. It was they who prompted on the one hand his affiliation with Conservative Reform and "Positive-Historical" Judaism, and on the other his involvement in advancing the Wissenschaft des Judentums movement as a means of inculcating reform and advancing the civilization of the Jews. In addition, Rabbi Baer Meisels, whom Jastrow met in Warsaw, may also be added to the list of those who influenced his views. It was he who taught Jastrow to strive for the fraternity of all people and instilled in him a love of freedom.

In his work as a rabbi and preacher, Jastrow sought to develop and promote all the ideas learned from his teachers, the Haskalah, and the experiences of the Reform movement of Judaism in Germany. He believed that Judaism was in jeopardy and that the only way forward was the path of progress and reform, which on the one hand would protect Judaism from petrification as totally incompatible with the modern world, and on the other would not necessarily lead to complete assimilation and departure from Judaism, which was often the case in Germany, where the Reform movement was treated as a step on the road to conversion to Christianity. Jastrow was aware of these threats and took up the challenge, striving to implement his vision of reform everywhere he came to work and to lead the Jewish community.

The motto of Jastrow's activity in Warsaw was "the promotion of education and culture." He took part in numerous initiatives which sought to improve the standard of education among the Jews in the Kingdom of Poland, and contributed to the establishment of many institutions, both formal and otherwise, mainly aimed at young people. As preacher of the progressive synagogue at Daniłowiczowska Street, he supported progress through reformed liturgy and rituals, as well as the introduction of the Polish language in place of German. Already in Warsaw his sermons contained the essence of his vision of reform, which was based on respect for all people, belief in Israel's mission of transmitting divine revelation to the world, and rejection of belief in the rebuilding of the Temple and the renewal of the sacrificial cult. On the basis of these religious doctrines, Jastrow also strove to advocate the Polish-Jewish dialogue and fraternity that took root during the years preceding the January Uprising, for which he paid with imprisonment in the Warsaw Citadel and exile. He was a precursor of interreligious dialogue in Poland, though his contribution to building Polish-Jewish, Christian-Jewish, and Polish-German understanding has not yet been fully researched by historians.

By the time Jastrow returned to Germany, after his banishment from Warsaw, to serve as a rabbi in Mannheim and Worms, he was already a well-known figure, famous for being both a revolutionary and a rabbi who had suffered for his beliefs. In both towns he focused on implementing reforms focused on promoting human dignity and improving morality and spiritual life, with the aim of protecting the communities from stagnation or departure from Judaism.

A new chapter in Jastrow's career began when he arrived in America in 1866. He combined his rabbinical post in Congregation

Rodeph Shalom with participation in the work of numerous Jewish organizations, though his main efforts were in sensitizing others to the fundamental values of Judaism and teaching respect for them. There were many attempts to reform Judaism in America, and Jastrow joined groups which strove for reforms promoting unity rather than division, sometimes requiring personal compromise (hence his collaboration with Wise and his Reform camp). Despite such personal conflicts, Jastrow remained intransigent whenever what he regarded as the fundamental values of Judaism were threatened, and this was an attitude he expressed in numerous disputes and controversies. It was in such conflicts that his vision of reform was articulated most comprehensively. Jastrow's affiliation and collaboration with people who Moshe Davis classified as advocates of the "Historical School," and his co-organization of the Jewish Theological Seminary, unequivocally corroborate his affiliation with "Positive-Historical" Judaism, the forerunner to Conservative Judaism. Unfortunately, Jastrow's achievements in this field have often been ignored in modern Jewish-American historiography.

Jastrow's activity in the United States was not limited to work in the religious sphere. He was a co-founder of the most important academic and educational institutions of American Judaism, from Maimonides College to the Jewish Publication Society and the compilation of the first Jewish encyclopedia. Nevertheless, his greatest achievement in the Wissenschaft des Judentums movement in America was *A Dictionary of the Targumim, The Talmud Babli and Yerushalmi, and the Midrashic Literature,* with which he left an indelible imprint in the field of Jewish Studies.

Let us try to define Jastrow's vision of the reform of Judaism. His understanding of the process was rooted in his education and experience as preacher and rabbi. He supported the idea of a reform that would break down the barriers of the "ghetto," bring the Jews closer to the world, and help them fully participate in the lives of their countries of residence. Equality and good relations with their neighbors were its essential conditions.

Jastrow believed that the basis of Judaism lay in Revelation, the Bible, and the Talmud. Its reform needed to be pursued with respect and full appreciation for the tradition and history of the Jews. He maintained that the Bible and the Talmud originated in a certain set of historical circumstances which should not be thoughtlessly transposed to modern times. Thus, in his view, critical knowledge of the whole history of the Jews and Judaism was crucial to implementing reform.

Jastrow held that reform should be undertaken with an awareness that its goal was the spiritual development of worshippers, and that the overall level of education and knowledge of Jewish identity had to be improved in order to implement it. At the same time, he believed, it was crucial to ensure that religious crises or departures from Judaism were not caused by the rejection of certain traditional ideas, such as the beliefs in the Messiah, the rebuilding of the Temple, and resurrection. According to him, reform should not be based on passing fashions and imposed externally, but ought to be well thought out, accepted, and implemented with moderation so that it served spiritual development and not conformism. Jastrow followed these principles in Warsaw, Mannheim, Worms, and Philadelphia.

Jastrow's work serves as an excellent study in the history of Judaism in Europe and the United States in the second half of the nineteenth century, including all its main problems and events, which may be considered from a comparative perspective. It may cast new light on a number of issues, one of the most important being the extent of the impact of the Reform movement on Judaism in the Polish lands, particularly in Warsaw, which is a much-disputed matter.

Should the Polish rabbis and preachers referred to in Polish historiography as advocates of assimilation, acculturation, and integrationism be called instead Reformers? Jastrow's views in Warsaw were no different from his views in Worms or Philadelphia. Moreover, by the time he embarked on his mission to reform Congregation Rodeph Shalom, the second generation of progressive and perhaps even more reformed Jews sat in the pews of the synagogues at Daniłowiczowska and Nalewki streets. However, the answer to the question of why the Reform movement in Judaism and, later, Reform Judaism were not as successful in the Polish lands as they were in Germany or the United States, is a topic for another book.

I do hope, however, that this book will encourage further research on the religious views of rabbis and preachers of progressive synagogues in the Polish lands, and that the findings will "reform" our knowledge on this topic.

As mentioned in the foreword, this book does not claim to offer a presentation of Jastrow's full biography, but focuses on emphasizing his religious views. Some aspects of Jastrow's activity have been deliberately omitted as irrelevant, or passed over due to the lack of sources.

A complete biography, which will hopefully be written in the future, should include chapters on Jastrow's involvement in the conspiracy and preparations for the January Uprising and in the event itself, and his work with the numerous Jewish organizations in America, and particularly in Philadelphia, in which he held important positions. However, this lies outside the scope of this project.

Appendix I

Jastrow's letter to Rabbi Jacob S. Raisin

American Jewish Archives, Small Collection no. 5686 [no date].

To Rabbi Jacob S. Raisin,

                                                                            139 W. Upsal St.

Your letter of the 8th inst. received. The pamphlet you announce has not come yet; I thank you for it in advance, and shall in return make such remarks as may suggest themselves to me. I hasten to reply that I am the author of "BELEUCHTUNG" etc.

    The origins of that pamphlet may be of interest to you. The central government in St. Petersburg asked the government in Warsaw for an opinion how to ameliorate the condition of the Jews. Muchanow at that time the Secretary of the Interior and Church Department, and virtually the head of the government, the Viceroy, Gorczakow being a decrepit old soldier, appointed a commission for the purpose, the head of which was a liberal-minded Pole, befriended to or could rather say by influential Jews in Warsaw. The propositions worked out by that commission, under the guidance of those influences were narrow enough, yet an improvement upon the miserable laws then prevailing. The Hassidim getting wind of these negotiations and fearing innovations which might favor education, employed good services of the Censor and Director of the Rabbinical School, Jakub Tugendhold (...a non lucendo) to counteract their influences—without avail as far as the Commission was concerned. But when the report came before Muchanow, the latter said, "This has been written by Epstein." (the foremost of the Jews with whom the President of the Commission was on terms of friendship) and tore it to pieces, and appointed his own tool to make a report to his liking, the result of which you see in the "Beleuchtung". Though kept in Muchanow's private chest we got hold of it, i. e. we got a verbatim copy—ask not by what means—you can guess.

    I, being a perfect stranger in Poland at that time (I came to Warsaw in 1858), had to get the advice of natives, and from week to week we had meetings to that effect, and for similar purposes,— all this in secret, at the risk of liberty if not life, for a sojourn in some fortress or in Siberia is not conducive to health. Thus I translated my report and made my annotations, as you see. We had our special agent in St. Petersburg to watch our affairs: we had direct or indirect communication with the Russian ambassadors at European courts, and care was taken that the Emperor should receive the pamphlet personally. A similar brochure to mine was issued in French by M. Lubliner in Brussels, an emigrant from the revolutionary days of 1831, and lawyer in Brussels.

I thought these "inwardnesses' might be of use to you, and, not being much at leisure, I dropped these lines in haste, and you will please excuse the carelessness in style and presentation of the subject. Let me have your article on Haskalah in due time, if you please.

With best wishes for your success in life.
Yours truly,
M. JASTROW.

Appendix II

Aleksander Kraushar,
"Kartka z niedawnej przeszłości"

From *Książka jubileuszowa dla uczczenia pięćdziesięcioletniej działalności literackiej J.I. Kraszewskiego* (Warsaw, 1880), 507–510, 524–525.

At that time, a Jewish youth club formed to meet periodically in order to read and discuss new literary and academic works, or its members' own essays, on subjects from the fields of literature, history, and the natural sciences.

The club met one evening a week, and after a few hours of discussion on the works currently being read, the rest of the evening was dedicated to music. At first, the club comprised but a few members, but before long, new people from various Jewish circles, both the younger and the older generation, began to join. (…)

When the club organized itself upon firmer foundations, and, having established its statutes, decided to enhance its activity by inviting persons of more mature age and function, it was decided that the noble Preacher Dr. J[astrow] would be asked to take upon himself the moral protectorate of the club, and with the weight of his name endow it with the quality of an educational institution.

The other person besought to participate in the meetings was Henryk T[oeplitz].

He cordially accepted the invitation and, to show the young people how much he appreciated the trust bestowed upon him, offered them his premises as the venue for their periodic meetings.

From that time, the familiar little rooms at Danielowiczowska Street pulsated with life and uncommon activity every Wednesday evening.

The program of the evenings was very diverse. After an initial chat about current events and the news of the day, one of the members usually sat down at the table with a manuscript on a subject from the field of history or literature, read it to the members present, and then a discussion commenced, during which the reader supported the opinions they had just expressed.

Appendix 2

The discussions were lively at times, and the last word belonged to the chairman of the meeting—it was [sometimes] the host, T[oeplitz], who was chosen as chairman, though most often it was Dr. J[astrow]. (...)

During one of those evening meetings, a treatise was read on the attitudes of Polish writers to the Jewish question, and on Jewish characters in novels written by the most prominent novelists.

The aim of the treatise was to demonstrate that Jewish characters in Polish novels were depicted negatively on the whole; and that, with some few exceptions, whenever our novelists introduced Jewish characters and their actions, without knowing Jewish society at all, and as if their aim was to cater to the prejudice and unrefined taste of their readers, they depicted the Jews as loathsome fanatics or usurers jabbering in their own jargon...

A reflection of that view of the leaders of the nation's intellectual life was the prejudice prevalent in our society at the time towards one of its constituent elements.

The novel, as the most easily accessible chair for the leaders of the nation from which to speak to thousands of hearts and minds, and implant in them healthy seeds or weeds, was the more remarkable in its position, and was able to exert the more effective influence on the reading masses, in that for a long time it was the only form of manifestation of the national spirit to the outside. And this form, the novel—it was said—instead of employing its solemn importance to thwart the prejudice against the Jews ingrained in the nation, by doubling their good virtues and awakening neighborly feelings between the Jews and the society they lived in, always took an unamicable stance toward the Jews. By ridiculing and passing over them, and humiliating their dearest feelings, novels always depicted them as a tumor harmful to society, and the whole periodical press fell into line with these views...

"These observations are valid enough," said Dr. J[astrow] with his usual weightiness during the discussion. "Undeniably, however, the Jews themselves must accept part of the blame for this unpleasant treatment of Jewish characters and their whole community with pen and word. However do you expect Polish writers, who know little of the Jews, knowing them only inasmuch as the immediate (and, it must be admitted, not very appealing) surroundings have enabled them to observe, to have a good opinion of the Jews when the Jews themselves, or at least their more enlightened class, know so little of their spiritually more impoverished co-religionists, so little effort do they make to learn about their past, present, and desires for the future. You, who are lucky in that through random circumstances and without contributing thereto in any way, have reached the shore and experienced the benefits of superficial civilization, put all your pride and worth into shrugging off the solidary responsibility for the ignorance, superstitions, and absenteeism of your younger brethren in faith... A measure of worth and merit in your eyes is to keep as much distance as possible from your co-religionists, leave them to their fate... You do not found schools, do not train leaders of education, do not know your past, traditions, or customs, the history of your own tribe. In your community, the largest in the country, there has not been even the germ of an idea of starting a special journal to influence the Jews and reduce prejudice against them in the society that surrounds them. And small wonder, then, if this nation's intelligentsia, not seeing among you people with the courage of their own convictions, judges you on the basis of the appearances with which you supply it, if from time to time you read lucubrations offensive to you in the press. If there is to be a change for the better here in this respect, we must needs set about the great work of reviving the Polish Jews and making them citizens of this country in the true meaning of the word, with a courage characteristic of truly higher minds and genuinely sentient hearts. Such a reform must take its beginning in us ourselves, and the time will come when today's prejudices wane, the obstacles which block our path to self-development disappear, and a radical legislative change in relations puts an end to the problems that constrain us. I see positive symptoms in the current attitude, however hostile toward the Jews it is. In the past we were despised and disdained. Today, they truly hate us. It is easier to turn hatred into a more positive attitude. Disdain does not even allow one to resent the opponent..."

The epoch in which Dr. J[astrow] spoke in more or less these words to the young people surrounding him was a breakthrough era in the history of the Polish Jews, something indefinite, which to some seemed to herald brightness and progress, and to others to portend ignorance and backwardness. [...]

The first glimmers of progressive notions reached the Polish Jews—and this fact can be explained historically—not from the society in which they lived, but from Germany. At the beginning of this century, the Polish Jews, rejected from relations with their immediate environment, with the gates to general schools closed to them, were forced to turn to the source, which forecasted spiritual revival and freedom from the superstitions hindering their intellectual development.

The influence of Mendelssohn's school awoke in the Polish Jews the drive to become acquainted with the coryphees of German literature, who in the words of Nathan the Wise predicted a better fate for the Jews, and a humanitarian attitude toward their religious denomination. [...]

But let us return to the interrupted story. The first step made by Kraszewski in the field of bravely touching upon the delicate issue of granting the Jews social privileges in the minds of the nation stimulated the Jewish Warsaw intelligentsia into more energetic action.

The literary youth group gathered in T[oeplitz]'s apartment around their spiritual leader, Dr. J[astrow], recognized the full gravity of the situation, and, with redoubled vigor, began to ponder the consolidation of their current ephemeral existence.

The idea was born to organize periodical readings on subjects related to history and literature. Dr. J[astrow] took upon himself the responsibility of compiling a series of stories on Jewish history, and biographies of the most eminent activists and advocates of Jewish emancipation.

The members of the club undertook to give occasional presentations of their own literary fiction on various topics, and works on subjects from the field of the natural sciences. A tempting topic was announced: Kraszewski and Korzeniowski as novelists.

One of the members satirically described the meeting of the ghosts of Herzberg and one of his editors on the Champs-Élysées. Biographies of Mendelssohn and Czacki were compiled, etcetera.

An article by Neufeld, a writer still unknown at the time, entitled "Chasyd" and published in *Samuel Orgelbrand's Universal Encyclopedia with Illustrations and Maps*, made a lasting impression. The author, who was temporarily staying in Warsaw, was invited to one of the evening meetings at T[oeplitz]'s.

Appendix III

Selections from Jastrow's March 1, 1861, Sermon

Dokończenie mowy Jastrowa mianej na ulicy Daniłowiczowskiej w bóżnicy 1.3.1861 r. (Concluding Part of the Sermon Delivered in the Synagogue on Daniłowiczowska Street on March 1, 1861), Zakład Narodowy im. Ossolińskich, manuscript, call no. 13079/II, 26–28.

…It is real tolerance and forbearance not to condemn, deprecate, and curse a community that followed the path of the sinful in its arduous thralldom, but, like Abraham, to fight and pray for it, to hope that the good and rightful law and truth will speak out again—this is real tolerance indeed. This is what I said recently, when disagreement and contention still reigned between us and our brethren. And that hope did not fail us because the good and rightful law and truth spoke, and the spirits of love and forbearance have blown among us.

Thanks be to the highest for this. But think not, brethren, that the deed of conciliation is already done; think not that when the most fervent wishes of ourselves and all of our noble compatriots are granted, it will befit us to stop there.

Oh no, all you whose calling it is to act by deed, word, and example, maintain among your co-religionists the noble spirit which has so marvelously seized the entire nation; all you witnesses of the mistakes and weaknesses of bygone days, be forbearing to others, do not be forbearing to yourselves.

Education and learning are means of making good mistakes and eradicating weaknesses. Brothers in Israel, the time has come to educate and teach our children more than ever before. […]

The advancement of the whole of society lies in the gradual development of this truth, while the advancement of the people manifests itself in its sudden inspiration. This inspiration is constant repetition of the divine inspiration, and a foretaste of the era of universal peace, accord, and happiness predicted by the prophets. Is this not a revelation of the divine spirit among us, this spirit of love and accord? Is this not the voice of the mighty God that drowned out base whispers of passion? Is this not the unbeatable power of progress, true divine power, the power of the truth that brought down the barriers of prejudice and wrongheadedness? With this power of truth, this power of love, this divine power, let us stand against mistakes and lies, because they defend not by violence, but by the strength of my Spirit, says the Lord of Hosts. Amen.

Appendix IV

Jastrow's Letter to the Synagogue Council of Mannheim

Markus Jastrow, *Offenes Schreiben an den Großh. Synagogenrath in Mannheim* (Mannheim, 1862).[1]

I am taking the liberty to humbly present the Honorable Council of the Synagogue with the following explanation:

You are aware of the circumstances—and the internal dilemmas—under which I decided at a certain point to leave the Warsaw community, of which I had been a member until my banishment from the Kingdom of Poland, and to accept the post of rabbi in your reputable community, offered me in so noble a manner. It was a difficult decision, not only due to the hopelessness of my former community in regard to finding someone for my post there—to this day no academically educated Jewish theologian has been able to preach the Word of God in Polish; it was a difficult decision, not only due to the fact that I was showered with countless manifestations of love and attachment by the members of my community in Warsaw and the whole Polish land, for which I am deeply grateful, but also that parting with my previous area of work seemed to be an injustice to myself because I rejected the great calling entrusted to me by Providence—a calling which first of all befits those who have given themselves the task of educating their highly talented but long neglected, both spiritually and materially, brothers in faith as useful people and fellow countrymen.

I overcame all these weighty scruples, convinced, firstly, that my return to Warsaw and to my work begun there was connected with immediate danger to me, and secondly, that there can be little hope of unrestricted organizational work in the Kingdom of Poland due to the

---

[1] The original text was published in Michał Galas, "Einmal Warschau—Mannheim und zurück. Rabbiner Marcus Mordechaj Jastrow zum hundertsten Todestag," *Judaica. Beiträge zum Verstehen des Judentums* 4 (2003): 289–298.

current political relations. In this political situation, I had to sacrifice my inner calling for the peace and safety of my family, and I did so by accepting the post of town rabbi in Mannheim which you offered me.

However, my perception of the situation in Poland was exaggerated at the time, as I later learned from competent and reliable sources, and thus my decision to accept the honorable choice of my person as town rabbi here was made in such circumstances. During the move from Colberg in order to assume my office here, I was presented with the letter of appeal of September 16 of which the Honorable Council of the Synagogue is aware, from the committee of the synagogue in Warsaw, by a deputy of theirs, who also convinced me that my abovementioned concerns were unjustified. I did not neglect to send the Honorable Council of the Synagogue a certified translation of the abovementioned letter on September 21, at the same time expressing a request to have my appointment postponed until relations with my previous congregation were settled in one way or another.

I admit, with an openness that befits especially a religion teacher, that my greater decisiveness would have spared all the turbulence that ensued both in my community in Warsaw and your congregation, which I already adopted with love during my short stay here. I feel a duty to confess frankly to the Council of the Synagogue that my conscience forbids me to break off contact with the Warsaw community, which I renounced at one point when I believed it impossible to recreate the old arrangements. Instead of this open declaration, I entrusted the Honorable Council of the Synagogue, by means of the abovementioned letter of September 21, with the decision on my fate, as there was no reason for the Council to suffer damage in the interest of a foreign country.

In response to my request for postponement, the Honorable Council of the Synagogue entreated me in a letter of September 23, delivered by one of its members at the request of the whole council and on behalf of the congregation, or at least in that sense, to come to Mannheim without delay, as soon as my family, who fell ill in Berlin, were well enough to travel. I responded on Sept. 24 that I would obey the summons in accordance with my duty, but I took the liberty to repeat my request for the postponement of my formal appointment. Having arrived here on September 30, I announced to the Honorable Council of the Synagogue that I would like to postpone the final decision on my situation with the two communities in question until after the holiday, so that the community would not be unnecessarily upset during the holiday.

On October 16 a meeting of the Honorable Council of the Synagogue took place, to which I was kindly invited. I sought to explain to you my moral obligations to the Warsaw community and the Israelite people of the Kingdom of Poland, as well as the misguided circumstances in which I expressed my readiness to accept the rabbinical position here. I also requested that the Honorable Council of the Synagogue release me from my duty to the congregation in Mannheim for the good of my previous congregation.

If the reason for my request had been dissatisfaction with my new congregation, the Honorable Council of the Synagogue would have surely not hesitated to dismiss me, because free will and mutual sympathy between the teacher of the people and the congregation are the most important requirements of the blessed work of the First [superior]. No such dissatisfaction was the case. On the contrary, I made clear during the meeting that this was not so, and that I appreciate this rare love to me, still a stranger, demonstrated by all strata of the local Israelite community.

The Honorable Council of the Synagogue responded to my verbal request for dismissal with a declaration that it was not obliged or authorized to do so, but that it did not want to stand in my way if I decided that it was justifiable for me to leave the office with which I was recently entrusted.

I found myself in an awkward situation—I could either follow my heart to Warsaw and leave the office here without the consent of the Honorable Council of the Synagogue, or stay here and fight with the scruples of my conscience. I considered the former dishonorable and the latter impossible. In the meantime, the committee of the synagogue in Warsaw informed me of its decision to send their deputy to Mannheim for verbal negotiations with the Honorable Council of the Synagogue. I then suggested to the First [superior] that a court of arbitration with intermediaries should be appointed to decide on my legal and moral obligations to both communities in question. The Honorable Council of the Synagogue agreed to this method of resolving the issue with commendable readiness and amenability. I admit that individual members of the Honorable Council of the Synagogue asked me multiple times if I could possibly stay here with the peaceful soul that is much needed by a rabbi. Only then did I understand that these men discerned me better than I did myself. I believed that my peace would return with the decision of the court of arbitration in favor of Mannheim; that I would feel exempt from my obligation toward the community in Warsaw. Speculations about the possible dangers to which I might be exposed in the Kingdom of Poland must have vanished from my head, but not from my soul, and I was hoping that consideration for my family would balance the yearning for my previous activities. I expressed these thoughts to the individual members of the Honorable Council of the Synagogue and the deputy from Warsaw, who had arrived here in the meantime.

On October 20 the court of arbitration, comprising my respectable friend Rabbi [Benjamin] Willstätter, the bookseller Mr. [Adolf] Bielefeld, and the attorney Dr. [Jakob] Guttmann, passed judgment that I had no obligation to return to Warsaw following the amnesty; therefore I was legally and morally obliged to accept the post offered me in Mannheim. However, the answer to the question of whether this decision could be modified due to important issues that needed my active support in Warsaw was negative, the decision being justified by the uncertainty of the situation in the Kingdom of Poland. So much for a brief summary of the facts.

On receiving the arbitration verdict, my inner spiritual battle grew more intense and led me to believe that I was at a stage of dangerous self-deception, believing that I could cut those many threads which bound me to my brothers in faith in the country that has become even dearer to me through its suffering. I understood that in parting from my beloved community with a bleeding heart in the best interests of my family, I was causing greater harm with that sacrifice, as I was sacrificing myself. I understood that my heart must bleed, my strength must weaken. Only after the seeming separation did I realize where the homeland for my spiritual strength lies and where the land in which it is rooted.

Finally, after a difficult battle, I decided to come forward with the declaration to the Honorable Council of the Synagogue and the general public that my duty (to save myself) orders me to return to Warsaw to my previous work.

Although I am aware that I may be misunderstood by some, I shall bear it with calm, for this is a consequence of my indecisiveness, which prevented me from making the only right decision at the right moment.

I am admittedly harming the congregation in Mannheim and it really does not deserve it! But I find consolation in the thought that such a noble-minded congregation will be able to demonstrate the virtue of forgiveness. And I bid farewell to you, Honorable Council of the Synagogue, whose members I came to value highly during the few days we were together. May God reward you for your earnest endeavors for the good of your community and may you receive your payment through the welfare of this community!

I bid farewell to you, community that so generously showered me with your love. I will never forget it or cease to appreciate it. May God reward you for your ardent enthusiasm and spiritual kindness with a happy teacher able to accept your love with an unbroken heart, and respond to your affection.

Mannheim, November 2, 1862
Dr. M. Jastrow

Appendix V

Jastrow's Farewell Sermon

Marcus Jastrow, *A Warning Voice: Farewell Sermon Delivered on the Occasion of his Retirement by Rev. Dr. M. Jastrow, Rabbi Emeritus of the German Hebrew Congregation Rodeph Shalom at Philadelphia* (Philadelphia, 1892), 6–12.

[...] It has been said that the majority of this congregation are no longer in sympathy with their teacher, and therefore a severance is required. If that were true, then would I stand before my God and say, "Not me do they reject, they reject my principles; they reject the truth by which I stand." What else can be done when congregation and teacher are no longer in sympathy?

But is this so? No, by far the vast majority in our congregation is in full sympathy with the truth I have been trying to impress upon their hearts. You are, in plain words, conservatively inclined at heart. There are some among you even more conservative than myself, and the few progressists among you would have no power to swerve you from your positions. What was this congregation's position heretofore? It stood before the world as a representative of progress, of due regard for the demands of time, combined with a faithful adherence to Israel's truths and to those forms which tradition and time have sanctioned as visible expressions of these truths. It had taken a firm stand in conjunction with other communities as a powerful agent in defense of the regard due to our religion and its mission, in contributing to human culture and civilization as a co-worker in all enterprises, Jewish or patriotic, which tended to increase the spiritual treasures and the happiness of mankind. So we stood before the country, a type of conservative Judaism. ...

You cried: "We will go to ruin; we must have a change both in the person and the form of government. We must introduce such a form of things that we may be enabled to retrieve our financial losses and win back our deserters!" I know, the leading men and women among you regret the condition of affairs as they exist. The intelligent and thoughtful regret that a time has come when, in our pulpits, thought must cede to tongue, learning yield to elocution, earnestness to frivolity; a time when the creation of noble discontent with one's self which is the awakening power of the best energies within man, and which, if anything, is the legitimate privilege and duty of the pulpit, is disliked and the appeal to what is noblest in man is called "scolding." Religion is not wanted from our pulpits; a quasi-science must take its place, and if religion be treated at all, it must be trampled under foot. The past must be ridiculed, earnestness derided, in order to give the hearer the full enjoyment of his self-conceit, of the consciousness of his superiority over his ancestors, of his great enlightenment and high standard education.

The earnest among you deeply regret the existence of such a condition of affairs. They know that this is not a foundation on which a future can be built, but they say, "What can we do? The congregation must be upheld; the establishment has to be kept up, and if the goods hitherto offered are no longer in demand, what can we do? We must lay them upon the shelf and have fresh attractions to offer to our customers." Is this not, alas, a true description of congregational affairs in our present day? Tell me, do I exaggerate?...

You said that you would guard the conservatism of our congregation, and I cautioned you that this was a dangerous illusion. I used a very common illustration of one seated in a carriage and in a critical moment, seizing the driver's hand to prevent him from exceeding the limits of discretion; surely, an accident will happen and the vehicle will be upset. When the true relation exists between congregation and minister, the former presses onward while the latter acts as the restraining power. Only in this way can rash and subversive measures be prevented and a conservative onward movement be secured. By such means, congregations will develop in a healthy way. Other means are revolutionary in tendency. I told you all this; I cautioned you: but you would not listen to my voice, and now the king that has been chosen will soon be among you. ...

I beg you, see to it that devotion be restored to us both in synagogue and home, for, alas, the truth must be said, we have ceased to be a praying nation. We do not enter our house of worship with that reverence on our lips and in our hearts which our forefathers felt and which they expressed, when on the threshold of the sanctuary they whispered the words, "How fearful is this place! Surely, this is none other but the House of God, and this is the gate of heaven!" We have ceased to be a praying people; in spite of all the improvements introduced to make our services attractive, we have not succeeded. Why not? For the reason that where the spark of devotion is not slumbering within the heart, all efforts to fan it into a flame are vain. The serpent of skepticism has eaten away our hearts. We have no devotion any more, and what is worse, many of us want none. In the house of God, many seek diversion, entertainment, or at best so-called scientific instruction, and this on any subject rather than religion. This is not the case with you. You want the fire of religion to be maintained on the altar of your own and your children's hearts. You desire to live and stand before the world as representatives of true religious earnestness. Therefore, I beg of you, try your utmost in conjunction with him who henceforth will lead you in your religious affairs to restore devotion to the house of worship. Exert yourselves and call upon your children to exert themselves to manifest their love of Israel's God, both in prayer and in demeanor, both within and without this house of assembly. Let it no longer be an empty word when we recite, "Thou shall love the Lord thy God with all thy heart, with all thy soul and with all thy might." Let it become a truth again as it was though the many ages of Israel's existence, in suffering and martyrdom. Let us be grateful to the Leader of mankind that we, especially in this blessed refuge of the oppressed, can again freely wave our banner of the Unity of God without fear of civil disabilities or social ostracism. But let us be mindful that a religion which demands no sacrifice is no religion. Self-conquest is the essence of all religion. There is no love of God, in fact there is no sentiment of devotion in our bosoms, but urgently demands to be made perceptible to ourselves, to be manifested by sacrifice. There is no filial love that is not anxious to prove its existence by acts of self negation. There is no relation of man to man, but is founded on sacrifice, and surely the highest relation of man must claim sacrifices of the sublimest nature. And yet, the least of all sacrifices is that which the American Jew is most reluctant to lay down on the altar of his religion—CONVENIENCE.

"Fear ye the Lord and serve him in truth with all your heart, for see what great things he has done with you." I beg you, see what has become of us American Jews in our land of freedom! See the oppressed and down-trodden of fifty years ago, how they stand here, prosperous and respected, the peers of the best in the land! See what great things the Lord has done for us! Therefore, listen to your leader's parting voice. Do not forsake the banner of Israel's ancient faith, turn not aside towards those vanities of false enlightenment and upstart self-sufficiency,—for vanities they are. Serve ye the Lord with all your heart. I care not in what language you pray, although the truly prayerful heart is satisfied with any language even though it be one only half-understood, drawing inspiration from its very antiquity and its sacred associations. Look at the child in prayer, it scarcely understands, it only divines what it stammers, and yet we envy its sacred happiness and would give our life's blood, could we re-conquer it but for one moment!

But I shall not detain you any longer. Whenever I shall be asked and my physical strength will permit, I shall teach you the good and the right way according to what light I possess. I shall support him whom you have chosen to be your king, whenever my conscience will allow me to do so. In everything that is good, in everything that is conducive to the welfare of the congregation, to the welfare of Israel according to my convictions, he shall have my full support. I have delivered this, my farewell, address to you in order to satisfy myself and you that you have found no wrong in me, and again, I call upon the Lord as my witness, that, to my knowledge, I have not done any wrong to any one of you. I part with you, not in grudge, not even in bitterness, though that might be justifiable under the circumstances. I part with you as a friend from friends. I shall never forget what this congregation has been unto me; how in every trying moment you came to my rescue. When sickness befell me, you were helpful to me in giving me the means of restoring my health. When affliction entered my house, you came to me and sympathized with me and consoled me, as I have tried to console you in your hours of bereavement. I part with you as a grateful friend from friends who have honored him and who have loved him, and I dare say, still do love him. God bless you! Only fear the Lord and serve Him with all your hearts. Do not follow those vanities which are the fashion of our day, for they will neither save nor profit. And as for the future of Israel, I am not afraid, and be you not disheartened. "The Lord will not forsake His people for the sake of His great name. For the Lord has been pleased to make you His people."

List of Abbreviations

AGAD—Archiwum Główne Akt Dawnych (Central Archive of Historical Records)

AJA—American Jewish Archives

AJAJ—*American Jewish Archives Journal*

APP—Archiwum Państwowe w Poznaniu (The State Archive in Poznań)

AZJ—*Allgemeine Zeitung des Judenthums*

Biuletyn ŻIH—*Biuletyn Żydowskiego Instytutu Historycznego* (Jewish Historical Institute Bulletin)

CJA—Centrum Judaicum Archiv, Berlin

CWW—Centralne Władze Wyznaniowe (Central Religious Authorities)

KRSW—Komisja Rządowa Spraw Wewnętrznych (Government Committee for Internal Affairs)

MGWJ—*Monatsschrift für Geschichte und Wissenschaft des Judentums*

MS—Manuscript Collection

NPF—Marcus Jastrow Near Print File

PAJHS—*Publications of the American Jewish Historical Society*

REJ—*Revue des études juives*

SC—Small Collection

ŻIH—Żydowski Instytut Historyczny, Warsaw (Jewish Historical Institute).

List of Illustrations

1. Bertha Wolfssohn-Jastrow (1834–1908). American Jewish Archives, Cincinnati.
2. Reconstruction of the synagogue at Daniłowiczowska Street. Eleonora Bergman, "Synagoga na ulicy Daniłowiczowskiej (1800–1878)—próba rekonstrukcji," in *Rozdział wspólnej historii. Studia z dziejów Żydów w Polsce ofiarowane profesorowi Jerzemu Tomaszewskiemu w siedemdziesiątą rocznicę urodzin* (Wydawnictwo Cylkady: Warsaw, 2001), 128.
3. Jastrow in Warsaw (1). Muzeum Narodowe w Krakowie (National Museum in Krakow).
4. Jastrow in Warsaw (2). Muzeum Historyczne Miasta Stołecznego Warszawy (Historical Museum of Warsaw).
5. Henryk Pillati, *Pogrzeb pięciu ofiar manifestacji w Warszawie w 1861 roku*, Muzeum Narodowe w Krakowie. (National Museum in Krakow).
6. Aleksander Lesser, *Pogrzeb pięciu ofiar manifestacji w Warszawie w roku 1861*, Muzeum Narodowe w Krakowie (National Museum in Krakow).
7. Synagogue in Mannheim. Stadtarchiv Mannheim.
8. Jastrow's contract with Congregation Rodeph Shalom in Philadelphia. American Jewish Archives, Cincinnati.
9. The front page of *Programme der Einführungs-Feier, des Rev. Dr. Jastrow, Rabbiner der Rodef Sholem Gemeinde in Philadelphia* (Philadelphia, 1866).
10. The front page of *Programme of the Consecration Services of the Synagogue of the Congregation "Rodef Sholem"* (Philadelphia 1870).
11. Morris Jastrow (1861–1921). American Jewish Archives, Cincinnati.
12. Joseph Jastrow (1863–1944). American Jewish Archives, Cincinnati.
13. Plaque commemorating Rabbis Marcus Jastrow and Henry Berkowitz, Philadelphia. Photographed by Michał Galas.
14. Portraits of twelve distinguished rabbis in America. *American Phrenological Journal*, April 1868.
15. Jastrow on the steps of the Rodeph Shalom synagogue. American Jewish Archives, Cincinnati.
16. Jastrow with his dog, Knell. American Jewish Archives, Cincinnati.

17. Jastrow in the 1880s. American Jewish Archives, Cincinnati.
18. The front page of *A Dictionary of the Targumim, The Talmud Babli and Yerushalmi, and the Midrashic Literature*, compiled by Marcus Jastrow, Ph.D. Litt. D. with an Index of Scriptural Quotations, Volume I–II (London: W.C. Luzac & Co., New York: G.P. Putnam's Sons, 1903).
19. The editorial board of *The Jewish Encyclopedia*. *The Launching of a Great Work: The Jewish Encyclopedia* (New York, 1901).
20. Ex libris of the Marcus Jastrow Memorial Library. Van Pelt Library University of Pennsylvania, Philadelphia.
21. The Tombstone at the Cemetery, Philadelphia. Photographed by Michał Galas.

Bibliography

I. Archival sources

Archiwum Główne Akt Dawnych:
    Centralne Władze Wyznaniowe.
    Komisja Rządowa Spraw Wewnętrznych.

Archiwum Państwowe w Poznaniu:
    Akta stanu cywilnego gminy żydowskiej Rogoźno
    Księga metrykalna gminy żydowskiej Rogoźno
    Friedrich Wilhelms Gymnasium zu Posen—Gimnazjum im. Fryderyka Wilhelma w Poznaniu (1834–1920)

Archiwum Żydowskiego Instytutu Historycznego, Warsaw:
    Zespół Prace Magisterskie
    Jewish Community/Gmina Warszawska, syg. 199/1.

Archiwum Biblioteki Jagiellońskiej, Krakow:
    Korespondencja J.I. Kraszewski
    Manuscript 6470; 6508.

Muzeum Regionalnego im. Wojciechy Dutkiewicz w Rogoźnie:
    Dokumenty z historii miasta

Zakład Narodowy im. Ossolińskich:
    Manuscript 13079/II.

American Jewish Archives:
    Small Collections no. 3886; 5055; 5686; 5685; 5688; 5690; 5686; 5692; 13012; 6390; 5687; 9648; 9585.
    Manuscript Collections nr 425.
    Photograph Collections: Markus Jastrow; Jastrow's Family.

Jewish Theological Seminary Archives:
    Solomon Schechter Collection.

Leo Beck Institute Archives New York:
   Jacob Jacobson Collection.

Philadelphia Jewish Archives Center at the Balch Institute (The Philadelphia Jewish Archives, were moved to Temple University in Philadelphia):
   Rodeph Shalom Congregation Papers.
   Jewish Publication Society Papers.

University of Pennsylvania:
   The Universiy Museum Archives—Morris Jastrow Papers.
   Penn University Archives—Marcus and Morris Jastrow Papers.

Centrum Judaicum Archiv, Berlin
   1,75 A Ro 2, Nr 2, Ident. 6639; 75 A Ro 2, Nr 5, Ident. Nr 6642, 6646; 6638; 6643; 6645.

Universitätsarchiv Halle:
   Rep. 21 I nr 35; Rep. 21 II nr 84.

Universitätsarchiv Humboldt-Universität zu Berlin:
   Abgangszeugnis 16. Mai –3. August 1855.

Stadtarchiv Mannheim:
   Familienbogen (Polizeipräsidium Zug. —/ 1862).

Stadtarchiv Worms:
   Abt. 5, nr 5741, 5759.
   Abt. 12, Geburtsregister 1864, 1866.
   Abt. 13, nr 477.

Central Archives of Jewish People, Jerusalem:
   P. 38, Brief aus Erfurt vom 30. Sept. 1862.

II. Journals and periodicals" "

"Allgemeine Zeitung des Judentums' (AZJ), Berlin 1852–1903.
"Die Deborah," Cincinnati, OH, 1866–1902.

"Hebrew Leader," New York 1866–1882.
"Jutrzenka," Warsaw 1861–1863.
"Mannheimer Anzeiger," Mannheim 1862.
"Mannheimer Journal," Mannheim 1862.
"Monatsschrift für Geschichte und Wissenschaft des Judentums' (MGWJ), Breslau 1856–1903.
"Occident and American Jewish Advocate," Philadelphia 1865–1869.
"Revue des études juives," Paris 1883–1886.
"The Israelite = The American Israelite," Cinncinnati, OH, 1866–1885.

III. Jastrow's published works

Beleuchtung eines ministeriellen Gutachtens über die Lage der Juden im Königreich Polen. Veranlasst durch kaiserlichen Willen und bureaukratische Willkühr. Hamburg: Hoffmann und Campe, 1859.

Israels Auserwählung. Zwei Predigten am ersten und zweiten Tage des Wochenfestes (Schabuot) 5620 in der Synagoge zu Warschau (genannt: Synagoga przy Ulicy Daniłowiczowskiej) gehalten und auf dringendes Bitten vieler Gemeinde-Mitglieder herausgegeben von Prediger Dr. M. Jastrow. Berlin: Louis Gerschel, 1860.

Techynoth. Modlitwy dla Polek wyznania Mojżeszowego przez Rozalię z Felixów M.S[aulsową], [Forword by] Dr. M. Jastrow, V–VI. Warsaw, 1861.

Mowa — podczas nabożeństwa żałobnego w synagodze przy ulicy Daniłowiczowskiej w Warszawie. Warsaw, 1861.

Lejbe i Siora, czyli listy dwóch kochanków. Romans przez J. U. Niemcewicza. Nowe wydanie poprzedzone przedmową bezimiennego wydawcy. Warsaw, 1861, "Jutrzenka," 1861, no. 4, 26–28 [review].

Kazania miane podczas ostatnich wypadków w Warszawie. Poznań: Ludwik Merzbach, 1862.

Offenes Schreiben an den Grossh. Synagogenrath in Mannheim. Mannheim, 1862.

Die Vorläufer des polnischen Aufstandes. Beiträge zur Geschichte des Königreichs Polen von 1855 bis 1863. Leipzig: Otto Wigand, 1864.

Vier Jahrhunderte aus der Geschichte der Juden von der Zerstörung des Ersten Tempels bis zur makkabäischen Tempelweihe. Heidelberg: Ernst Carlebach, 1865.

Predigt, gehalten am Danksagungs-Tage, (29. November 1866) von Dr. M. Jastrow Rabbiner der Gemeinde Rodef Scholom zu Philadelphia. Philadelphia, 1866.

Offenes Schreiben an den Bundespräsidenten Herrn Schünemann-Pott, als Erwiderung auf dessen Vortrag: Jehova versus den Dreieinigen. Philadelphia, 1867.

Zweites und letztes offenes Schreiben an Herrn Schünemann-Pott als Erwiderung auf dessen Artikel: "Ein neuer Ritter Jehovah's' (Siehe: "Blätter für freies religiöses Leben," 12ter Jahrgang, No. 3). Philadelphia, 1867.

Antwort (an) Herrn I.M. Wise in Cincinnati, auf dessen Aufsatz betitelt "Das Pamphlet", "Deborah," 20. Sept., 1867, Nro. 12. Philadelphia. 1867.

Gegenerklärung auf die "Erklärung" des Herrn J.M. Wise in der "Deborah" Nro. 17. von M. Jastrow, Rabbiner in Philadelphia. Philadelphia, 1867.

Offene Erklärung an Herrn J.M. Wise, Rabbiner und Editor des "Israelite" und der "Deborah", von Dr. M. Jastrow in Philadelphia. Philadelphia, 1867.

Sermon Delivered in the Synagogue Rodef Shalom, Juliana Street on Thanksgiving Day, November 26th, 1868, by Rev. Dr. M. Jastrow, published by the Congregation. Philadelphia, 1868.

Awodat Israel. Israelitisches Gebetbuch für den öffentlichen Gottesdienst im ganzen Jahre, geordnet und übersetzt von Benjamin Szold, Rabbiner der Oheb Schalom-Gemeinde in Baltimore. 3. Aufl., revidiert von M. Jastrow, Rabbiner der Rodef-Schalom Gemeinde zu Philadelphia und H. Hochheimer, Rabbiner der Oheb Israel-Gemeide zu Baltimore. Baltimore, 1871.

Avodat Israel. Israelitish Prayer Book, for all the Public Services of the Year. Originally arranged by Rev. Dr. Benjamin Szold of Baltimore. Second Edition (Hebrew and German) Revised by Rev. Drs. M. Jastrow of Philadelphia, and H. Hochheimer of Baltimore. Hebrew and English Edition, in Text and Typographical Arrangement Fully Corresponding with the Revised Hebrew-German Edition, by M. Jastrow, rabbi of the Congregationn Rodef-Shalom. Philadelphia, 1873.

Songs and Prayers and Meditations for Divine Services of Israelites. Compiled by B. Szold, Rabbi of Congregation Oheb-Shalom, Baltimore. Translated from the German by M. Jastrow, Rabbi of the Congregation Rodef-Shalom. I–II. Philadelphia, 1873.

A Lecture on Temperance, Delivered March 28, 1874, at Broad Street Synagogue of Philadelphia. New York, 1874.

Israelitisches Gebetbuch für die häusliche Andacht, geordnet von Benjamin Szold. Zweite gänzlich umgearbeitete Auflage, herausgegeben von M. Jastrow. Philadelphia, 1875.

Gebete für Kinder für Haus und Schule, entworfen von Benjamin Szold, revidiert von M. Jastrow. Philadelphia: Verlag des Derausgebers [1875].

Kitsur Haggadah le-lel Pesaḥ. Family Service for the Eve of Passover. Hebrew and English, by M. Jastrow, Rabbi of the Congregation Rodeph Shalom. Philadelphia, 1878.

Shylock (A Lecture delivered before the "Deutsche Gesellschaft" of Philadelphia, translated by Miss Henrietta Szold). "The Penn Monthly," September 1880, 725–739.

[A sermon for *Simchat Torah*]. In *The American Jewish Pulpit: A Collection of Sermons by the Most Eminent American Rabbis*, 31–39. Cincinnati, 1881.

The Hebrew Reader for Schools, from the Prayer Book of Rev. Dr. B. Szold, revised by Rev. Drs. Jastrow and Hochheimer. Philadelphia, 1884.

Der ganze Mensch, Rede gehalten Samstag, den 28. April 1888, in Rodeph Shalom Synagoge in Philadelphia. Philadelphia, 1888.

"Prayer." In *Proceedings of the Commemorative Celebration of the Fiftieth Anniversary of the Founding of Hebrew Sunday Schools in America*, 9–10. Philadelphia, 1888.

The Causes of the Revived Disaffection against the Jews. By Rev. Dr. M. Jastrow. Address delivered before the Conference of the Jewish Ministers' Association in New York, Tuesday, May 27th, 1890. New York, 1890.

Turn Not to Folly Again. Sermon Delivered at the Synagogue Rodeph Shalom, on Thanksgiving Day (Nov. 27, 1890). Philadelphia [1890].

Transposed Stems in Talmudic Hebrew and Chaldaic, Dedicated in Reverence and Admiration to M. Joseph Derenburg in Commemoration of his Eightieth Birthday, by Dr M. Jastrow. Leipzig: W. Drugolin, 1891.

A Warning Voice. Farewell Sermon Delivered on the Occasion of his Retirement by Rev. Dr. M. Jastrow, Rabbi Emeritus of the German Hebrew Congregation Rodef Shalom at Philadelphia [delivered Nov. 27, 1892]. Philadelphia, 1892.

"Religion and Superstition." In *Addresses Delivered at the Opening Ceremonies of the Exhibition of Objects Used in Worship,* by William

Pepper. John S. MacIntosh, Marcus Jastrow, Charlemagne Tower. University of Pennsylvania, Department of Archaeology and Paleontology, April 16th, 1892, 12–15. Philadelphia, 1892.

"The Minister and Public Movement." In *The Activities of the Rabbi: A Course of Lectures Delivered under the Auspices of the Jewish Theological Seminary*, February-May, 5652, 65–72. New York: Jewish Theological Seminary Association, 5652–1892.

Der Neunzigste Psalm, übersetzt und erläutert von Dr. M. Jastrow. Leipzig, 1893.

"An Interpretation of Two Psalms. Psalm LXXIII and Psalm XC." In *Oriental Studies: A Selection of the Papers Read before the Oriental Club of Philadelphia 1888–1894*, 35–51. Boston, 1894.

Hymns and Responses from Jastrow's Prayer Book especially adapted for congregational singing in Congregation Rodeph Shalom by Wm. Loewenberg. [Philadelphia,] 1894.

"A Jewish English Version of the Bible." *The Peculiar People: A Christian Monthly Devoted to Jewish Interests* 9, no. 2 (May 1896): 40.

"An Analysis of Psalms LXXXIV and CI", [in:] *Semitic Studies in memory of Rev. Dr. Alexander Kohut*, (Berlin: S. Calvary & co, 1897), 254–263.

The History and the Future of the Talmudic Text. A lecture delivered before the Gratz College of Philadelphia December 9, 1895 by Marcus Jastrow, Ph.D. Rabbi Emeritus of the Congregation Rodef Shalom (Reprinted from "Gratz College Publication" No.1), (Philadelphia 1897), 75–103.

A Dictionary of the Targumim, The Talmud Babli and Yerushalmi, and the Midrashic Literature, compiled by Marcus Jastrow, Ph.D. Litt. D. with an Index of Scriptural Quotations, Volume I–II. London: Luzac & Co.; New York: G. P. Putnam's Sons, 1903.

III/1. Jastrow's articles published in periodicals and journals — a selection

"Der Besuch in der Synagoge." *Sippurim* (Prag) (1854): 173–175.

"Chmel." *Sippurim* (Prag) (1854): 201–209.

"Das Zusammenwirken Esra's und Nehemia's." *MGWJ* VII (1858): 72–80.

"Erklärung des vierunddreißigsten Kapitels im Jecheskeel." *MGWJ* X, (1861): 111–117

"Saisset über die Philosophie der Juden [review]." *MGWJ* XI (1862): 204–205.

"Die Israeliten zu Mekka von Davids Zeit bis in's fünfte Jarhundert unserer Zeitrechnung [review]." *MGWJ* XIII (1864): 313–317.

"Bear Meisels, Oberrabbiner zu Warschau. Ein Lebensbild auf historischem Hitergrunde nach einiger Anschauung entworfen." *Hebrew Leader*, April-June 1870 (1870: vol. 15 no. 25 [1.04], no. 26 [8.04], vol.16 no. 1 [15.4], no. 2 [22.04], no. 3 [29.04], no. 4 [6.05], no. 5 [12.05], no. 6 [20.05], no. 7 [27.05], no. 8 [3.06], no. 9 [10.06], no. 10 [17.06], no. 11 [24.06]. [This text was translated into Hebrew by M.N. Gelber and published in *He-Avar*, no. 13 (1966): 210–222, and was later on translated into Polish by Agata Paluch and published under the title Mordechaj (Markus) Jastrow, "Ber Meisels naczelny rabin Warszawy i jego życie na tle wydarzeń historycznych", trans. Agata Paluch, in *Żydzi szczekocińscy. Osoby, miejsca, pamięć*, eds. Michał Galas i Mirosław Skrzypczyk (Kraków: Wydawnictwo Austeria, 2008), 231–256].

"Biblische Analekten." *MGWJ* XX (1871): 241–248; XXI (1872): 1–7; 145–150.

"Einiges über den Hohepriester Onias IV in Ägypten und die Gründung des Tempels zu Heliopolis." *MGWJ* XXI (1872): 150–155.

"Eine angeblich griechische Stelle im Midrasch." *MGWJ* XXX (1881): 176–178.

"Einiges zur talmudischen Etymologie: I. Ein alter Copistenfehler; II. Eine wandernde Corruption." *MGWJ* XXXI (1882): 183–187.

Traditions mal comprises par le Talmud de Babylone, REJ, 1883, vol. 8, 149–152.

"'Alima" et "eluli", zur "ilmale"." *REJ* 7 (1883): 157–158.

"Im Midrasch zur Hohenliebe." *Magazin für die Wissenschaft des Judentums* XI (1884): 159.

"Eine eigenthümlich corrumpirte Midraschstelle." *Magazin für die Wissenschaft des Judentums* XII (1885): 143–145.

"Les Juifs et les jeux olympiques." *REJ* 10 (1885): 124–126.

"Hebräische und Chaldäische Wortbildungen in der talmudischen Zeitperiode," *Magazin für die Wissenschaft des Judentums* XIV (1887): 18–28.

"Note ser les mots "qwaqi u-dimoniki"," *REJ* 14 (1887): 277–279.

"On transposed stems in the Talmudic, Hebrew and Chaldaic," *Journal of the American Oriental Society* 14 (1888): 40–42.

"The Talmud on Roman and Greek Shows." *Sunday School Times*, August 3, 1889, 483.
"Light Thrown on Some Biblical Passages by Talmudic Usage." *Journal of Biblical Literature* 11, no. 1 (1892): 126–130.
"Les Ludim ou Ludaï." *REJ* 23 (1896): 308–310.
"Scénes de chasse dans le Talmud." *REJ* 23 (1896): 147–149.

Jastrow published also in other periodicals, such as: *Allgemeine Zeitung des Judenthums, American Hebrew, American Jewish Pulpit, Association Bulletin Y.M.H.A., Deborah, Israelite, Hebraica, Hebrew Leader, Jewish Exponent, Jewish Messenger, Jewish Record, Jewish Review, Jewish Times, Jüdische Literaturblatt, National Zeitung, Occident and American Jewish Advocate, Sunday School Times,* and *Young Israel.*

IV. Other published source materials and monographs.

75 Jahre (1834–1909) Friedrich-Wilhelms Gymnasium in Posen. Poznań, 1908.
Abraham Geiger and Liberal Judaism: The Challenge of the Nineteenth Century, compiled with a biographical introduction by Max Wiener. Translated from German by Ernst J. Schlochauer. Philadelphia: Jewish Publication Society of America, 1962.
Abramsky, Chimen, Maciej Jachimczyk, and Antony Polonsky, eds. *The Jews in Poland.* Oxford: B. Blackwell, 1986.
Adler, Cyrus. *Lectures, Selected Papers, Addresses.* Philadelphia, 1933.
———, ed. *The Jewish Theological Seminary of America: Semi-Centennial Volume.* New York: The Jewish Theological Seminary of America, 1939.
———. *I Have Considered the Days.* Philadelphia: The Jewish Publication Society of America, 1941.
Afra, Cyrus. *Attitudes of the American Reform Rabbinate toward Zionism 1885–1948.* PhD diss., New York University, 1978.
Altman, Aleksander. *Moses Mendelssohn: A Biographical Study.* Tuscaloosa: University of Alabama Press, 1973.
Amram, Dawid W. *Memorial Address on the Tenth Anniversary of the Reverend Doctor Marcus Jastrow Rabbi Emeritus of the Congregation Rodef Shalom by...* Delivered at the Synagogue of the Congregation Rodef Shalom, Shemini Atsereth 5674-October 23, 1913. [Philadelphia,] 1913.

Appel, John J. "The Trefa Banquet." "Commentary," (February 1866): 75–78.
Ariel, Yaakov. "American Judaism and Interfaith Dialogue." In *The Cambridge Companion to American Judaism*, edited by Dana Evan Kaplan, 327–344. Cambridge: Cambridge University Press, 2005.
Bałaban, Majer. *Historia projektu szkoły rabinów i nauki religii mojżeszowej na ziemiach polskich*. Lviv: Nakładem Przełożeństwa Zboru Izraelickiego, 1907.
———. "W przededniu powstania styczniowego." In his *Studia historyczne*, 182–187. Warsaw: M.J. Freid, 1927.
———. *Historia Żydów w Krakowie i na Kazimierzu*, vol. 2. Kraków: "Nadzieja," 1936.
———. *Historia lwowskiej Synagogi Postępowej*. Lviv: Nakł. Zarządu Synagogi Postępowej, 1937.
———. *Cylkow Izaak*. Polski Słownik Biograficzny, vol. IV, 122–123. Krakow: Akademia Umiejętności, 1938.
———. "Żydzi w powstaniu 1863." *Przegląd Historyczny*, no 2 (1938): 564–599.
Barkai, Avraham. *Branching Out: German-Jewish Immigration to the United States 1820–1914*. New York: Holmes & Meier, 1994.
Barth, Nancy L. *History of the Publication of the Jewish Encyclopedia*. MA diss., University of Chicago, 1969.
Barton, George A. "The Contributions of Morris Jastrow Jr. to the History of Religion." *Journal of the American Oriental Society* 41 (In Memoriam Morris Jastrow, Jr.) (1921): 327–333.
Bartoszewicz, Kazimierz. *Wojna żydowska w roku 1859. (Początki asymilacji i antysemityzmu)*. Kraków: Gebethner, 1913.
Beit-Arie, Malachi, ed. *The Worms Maḥzor: The Jewish National & University Library in Jerusalem, Ms. Heb. 4° 78¹/₁*. Jerusalem: Jewish National University Library of the Hebrew University, 1985.
Bentwich, Norman. *Solomon Schechter: A Biography*. Philadelphia: Jewish Publication Society of America, 1938.
Berg, Julian. *Historia założenia chórów synagogalnych w Warszawie przy ul. Daniłowiczowskiej*. Warsaw, 1903.
Berg, Mikołaj. *Zapiski o powstaniu polskim 1863–4*. Kraków: Spółka Wydawnicza Polska, 1898.
Bergman, Eleonora. "Synagoga na ulicy Daniłowiczowskiej (1800–1878) — próba rekonstrukcji." In *Rozdział wspólnej historii. Studia z dziejów Żydów w Polsce ofiarowane profesorowi Jerzemu*

Tomaszewskiemu w siedemdziesiątą rocznicę urodzin, 113–128. Warsaw: Cyklady, 2001.

— — —. " *Złota Księga* Wielkiej Synagogi w Warszawie." In *Izaak Cylkow. Życie i dzieło*, edited by Michał Galas, Krakow-Budapest: Wydawnictwo Austeria, 2010, 57-70.

Berkowitz, Henry. "Notes on the History of the Earliest German Jewish Congregation." *PAJHS* 9 (1901): 123–127.

Berkowitz, Max E. *The Beloved Rabbi: An Account of the Life and Works of Henry Berkowitz*. New York: The Macmillan Company, 1932.

Berliner, A. "Dr. Marcus Jastrow." *Israelitischer Lehrer und Cantor*, no. 10 (1903): 37–38.

Bibliography of Morris Jastrow Jr., Professor of Semitic Languages in the University of Pennsylvania, 1885–1910. Philadelphia, 1910.

Bloch, Joshua. [Review] "Yahadut Amerika be-Hitpatuta (The Shaping of American Judaism) by Moshe Davis." *PAJHS* XLII, no. 1 (1951): 91–107.

Book of Job, The: Its Origin, Growth and Interpretation; together with a New Translation Based on a Revised Text by Morris Jastrow. Philadelphia: J.B. Lippincott Co, 1920.

Boras, Zygmunt, ed. *Dzieje Rogoźna*. Poznań: Wydawnictwo Lega, 1993.

Borzymińska, Zofia. "Przyczynek do dziejów szkolnictwa żydowskiego w Warszawie w XIX wieku, czyli jeszcze o Szkole Rabinów." *Biuletyn ŻIH*, no. 3–4 (1984): 183–196.

— — —. *Szkolnictwo żydowskie w Warszawie 1831–1870*. Warsaw: ŻIH, 1994.

Brann, Marcus. *Geschichte des Jüdisch-Theologischen Seminars (Fraenkel'sche Stiftung) in Breslau: Festschrift zum Fünfzigjährigen Jubiläum der Anstalt*. Breslau: T. Schatzky, 1904.

Brenner, Michael, and Stefan Rohrbacher, eds. *Wissenschaft vom Judentum. Annäherungen nach dem Holocaust*. Göttingen: Vandenhoeck and Ruprecht, 2000.

Breuer, Jacob, ed. *Fundamentals of Judaism: Selections from the Works of Rabbi Samson Raphael Hirsch and Outstanding Torah-true Thinkers*. New York: Published for the Rabbi Samson Raphael Hirsch Society by P. Feldheim, 1969.

Breuer, Mordechai. *The "Torah-im derekh-eretz" of Samson Raphael Hirsch*. Jerusalem: Feldheim, 1970.

Brickman, William W. *The Jewish Community in America: An Annotated and Classified Bibliographical Guide*. New York: B. Franklin, 1977.

Brilling, Bernhard. "Adoption of Family Names by Jews in Prussia (1804)." *Avotaynu: The International Review of Jewish Genealogy* 1, no. 2 (1985): 23–25.

Brisman, Shimeon. *A History and Guide to Judaic Encyclopedias and Lexicons: Volume Two of Jewish Research Literature.* Cincinnati: Hebrew Union College Press, 1987.

— — —. *History and Guide to Judaic Dictionaries and Concordances: Volume Three, Part One of Jewish Research Literature.* Hoboken NJ: KTAV, 2000.

Brocke, Michael, and Julius Carlebach, eds. *Biographisches Handbuch der Rabbiner*, Teil 1. *Die Rabbiner der Emanzipationszeit in den deutschen, böhmischen und großpolnischen Ländern 1781–1871.* Bearbeitet von Carsten Wilke, Band 1–2. München: K.G. Saur, 2004.

Brust, Mieczysław. *Zarys dziejów rzemiosła rogozińskiego 1248–1998.* Rogoźno: Cech Rzemiosł Różnych w Rogoźnie, 1998.

Bussgang, Julian. "The Progressive Synagogue in Lwów." In *Polin: Studies in Polish Jewry*, vol. 11, edited by Antony Polonsky, 127–153. Oxford: Littman Library of Jewish Civilization, 1998.

Butler, Menachem. "The History and Future of the Jastrow Dictionary." *The Commentator* LXVIII, no. 3 (2003).

Cain, Ehud M.Z. (Chaikin). *From Prussia with Love.* Jerusalem: n. p., 2002.

Cała, Alina. *Asymilacja Żydów w Królestwie Polskim (1864–1897).* Warsaw: PIW, 1989.

Chwalba, Andrzej. *Historia Polski 1795–1918.* Kraków: Wydawnictwo Literackie, 2000.

Clark, Christopher M. *The Politics of Conversion: Missionary Protestantism and the Jews in Prussia 1728–1941.* Oxford: Clarendon Press and Oxford University Press, 1995.

Clasper, James W., and Carolyn M. Dellenbach. *Guide to the Holdings of the American Jewish Archives.* Cincinnati: The American Jewish Archives, 1979.

Clay, Albert T., and James A. Montgomery, eds. "Bibliography of Morris Jastrow, Jr." *Journal of the American Oriental Society* 41 (In Memoriam Morris Jastrow, Jr.) (1921): 337–344.

Clay, Albert T. "Professor Jastrow as an Assyriologist." *Journal of the American Oriental Society* 41 (In Memoriam Morris Jastrow, Jr.) (1921): 333–336.

Cohen, Gerson. *Esau as Symbol in Early Medieval Thought*. In *Jewish Medieval and Renaissance Studies*, edited by Alexander Altman, 19–48. Cambridge, MA: Harvard University Press, 1967.

Cohen, Naomi Wienner. "The Reaction of Reform Judaism in America to Political Zionism, 1897–1922." *PAJHS* XL, no. 4 (1951): 361–394.

Cohon, Samuel S. "The History of the Hebrew Union College." *PAJHS* XL, no. 1 (1950–51): 17–55.

Corrsin, Stephen D. "Progressive Judaism in Poland: Dilemmas of Modernity and Identity." In *Cultures and Nations on Central and Eastern Europe: Essays in Honor of Roman Szporluk*, edited by Z. Gitelman, L. Hajda, J-P. Himka, and R. Solchanyk, 89–99. Cambridge, MA: Harvard University Press, 2000.

Dash, Joan. *Summoned to Jerusalem: The Life of Henrietta Szold*. New York: Harper & Row, 1979.

Davidson, Israel. "The Academic Aspect and Growth of the Rabbinical Department—the Seminary Proper." In *The Jewish Theological Seminary of America: Semi-Centennial Volume*, edited by Cyrus Adler. New York: The Jewish Theological Seminary of America, 1939.

Davis, Edward. *The History of Rodeph Shalom Congregation Philadelphia: 1802–1926*. Philadelphia: n. p., 1927.

Davis, Moshe. *Emergence of Conservative Judaism: The Historical School in 19th Century America*. Philadelphia: Jewish Publication Society of America, 1963.

———."Sabato Morais: A Selected and Annotated Bibliography of His Writings." *PAJHS* XXXVII (1947): 55–87.

———.*Yahadut Amerikah be-hitpathutah*. New York: n. p., 1951.

Diamant, Adolf. *Chronik der Juden in Dresden*. Darmstadt: Agora, 1973.

Diner, Hasia R. *A Time for Gathering: The Second Migration, 1820–1880*. Baltimore–London: Johns Hopkins University Press, 1992.

———. "Like the Antelope and the Badger: The Founding and Early Years of the Jewish Theological Seminary, 1886–1902." In *Tradition Renewed: A History of the Jewish Theological Seminary*. Volume I: *The Making of an Institution of Jewish Higher Learning*, edited by Jack Wertheimer, 3–42. New York: Jewish Theological Seminary, 1997.

Dohrn, Verena. "The Rabbinical Schools as Institutions of Socialization in Tsarist Russia, 1847–1873." In *Polin: Studies in Polish Jewry*, vol.14, edited by Antony Polonsky, 83–105. Oxford: Littman Library of Jewish Civilization, 2001.

Drachman, Bernard. *The Unfailing Light: Memories of an American Rabbi.* New York: Rabbinical Council of America, 1948.

Duker, Abraham. "Jewish Participants in the Polish Insurrection of 1863." In *Studies and Essays in Honor of A.A. Neuman*, 144–153. Philadelphia: Brill (for the Dropsie College), 1962.

Eisenbach, A., D. Fajnhauz, and A. Wein, eds. *Żydzi a powstanie styczniowe. Materiały i dokumenty.* Warsaw: ŻIH, 1963.

Eisenbach, Artur, and Eligiusz Kozłowski. "Jastrow Marcus." In *Polski Słownik Biograficzny,* vol. XI, 70–71. Wrocław: Ossolineum, 1964–1965.

Eisenbach Artur, *Kwestia równouprawnienia Żydów w Królestwie Polskim.* Warsaw: Książka i Wiedza, 1972.

———. *Emancypacja Żydów na ziemiach polskich 1785–1870 na tle europejskim.* Warsaw: PIW, 1988. [English edition: *The Emancipation of the Jews in Poland, 1780–1870,* edited by Antony Polonsky, translated by Janina Dorosz. Oxford: B. Blackwell, 1991].

Elazar, Daniel J., and Rela Mintz Geffen. *The Conservative Movement in Judaism: Dilemmas and Opportunity.* Albany, NY: State University of New York Press, 2000.

Ellenson, David. "The Mannheimer Prayerbooks and Modern Central European Communal Liturgies: A Representative Comparison of Mid-Nineteenth Century Works." In his *Between Tradition and Culture: The Dialectics of Modern Jewish Religion and Identity*, 59–78. Atlanta, GA: Scholars Press, 1994.

Esman, Janusz. *Opis Rogoźna z 1794 roku.* Rogoźno: n. p., 1989.

Feiner, Shmuel, and David Sorkin, eds. "Między Lesznem a Berlinem. Pierwszy spór ortodoksji z haskalą i jego religijne oraz społeczne implikacje." In *Duchowość żydowska w Polsce. Materiały z międzynarodowej konferencji dedykowanej pamięci profesora Chone Shmeruka,* edited by Michał Galas, 279–286. Kraków: Księgarnia Akademicka, 2000.

———. *New Perspectives on the Haskalah.* London: Littman Library of Jewish Civilization, 2001.

———. *Haskalah and History: The Emergence of a Modern Jewish Historical Consciousness,* transl. Ch. Naor and S. Silverston. London: Littman Library of Jewish Civilization, 2002.

Feingold, Henry L. *Zion in America: The Jewish Experience from Colonial Times to the Present.* New York: Twayne Publishers, 1981.

Fierstien, Robert E. "A Noble Beginning: The Seminary Alumni Association: 1901–1918." In his *A Century of Commitment: One*

Hundred Years of the Rabbinical Assembly, 1–20. New York: Rabbinical Assembly, 2000.

———. *A Different Spirit: The Jewish Theological Seminary of America, 1886–1902*. New York: Jewish Theological Seminary of America, 1990.

Fineman, Irving. *Woman of Valor: The Life of Henrietta Szold, 1860–1945*. New York: Simon and Schuster, 1961.

"First Ordination and the Terefa Banquet 1883, The." *AJAJ* (November 1974): 129.

Frank, Yitshak. *The Practical Talmud Dictionary*. Jerusalem: Feldheim Publishers, 1991.

Freidenberg, Albert M. "A List of Jews Who were Grand Masters of Masons in Various States of this Country." *PAJHS*, no. 19 (1910): 95–101.

Friedland, Eric L. *"Were Our Mouths Filled with Song": Studies in Liberal Jewish Liturgy*. Cincinnati: Hebrew Union College Press, 1997.

———. *The Historical and Theological Development of the Non-Orthodox Prayerbooks in the United States*. PhD diss., Brandeis University, 1967.

———. "Marcus Jastrow and Abodath Israel." In *Texts and Responses: Studies Presented to Nahum N. Glazer on the Occasion of his Seventieth Birthday by his Students*, edited by Michael A. Fishbane and Paul M. Flohr. 186–200. Leiden: Brill, 1975.

———. "Hebrew Liturgical Creativity in Nineteenth-Century America" *Modern Judaism* 1, no 3 (1981): 323–336.

Friedländer, David. *Über die Verbesserung der Israeliten des Königreich Pohlen. Ein von der Regierung daselbst im Jahr 1816 abgefordertes Gutachten*. Berlin: Nicolaische Buchhandlung, 1819.

Friedman, Murray, ed. *Jewish Life in Philadelphia, 1830–1940*. Philadelphia: Institute for the Study of Human Issues, 1983.

———, ed. *When Philadelphia Was the Capital of Jewish America*. Philadelphia: Balch Institute Press; London: Associated University Presses, 1993.

Galas, Michał. "Aleksander Kraushar als Erforscher des Frankismus." *Judaica. Beiträge zum Verstehen des Judentums*, no. 1 (1999): 42–53. transl. S. Schreiner.

———. "Einmal Warschau—Mannheim und zurück. Rabbiner Marcus Mordechaj Jastrow zum hundertsten Todestag." *Judaica. Beiträge zum Verstehen des Judentums*, no. 4 (2003): 289–298. transl. S. Schreiner.

———. "Chasydyzm—od herezji do ultraortodoksji" [Hasidism: From Heresy to Ultra-Orthodoxy]. In *Czas chasydów* [Time of the Hasidim], 11–41. Krakow: Muzeum Historyczne Miasta Krakowa, 2005.

———. "Rabbi Marcus Jastrow: A Symbol of Polish-Jewish Relations in the 19th Century." In *Newsletter of the Skalny Center for Polish and Central European Studies*, 5. Rochester, NY: University of Rochester, 2006.

———. *Rabin Markus Jastrow i jego wizja reformy judaizmu. Studium z dziejów judaizmu w XIX wieku*. Krakow: Wydawnictwo Austeria, 2007.

———. "Rabbi Marcus Jastrow (1829–1903)." In *YIVO Encyclopedia of Jews in Eastern Europe*, edited by Gershon Hundert, 819. New Haven: Yale University Press, 2008.

———. "Rabbi Ber Meisels i jego działalność w Warszawie." In *Żydzi szczekocińscy. Osoby, miejsca, pamięć*, edited by Michał Galas and Mirosław Skrzypczyk, 157–169. Kraków: Wydawnictwo Austeria, 2008, 157–169.

———, ed. *Izaak Cylkow. Życie i dzieło*. Krakow-Budapest: Wydawnictwo Austeria, 2010.

———. "Jewish-Polish Relations in the writings of Rabbi Marcus Jastrow." *Jewish Studies at the Central European University* 6 (2011): 39–53.

———. "Rabin Markus Jastrow (1829–1903) i jego droga z Rogoźna do Warszawy." *Studia Historica Slavo-Germanica* 28, 2008–10 (2011): 155–174.

———. "Ozjasz (Jehoshua) Thon (1870–1936) —Prediger und Rabbiner in Krakau (Eine Erinnerung anlässlich seines 75. Todestages)." *Judaica. Beiträge zum Verstehen des Judentums*, no. 3 (2011): 311–321. transl. S. Schreiner.

———. "The Influence of Progressive Judaism in Poland: An Outline." *Shofar: An Interdisciplinary Journal of Jewish Studies* 29, no. 3 (2011): 55–67.

———. "Three Views of Jewish Acculturation to Polish Culture in the 19th and Early 20th Twentieth Century Kraków." In *Jewish Lifeworlds and Jewish Thought: Festschrift presented to Karl E. Grözinger on the Occasion of his 70th Birthday*, 245–251. Wiesbaden: Harrassowitz Verlag, 2011.

———, ed. *Synagoga Tempel i środowisko krakowskich Żydów postępowych*. Kraków—Budapest: Wydawnictwo Austeria, 2012.

Gąsowski, Tomasz. *Między gettem a światem. Dylematy ideowe Żydów galicyjskich na przełomie XIX i XX wieku.* Kraków: Księgarnia Akademicka, 1996.

Gelber, Natan M. "Zur Geschichte der Judenfrage." *Zeitschrift für Osteuropäische Geschichte* (1914): 483–512.

— — —. "Akt zbratania polsko-żydowskiego przed powstaniem styczniowym 1863–1864." In *Almanach żydowski na rok 5678.*Wien: n. p., 1918.

— — —. *Die Juden und der polnische Aufstand 1863.* Wien: R. Löwit, 1923.

— — —. "Dr. Mordechai (Markus) Jastrow." *He-Avar*, no. 11 (1964): 7–26. (Hebrew)

Ginzberg, Eli. *Keeper of the Law: Louis Ginzberg.* Philadelphia: Jewish Publication Society of America, 1966.

Glanz, Rudolf. *The German Jews in America: An Annotated Bibliography Including Books, Pamphlets and Articles of Special Interest.* Cincinnati: Hebrew Union College Press, 1969.

Glazer, Nathan. *American Judaism.* Chicago: University of Chicago Press, 1972.

Gordis, Robert. *Understanding Conservative Judaism.* New York: The Rabbinical Assembly, 1978.

Gottheil, Richard. "Morris Jastrow, Jr." *PAJHS*, no. 29 (1925): 170–73.

Greatz, Heinrich. *Tagebuch und Briefe*, (hrsg.) Reuven Michael. Tübingen: Mohr, 1977.

— — —. *Dr. M. Jastrow, Vier Jahrhunderte aus der Geschichte der Juden von der Zerstörung des ersten Tempels bis zur makkabäischen Tempelweihe. Iv, und 206 S., Heidelberg 1865*, MGWJ, XV, 1b66, 237–238.

Gurock, Jeffrey S. "Resisters and Accommodators: Varieties of Orthodox Rabbis in America, 1886–1983." *AJAJ* XXXV, no. 1 (1983): 100–187.

Guterman, Alexander. "The Origin of the Great Synagogue in Warsaw on Tłomackie Street." In *The Jews in Warsaw: A History*, edited by Władysław T. Bartoszewski and Antony Polonsky, 182–211. Oxford: Basil Blackwell, in association with the Institute for Polish-Jewish Studies 1991..

Guterman, Alexander. *Me-hitbolelut la-leumiyut: perakim be-toldot Bet ha-keneset ha-gadol ha-Sinagogah be-Varshah 1806–1943.* Jerusalem: Karmel, 1993.

Halkowski, Henryk. [Introduction.] In *Tora. Pięcioksiąg Mojżesza*, tłumaczenie Izaak Cylkow, I–VII. Kraków: Wydawnictwo Austeria, 2006.

Heinemann, Isaak. *Manuel Joëls wissenschaftliches Lebenswerk. Festvortrag anlässlich der Gedächtnisfeier des Jüdisch-Theologischen Seminars am 31. Oktober 1926.* Breslau: n. p., 1927.

Heller, James G. *Isaac M. Wise: His Life, Work and Thought.* New York: Union of American Hebrew Congregations, 1965.

Hensel, Jürgen. "Wie "deutsch" war die "fortschrittliche" jüdische Bourgeoise im Königreich Polen? Antworten anhand einiger Beispiele aus Warschau und Lodz." In *Symbiose und Traditionsbruch. Deutsch-jüdische Wechselbeziehungen in Ostmittel- und Südosteuropa (19. und 20. Jahrhundert),* edited by Hans Hecker and Walter Engel, 135–172. Essen: Klartext, 2003.

Heppner, A., and J. Herzberg, *Aus Vergangenheit und Gegenwart der Juden und den jüdischen Gemeinden in den Posener Landen nach gedruckten und ungedruckten Quellen,* vol. II. Koschmin: Bromberg, 1909.

Hertzberg, Arthur, and Aron Hirt-Manheimer. *Żydzi. Istota i charakter narodu.* Transl. B. Paluchowska (Warsaw: Mada, 2001), 172. (English: Arthur Hertzberg and Aron Hirt-Manheimer, *Jews: The Essence and Character of a People.* San Francisco: HarperSanFrancisco, 1998.

Hinczewski, Jan. *Kalendarium dziejów Rogoźna.* Rogoźno: n. p., 1989.

Hirsch, Emil G. "Review of *A Dictionary of the Targumim, the Talmud Babli and Yerushalmi, and the Midrashic Literature. Compiled by M. Jastrow, Ph.D., New York, G. P. Putnam's Sons. (1888–1901, Parts I–XIV.)*" *The Alumni Register* (1901): 497–503.

Hirsch, Samson Raphael. *The Nineteen Letters,* newly translated by Karin Paritzky, revised and with a comprehensive commentary by Joseph Elias. Jerusalem: Feldheim Publishers, 1995.

Hirsch, Samuel. *Die Messias-Lehre der Juden in Kanzelvorträgen. Zur Erbauung denkender Leser.* Leipzig: Heinrich Hunger, 1843.

–––. *Dr. Jastrow und sein Gebaren in Philadelphia. Ein ehrliches, leider abgenötigtes Wort.* Philadelphia: n. p., 1868.

Hirszhorn, Samuel. *Historia Żydów w Polsce, 1788–1914.* Warsaw: B-cia Lewin-Epstein i S-ka, 1921.

Hochman, Andee. *Rodeph Shalom: Two Centuries of Seeking Peace.* Philadelphia: n. p., 1995.

Hońdo, Leszek. "Das Verhältnis der Juden in Westgalizien zur polnischen und deutschen Kultur an der Wende vom 19. zum 20. Jahrhundert." In *Symbiose und Traditionsbruch. Deutsch-jüdische Wechselbeziehungen in Ostmittel- und Südosteuropa (19. und 20.*

Jahrhundert), edited by Hans Hecker and Walter Engel, 81–94. Essen: Klartext, 2003.

Jastrow, Alice, et al., eds. *The History of the Young Women's Union of Philadelphia, 1885–1910* [no year or place].

Jastrow, Joseph. "Joseph Jastrow." In *A History of Psychology in Autobiography*, vol. I, edited by Carl Murchinson, 135–162. Washington, DC: American Psychological Association, 1961.

Jewish Theological Seminary of America: Documents, Charters and By-laws, The. New York: The Jewish Theological Seminary of America, 1903.

Jick, Leon A. *The Americanization of the Synagogue, 1820–1870*. Hanover: Published for Brandeis University Press by the University Press of New England, 1992.

Justus. "Żydzi w powstaniu 1863 r." *Rocznik Weteranów* (1925): 198–201.

Karkhanis, Sharad. *Jewish Heritage in America: An Annotated Bibliography*. New York: Garland Pub., 1988.

Karp, Abraham J. "The Origins of Conservative Judaism." *Conservative Judaism* 14, no. 4 (1965): 33–48.

———. "The Conservative Rabbi: "Dissatisfied but not Unhappy."'" *AJAJ* XXXV, no. 1 (1983): 188–262.

———. "A Century of Conservative Judaism in the United States." In *The History of Judaism in America: Transplantations, Transformations, and Reconciliations*, part. I, edited by J.S. Gurock, 213–272. New York: Routledge, 1998.

Kasowsky, Chaim, and Biniamin Kasowsky. *Otsar ha-shemot le-Talmud bavli. [Thesaurus nominus, quae in Talmude Babylonico reperiuntur]*. Jerusalem: The Ministry of Education and Culture, Government of Israel; New York: The Jewish Theological Seminary of America, 1976.

Keller, Volker. *Jüdisches Leben in Mannheim*. Mannheim: Edition Quadrat, 1995.

Kemlein, Sophia. "The Jewish Community in the Grand Duchy of Poznań under Prussian Rule, 1815–1848." In *Polin: Studies in Polish Jewry*, vol. 14, edited by Antony Polonsky, 49–67. Oxford: Littman Library of Jewish Civilization, 2001.

———. "Między tradycją a nowoczesnością — intelektualiści żydowscy w Poznaniu w pierwszej połowie XIX wieku." *Kronika Miasta Poznania*, no. 2 (1998): 77–90.

———. *Żydzi w Wielkim Księstwie Poznańskim 1815–1848. Przeobrażenia w łonie żydostwa polskiego pod panowaniem pruskim*, edited by

K. Makowski, translated by Zenona Choderny-Loew. Poznań: n. p., 2001.

— — —. "Żydzi wśród Niemców i Polaków (wzajemne stosunki, uprzedzenia i konflikty w Wielkim Księstwie Poznańskim w pierwszej połowie XIX wieku)." In *Żydzi w Wielkopolsce na przestrzeni dziejów*, edited by Jerzy Topolski and Krzysztof Modelski, 128–148. Poznań: Wydawnictwo Poznańskie, 1999.

Kieniewicz, Stefan. "Assimilated Jews in Nineteenth-Century Warsaw." In *The Jews in Warsaw: A History*, edited by Władysław T. Bartoszewski and Antony Polonsky, 151–170. Oxford: B. Blackwell, 1991.

— — —. *Powstanie Styczniowe*. Warsaw: PWN, 1983.

Kiron, Arthur, "'Dust and Ashes': The Funeral and Forgetting of Sabato Morais." *American Jewish History* 83, no. 3 (1996): 155–188.

— — —. *Golden Ages, Promised Land: The Victorian Rabbinic Humanism of Sabato Morais*. PhD diss., Columbia University, 1999.

Kisch, Guido, ed. *Das Breslauer Seminar. Jüdisch-Theologisches Seminar (Fraenkelsche Stiftung) in Breslau 1854–1938*. Tübingen: Mohr, 1963.

Kleczyńscy, F. I J., ed. *Liczba głów żydowskich w Koronie z taryf roku 1765*. Archiwum Komisji Historii Akademii Umiejętności, vol. VIII. Kraków: Akademia Umiejętności, 1898.

Klein, Esther M. *Guidebook to Jewish Philadelphia: History, Landmarks, Donors of the Jewish Community for the life of Philadelphia 1703–1965*. Philadelphia: Philadelphia Jewish Times Institute, 1965.

Kober, Adolf. "Jewish Religious and Cultural Life in America as Reflected in the Felsenthal Collection." *PAJHS* XLV, no. 1–4 (1955–56): 93–127.

Kohler, K. "Jastrow's Talmudic Dictionary." *Hebraica* V, no 1 (1888): 1–6.

Kohler, Max J. "The German-Jewish Migration to America." *PAJHS*, no. 9, (1901): 87–105.

— — —. "The Board of Delegates of American Israelites, 1859–1878." *PAJHS* XXIX (1925): 75–135.

Koltun-Fromm, Ken. *Abraham Geiger's Liberal Judaism*. Bloomington, IN: Indiana University Press, 2006.

Korn, Bertram Wallace. *Eventful Years and Experiences: Studies in Nineteenth Century American Jewish History*. Cincinnati: American Jewish Archives, 1954.

Korros, Alexandra Shecket, and Jonathan D. Sarna. *American Synagogue History: A Bibliography and State-of-the-Field Survey*. New York: M. Wiener Pub., 1988.

Kozińska-Witt, Hanna. *Die Krakauer Jüdische Reformgemeinde 1864–1874.* Frankfurt a. M.: Peter Lang Verlag, 1999.

— — —. "Stowarzyszenie Izraelitów Postępowych w Krakowie 1864–74." In *Duchowość żydowska w Polsce. Materiały z międzynarodowej konferencji dedykowanej pamięci profesora Chone Shmeruka*, edited by Michał Galas, 309–326. Kraków: Księgarnia Akademicka, 2000.

Kramsztyk, Izaak. *Kazania*, vol. 1–2. Kraków: Gebethner i Spółka, 1892.

Kraushar, Aleksander. "Kartki z niedawnej przeszłości." In *Książka jubileuszowa dla uczczenia pięćdziesięcioletniej działalności literackiej J.I. Kraszewskiego*, 505–527. Warsaw: J. Unger, 1880.

— — —. *Kartki z pamiętnika Alkara.* Kraków: Gebethnera i Spółka, 1910.

Kupfer, Franciszek. *Ber Meisels i jego udział w walkach wyzwoleńczych narodu polskiego (1846, 1848, 1863–1864).* Warsaw: ŻIH, 1953.

Łagiewski, Maciej. *Wrocławscy Żydzi 1850–1944.* Wrocław: Muzeum Historyczne, 1997.

Łastik, Salomon. *Z dziejów oświecenia żydowskiego. Ludzie i fakty.* Warsaw: PIW, 1961.

Levin, Alexandra Lee. *The Szolds of Lombard Street: A Baltimore Family, 1859–1909.* Philadelphia: Jewish Publication Society of America, 1960.

— — —. "The Jastrows in Madison: A Chronicle of University life, 1888–1900." *Wisconsin Magazine of History* 46, no. 4 (1963): 243–256.

— — —. *Henrietta Szold: Baltimorean.* Baltimore: Jewish Historical Society of Maryland, 1976.

Levitas, Irving. "Reform Jews and Zionism: 1919–1921." *AJAJ* XIV, no. 1 (1962): 3–19.

Lewin, Adolf. *Geschichte der badischen Juden seit der Regierung Karl Friedrichs (1738–1909).* Karlsruhe: Kommissionsverlag G. Braun, 1909.

Lubliner, Ludwik O. *De la condition politique et civile de Juifs dans le Royaume de Pologne: examen critique d'un rapport adressé en l'année 1858 à l'empereur.* Bruxelles: n. p., 1860.

Lucas, Franz D., and Frank Heike. *Michael Sachs. Der konservative Mittelweg. Leben und Werk des Berliner Rabbiners zur Zeit der Emanzipation.* Tübingen: Mohr, 1992.

Makowski, Krzysztof. "Verzeichnis der israelitischen Absolventen von Gymnasien im Großherzogtum Posen in den Jahren 1815–1848." *Nordost-Archiv*, NF Bd. 1, 1992, H. 2, 457–460.

— — —. "Ludność żydowska wobec wydarzeń Wiosny Ludów na ziemiach polskich." In *Żydzi w obronie Rzeczypospolitej, materiały konferencji w Warszawie 17 i 18 października 1993 r.*, edited by Jerzy Tomaszewski, 43–63. Warsaw: Cyklady, 1996.

———. "Gdy na ulicach Poznania, obok polskiego, powszechnie rozbrzmiewał język niemiecki i żydowski. Niemcy i Żydzi w Poznaniu w latach 1815–1848." *Kronika Miasta Poznania*, no. 3 (1996): 48–65.

———. "Żydzi wobec Wiosny Ludów w Wielkim Księstwie Poznańskim." In *Żydzi w Wielkopolsce na przestrzeni dziejów*, edited by Jerzy Topolski and Krzysztof Modelski, 149–167. Poznań: Wydawnictwo Poznańskie, 1999.

———. *Siła Mitu. Żydzi w Poznańskiem w dobie zaborów w piśmiennictwie historycznym*. Poznań: Wydawnictwo Poznańskie, 2004.

Malamed, Efim. "The Zhitomir Rabbinical School: New Materials and Perspectives." In *Polin: Studies in Polish Jewry*, vol.14, edited by Antony Polonsky, 105–116. Oxford: Littman Library of Jewish Civilization, 2001.

Marcus, J.R., and A.A. Pek, eds. *The American Rabbinate: A Century of Continuity and Change, 1883–1983*. Hoboken, NJ: KTAV, 1985.

Marcus, Jacob Rader. *United States Jewry, 1776–1985*, vol. II–III. Detroit: Wayne State University Press, 1991.

Marek, Lucjan. "Początki ruchu zawodowego wśród pracowników handlowych w Warszawie, 1856–1881." *Biuletyn ŻIH*, no. 58, (1966): 81–105.

Margolis, L. "Jastrow's Targumic-Talmudic-Midrashic Dictionary." *The American Journal of Semitic Languages and Literatures* XVIII (October 1901—July 1902): 56–58.

Markiewicz, Henryk, ed. *Żydzi w Polsce. Antologia literacka*. Kraków: Uniwersitas, 1997.

Maślak-Maciejewska, Alicja. *Życie i działalność Szymona Dankowicza (1834–1910)*. Kraków—Budapest: Wydawnictwo Austeria, 2013.

Memoire sur la situation des Israélites en Pologne. Paris: Typographie et Lithographie Lacour, 1858.

Merwin, Bertold. *Żydzi w powstaniu 1863*. Lviv: Jedność, 1913.

Meyer, Isidore S. ed. *Early History of Zionism in America*. New York: American Jewish Historical Socity and Theodore Herzl Foundation, 1958.

Meyer, Michael A, and W. Gunther Plaut, *The Reform Judaism Reader: North American Documents*. New York: UAHC Press, 2001.

Meyer, Michael A., and Michael Brenner, eds. *German-Jewish History in Modern Times*, vol. 1–2. New York: Columbia University Press, 1997.
Meyer, Michael A. *The Origins of the Modern Jew: Jewish Identity and European Culture in Germany, 1749–1824*. Detroit: Wayne State University Press, 1967.
— — —. *Response to Modernity: A History of the Reform Movement in Judaism*. Detroit: Wayne State University Press, 1995.
— — —. "The German Model of Religious Reform and Russian Jewry." In his *Judaism within Modernity: Essays on Jewish History and Religion*, 278–303. Deitroit: Wayne State University Press, 2001.
— — —. "Religious Reform." In *YIVO Encyclopedia of Jews in Eastern Europe*, www.yivoinstitute.org/pdf/reform.pdf.
Michałowska, Helena. *Salony artystyczno-literackie w Warszawie w 1832–1860*. Warsaw: PWN, 1974.
Millgram, Abraham E. *Jewish Worship*. Philadelphia: Jewish Publication Society of America, 1971.
Modlitwy dla Izraelitów na dni zwyczajne i uroczyste, translated by H[enryk] Liebkind, Warsaw: J. Rothwand, 1846.
Monasch, Bar Loebel. *1801–1879, Lebenserinnerungen. Memoirs. Pamiętnik*, introduction, compilation, and the critical edition of the German original and Polish translation by Rafał Witkowski, English translation by Peter Fraenkel. Poznań: Towarzystwo Miłośników i Badaczy Ziemi Krotoszyńskiej, 2004.
Morais, Henry Samuel. *The Jews of Philadelphia: Their History from the Earliest Settlements to the Present Time*. Philadelphia: Levytype Co., 1894.
Morgenstern, Julian. "Morris Jastrow Jr. as a Biblical Critic." *Journal of the American Oriental Society* 41 (In Memoriam Morris Jastrow, Jr.) (1921): 322–327.
Myers, David N. "The Ideology of Wissenschaft des Judentums." In *History of Jewish Philosophy*, edited by Daniel H. Frank and Oliver Leaman Oliver, 706–720. London—New York: Routledge, 1997.
Nadell, Pamela S. *Conservative Judaism in America: A Bibliographical Dictionary and Sourcebook*. Westport—London: Greenwood Press, 1988.
Nauen, Lindsay B., ed. *A Guide to the Philadelphia Jewish Archives Center*. Philadelphia: Philadelphia Jewish Archives Center, 1977.

Niemojewski, Jan Nepomucen. *Wspomnienia*, wyed. and with a foreword, commentaries, and index, by Stefan Pomarański. Warsaw: Gebethner, 1925.

Nulman, Macy. *The Encyclopedia of Jewish Prayer: Ashkenazic and Sephardic Rites*. Northale, NJ: Aronson, 1993.

Nussbaum, Hilary. *Szkice historyczne z życia Żydów w Warszawie od pierwszych śladów pobytu ich w tym mieście do chwili obecnej*. Warsaw: K. Kowalewski, 1881.

Olath Tamid. Gebetbuch für israelitische Reform-Gemeinden, (hrsg.) David Einhorn. Baltimore: n. p., 1856.

Olitzky, Kerry M., Lance Sussman, and Malcolm H. Stern, eds. *Reform Judaism in America: A Bibliographical Dictionary and Source Book*. Westport, CT: Greenwood Press, 1993.

———. *The American Synagogue: a Historical Dictionary and Sourcebook*. Westport, CT: Greenwood Press 1996.

Opalski, Magdalena. "Polish-Jewish Relations and the January Uprising: The Polish Perspective." In *Polin: A Journal of Polish-Jewish Studies*, vol. 1, edited by Antony Polonsky, 68–80. Oxford: Littman Library of Jewish Civilization, 1986.

Opalski, Magdalena, and Israel Bartal. *Poles and Jews: A Failed Brotherhood*. Hanover: University Press of New England, 1992.

Parzen, Herbert. *Architects of Conservative Judaism*. New York: J. David, 1964.

Petuchowski, Jakob J. *Prayerbook Reform in Europe: The Liturgy of European Liberal and Reform Judaism*. New York: World Union for Progressive Judaism, 1968.

Philipson, David. "The History of the Hebrew Union College." In *Hebrew Union College Jubilee Volume (1875–1925)*, 1–71. Cincinnati: HUC Press, 1925.

Philipson, David. *The Reform Movement in Judaism*. New York: KTAV, 1967.

Pięcioksiąg Mojżesza dla Żydów-Polaków (Chamissach Chumsze Torach). Vol. I. *Księga rodzaju, Genesis (Bereszyt). […] (Or Torach) Światło Zakonu. Uwagi i objaśnienia gramatyczne, leksykograficzne, historyczne, geograficzne i obrządkowo religijne, do tłumaczenia polskiego Pięcioksięgu Mojżesza*, tłómaczył z hebrajskiego i objaśnił komentarzem Daniel Neufeld. Warsaw: n. p., 1863.

Pilarczyk, Krzysztof. *Literatura żydowska od epoki biblijnej do haskali*. Kraków: Wydawnictwo UJ, 2006.

Pinkas ha-Kehilot: Encyclopedia of Jewish Communities, vol. VI, District Poznań and Pomerania. Jerusalem: Yad Vashem, 1999.

Plaut, Gunther W. *The Growth of Reform Judaism: American and European Sources until 1948*. New York: World Union for Progressive Judaism, 1965.

Polonsky, Antony. "Warszawska Szkoła Rabinów: orędowniczka narodowej integracji w Królestwie Polskim." In *Duchowość żydowska w Polsce. Materiały z międzynarodowej konferencji dedykowanej pamięci profesora Chone Shmeruka*, edited by Michał Galas, 287–308. Kraków: n. p., 2000.

— — —. *The Failure of Jewish Assimilation in Polish Lands and Its Consequences*. Oxford: Oxford Centre for Hebrew and Jewish Studies, 2000.

Posner, Raphael, Uri Kaploum, and Shalom Cohen, eds. *Jewish Liturgy*. Jerusalem: Keter Pub. House, 1975.

Programme der Einführungs-Feier, des Rev. Dr. Jastrow, Rabbiner der Rodef Sholem Gemeinde in Philadelphia. Philadelphia: n. p., 1866.

Programme of the Consecration Service of the Synagogue of the Congregation "Rodef Shalom." Philadelphia: n. p., 1870.

Pucker, Bernard H. "Review of *Emergence of Conservative Judaism: The Historical School in 19th Century America* by Moshe Davis," *American Jewish Historical Quarterly* LIV, no. 4 (1965): 481–483.

Quellen zur Geschichte der Juden in den Archiven der neuen Bundesländer, (hrsg.) Stefi Jersch-Wenzel and Reinhard Rürup, Band 6: *Stiftung "Neue Synagoge Berlin — Centrum Judaicum,"* Teil I–II. München: Saur, 2001.

Raisin, Jacob S. *The Haskalah Movement in Russia*. Philadelphia: Jewish Publication Society of America, 1913.

Raphael, Marc Lee. *Profiles in American Judaism: The Reform, Conservative, Orthodox, and Reconstructionist Traditions in Historical Perspective*. San Francisco: Harper & Row, 1988.

Reychman, Kazimierz. *Szkice genealogiczne*. Warsaw: n. p., 1936. Reprinted Warsaw: Wydawnictwo Artystyczne i Filmowe, 1985.

Rosenau, William. *In Honor of the Seventieth Birthday of Rev. gr. Benjamin Szold, November 15th, 1899. With compliments of Congregation Oheb Shalom*. Baltimore: Congregation Oheb Shalom, 1899.

Rosenau, William. *Benjamin Szold*. Baltimore: n. p., 1902.

Rosenbach, Hyman P. *History of the Jews in Philadelphia Prior to 1800*. Philadelphia: Edward Stern, 1883.

Rosenbaum, Jeanette W. "Hebrew German Society Rodeph Shalom in the City and County of Philadelphia (1800–1950)." *PAJHS* XLI, no.1–4 (1951–1952): 83–93.

Rosenbloom, Noah H. *Tradition in an Age of Reform: The Religious Philosophy of Samson Raphael Hirsch*. Philadelphia: Jewish Publication Society of America, 1976.

Rosenblum, Herbert. *The Founding of the United Synagogue of America, 1913*. PhD diss., Brandeis University, 1970.

Rosin, Dawid. *Reime und Gedichte des Abraham ibn Esra*, t. 1–2. Breslau: n. p., 1884–1888.

Rothschild, Samson. *Beamte der Wormser jüdischen Gemeinde (Mitte des 18. Jahrhundertes bis zur Gegenwart)*. Frankfurt a. M.: J. Kauffmann Verlag, 1920.

Rozenblit, Marsha L. "Jewish Identity and the Modern Rabbi: The Cases of Isak Noa Mannheimer, Adolf Jellinek, and Moritz Guedemann in Nineteenth-Century Vienna." *Leo Beck Institute Year Book* (1990): 103–131.

Sachs, Michael. *Religiöse Poesie der Juden in Spanien*. Berlin: n. p., 1845.

–––. *Die Festgebete der Israeliten*. Text und Übersetzung mit erläuternden Anmerkungen. 9 Bde. Berlin: n. p., 1855–56.

–––. *Das Gebetbuch der Israeliten mit vollständigem, sorgfältig durchgesehenem Texte*. Neu übersetzt und erläutert. Berlin: n. p., 1858.

–––. *Predigten*, (hrsg.) David Rosin, Bde. I–II. Berlin: n. p., 1866–1869.

Samuel, Hirsch. *Die Messias-Lehre der Juden in Kanzelvorträgen. Zur Erbauung denkender Leser*. Leipzig: Heinrich Hunger, 1843.

Sarna, Jonathan D. "The Debate over Mixed Seating in the American Synagogue." In *The American Synagogue: A Sanctuary Transformed*, edited by Jack Wertheimer, 363–394. Hanover–London: Brandeis University Press, 1987.

–––, and Nahum M. Sarna. "Jewish Bible Scholarship and Translations in the United States." In *The Bible and Bibles in America*, edited by E.S. Frerichs, 83–116. Atlanta: Scholars Press, 1988.

–––. *JPS: The Americanization of Jewish Culture 1888–1988*. Philadelphia: Jewish Publication Society of America, 1989.

–––. "The American Jewish Response to Nineteenth-Century Christian Missions." In *Essential Papers on Jewish-Christian Relations in the United States. Imagery and Reality*, edited by Naomi W. Cohen, 21–42. New York: New York University Press, 1990.

–––, ed. *The American Jewish Experience*. New York: Holmes & Meier, 1997.

―――. *American Judaism: A History*. New Haven: Yale University Press, 2004.
Sawicki, Aron. "Szkoła Rabinów w Warszawie (1826–1863)." *Miesięcznik Żydowski* 1–2 (1933): 244–274.
Schad, Margit. "Rabbiner Dr. Michael Sachs als Prediger: "Ich muß einen neuen Menschen für die alte Lehre fordern."'" In *Neuer Anbruch: Zur deutsch-jüdischen Geschichte und Kultur*, edited by Michael Brocke, Aubrey Pomerance, and Andrea Schatz, 191–204. Berlin: Metropol, 2001.
―――. *Rabbiner Michael Sachs: Judentum als höhere Lebensanschauung*. Hildesheim: Olms, 2007.
Schechter, Solomon, *A Man of Full Stature: Address of Prof. Schechter for Memorial Services of Dr. Jasstrow* (sic). Philadelphia, November 5, 1903.
―――. "Dr. Jastrow's Great Work: A Review of the Famous Jewish Scholar's Dictionary of the Talmud." *The New York Times*, January 30, 1904, pp. 65–66.
Schünemann-Pott, Friedrich. "Ein neuer Ritter Jehovah's." *Blätter für freies religiöses Leben*, no. 3 (1867): 40–45.
Schwartz, Shuly Rubin. *The Emergence of Jewish Scholarship in America: The Publication of the Jewish Encyclopedia*. Cincinnati: HUC Press, 1991.
Schwarz, Sidney H. *Law and Legitimacy: An Intellectual History of Conservative Judaism, 1902–1973*. PhD diss., Temple University, 1981.
Seder ha-Avodah—Israelitisches Gebetbuch für die öffentliche Andacht, zunächst für die israelitische Gemeinde zu Leipzig, vol. I (hrsg.) A.M. Goldschmidt. Leipzig: n. p., 1876.
Seder ha-Avodah—Israelitisches Gebetbuch für die öffentliche Andacht des ganzen Jahres, zunächst für die israelitische Gemeinde zu Leipzig, vol. II (hrsg.) A.M. Goldschmidt. Leipzig: n. p., 1874.
Seder ha-Avodah—Ordnung der öffentlichen Andacht für die Sabbat- und Festtage des ganzen Jahres. Nach dem Gebrauche des Neuen-Tempel-Vereins in Hamburg. Hamburg: n. p., 1819.
Sharfman, Harold I. *The First Rabbi: Origins of Conflict between Orthodox and Reform: Jewish Polemic Warfare in pre-Civil War America. A Biographical History*. Malibu, CA: Pangloss Press, 1988.
Sherman, Moshe, ed. *Orthodox Judaism in America: A Biographical Dictionary and Sourcebook*. Westport, CT: Greenwood Press, 1996.

Silverstein, Alan. *Alternatives to Assimilation: The Response of Reform Judaism to American Culture, 1840–1930*. Hanover: Published for Brandeis University Press by University Press of New England, 1994.

Sklare, Marshal. *Conservative Judaism: An American Religious Movement*. New York: Schocken Books, 1972.

Sokoloff, Michael. *A Dictionary of Judean Aramaic*. Ramat-Gan: Bar Ilan University Press, 2003.

———. *A Dictionary of Jewish Babylonian Aramaic of the Talmudic and Gaonic Periods*. Ramat-Gan: Bar Ilan University Press; Baltimore: Johns Hopkins University Press, 2002.

———. *A Dictionary of Jewish Palestinian Aramaic of the Byzantine Period*. Ramat-Gan: Bar Ilan University Press; Baltimore: Johns Hopkins University Press, 2002.

Solomon, Norman. *Judaizm*, tłum. Joanna Mytkowska. Warsaw: n. p., 1997.

Sperber, Daniel. *A Dictionary of Greek and Latin Legal Terms in Rabbinic Literature*. Ramat-Gan: Bar Ilan University Press, 1984.

Starke, Herman. *Zur Geschichte des Königlichen Wilhelms—Gymnasiums zu Posen*. Poznań: n. p., 1884.

Stern, Nathan. *The Jewish Historico-Critical School of the Nineteenth Century*. New York: n. p., 1901.

Streit, L. *Dzieje synagogi postępowej w Stanisławowie*. Stanisławów: Nakładem Zarządu Synagogi Postępowej w Stanisławowie, 1939.

Sussman, Lance J. *Isaac Leeser and the Making of American Judaism*. Detroit: Wayne University Press, 1995.

Szacki, Jakub. "Yidn un der Poylisher oyfshtand fun 1863." *Historishe shriftn. YIVOt. Historishe Sekcje* 1 (1929): 423–468.

———. *Geschichte fun Yidn in Warshe*, vol. II. New York: YIVO, 1948.

———. *Yidishe bildungs-polit̞ik in Poyln fun 1806 biz 1866*. New York: YIVO, 1943.

Szold, Benjamin. *Auch ein Wort über Jastrow und Hirsch, von…, Rabbiner der Oheb-Shalom-Gemeide zu Baltimore*. Baltimore: Gedruckt bei C. W. Schneidereith, 1868.

Szold, Henrietta. "Marcus Jastrow." In *The American Jewish Year Book 5665* (September 10, 1904, to September 29, 1905), 401–408. Philadelphia: Jewish Publication Society of America, 1904.

———. "Marcus Jastrow." *PAJHS*, no. 12 (1904): 181–183.

Tefilot Benej Jeszurun: Minhag Amerika. The Daily Prayers of American Israelites. Cincinnati: n. p., 1857.

Temkin, Sefton D. *Creating American Reform Judaism: The Life and Times of Isaac Mayer Wise*. London: Littman Library of Jewish Civilization, 1998.

Timmings, William T. *In the Eve It Will Be Light: Sacred Song for High Voice* (with piano), words translated from the Hebrew by Marcus M. Jastrow. New York: H. W. Gray, 1929.

Tomaszewski, Jerzy, ed. *Żydzi w obronie Rzeczypospolitej — materiały konferencji w Warszawie 17 i 18 października 1993 r*. Warsaw: Cyklady, 1996.

Tomczak, A., et al., eds. *Lustracja województw wielkopolskich i kujawskich 1564–1565*, part I. Bydgoszcz: Bydgoskie Towarzystwo Naukowe, 1961.

Tora. Pięcioksiąg Mojżesza, translated by Izaak Cylkow. Kraków: n. p., 1895 (reprinted Kraków: Wydawnictwo Austeria, 2006).

Tuwim, Julian, ed. *Księga wierszy pisarzy polskich 19-go wieku*. Warsaw: PIW, 1954.

Urbach, Janusz K. *Udział Żydów w walce o niepodległość Polski*. Warsaw, n. p., 1938.

Wachs, Sharona R. *American Jewish Liturgies: A Bibliography of American Jewish Liturgy from the Establishment of the Press in the Colonies through 1925*. Historical Introduction by Karla Goldman, Liturgical Introduction by Eric L. Friedland. Cincinnati: HUC Press, 1997.

Wawrzyniec, Surowiecki. *O upadku przemysłu i miast w Polszcze*. Warsaw: n. p., 1810.

Waxman, Mordecai. *Tradition and Change: The Development of Conservative Judaism*. New York: Burning Bush Press, 1958.

Wechsler, Harold S. "Pulpit or Professoriate: The Case of Morris Jastrow." *American Jewish History* 74 (June 1985): 338–355.

———. "Anti-Semitism in the Academy: Jewish Learning in American Universities, 1914–1939." *AJAJ* XLII, no. 1 (1990): 7–21.

Wertheimer, Jack, ed. *The American Synagogue: A Sanctuary Transformed*. Hanover: Brandeis University Press, 1995.

Whiteman, Maxwell. "Isaac Leeser and the Jews of Philadelphia: A Study in National Jewish Influence." *PAJHS* XLVIII, no. 4 (1959): 207–245.

Wiernik, Peter. *History of the Jews in America: From the Period of the Discovery of the New World to the Present Time*. New York: The Jewish Press Publishing Company, 1912.

Wistrich, Robert S. *The Jews of Vienna in the Age of Franz Joseph*. Oxford: Published for the Littman Library by Oxford University Press, 1989.

Wodziński, Marcin. "Jakub Tugendhold and the first Maskilic Defense of Hasidim." *Gal-Ed* XVIII (2001): 13–41.

———. *Oświecenie żydowskie w Królestwie Polskim wobec chasydyzmu. Dzieje pewnej idei*. Warsaw: Cyklady, 2003. English: *Haskalah and Hasidism in the Kingdom of Poland: A History of Conflict*. Oxford: The Littman Library of Jewish Civilization, 2005.

Wolf, Edwin II, and Maxwell Whitman. *The History of the Jews in Philadelphia from Colonial Times to the Age of Jackson*. Philadelphia: Jewish Publication Society, 1975.

Z dziejów Gminy Starozakonnych w Warszawie w XIX stuleciu, tom I, *Szkolnictwo*. Warsaw: n. p., 1907.

Zarchin, Michael M. *Jews in the Province of Posen: Studies in the Communal Records of the Eighteenth and Nineteenth Centuries*. Philadelphia: The Dropsie College for Hebrew and Cognate Learning, 1939.

Zeitlin, Rose. *Henrietta Szold: Record of a Life*. New York: Dial Press, 1966.

Ziątkowski, Leszek. *Dzieje Żydów we Wrocławiu*. Wrocław: Wydawnictwo Dolnośląskie, 2000.

Zilbersztejn, Sara. "Postępowa Synagoga na Daniłowiczowskiej." *Biuletyn ŻIH*, no. 74 (1970): 31–57.

Żmichowska, Narcyza. *Pisma Gabryelli, vol. II*. Warsaw: Jan Jaworski, 1861.

Index

Aaron, Israel 123
Adamkiewicz, Filip 68
Adler, Cyrus 170, 180, 183, 184
Adler, Jakub 28, 28n30
Adler, Samuel 136
Alexander II 64
Alkabetz, Shlomo 105n9
Alter, Izaak Meir 57
Amram, David xii, xiv
Arcichiewicz, Michał 68
Auerbach, Isaac 7
Bałaban, Majer 21n1
Bartoszewicz, Kazimierz 84n227
Berg, Ludwik 29, 29n32
Bergman, Eleonora xvi, 25n20, 26, 27
Berkowitz, Henry 123, 126–129, 156
Bernays, Jacob xxv
Bernhard, Adolf 22, 30, 33, 50, 93, 203
Bernstein, Ignacy 50
Bershon, Mejer 28
Bettelheim, Aaron S. 160, 164
Bielefeld, Adolf 93, 203
Blumenthal, Joseph 160
Bona, the queen 2
Bondi, Jonas 160
Borzymińska, Zofia 56, 56n137
Brann, Marcus xxv, 52n120
Brendel, Karol 68
Brünner, Izydor 53
Buttenwiesser, Laemmlein 164
Centnerszwer, Jakub 22, 23, 24, 33
Chojnacka, Kazimiera 14
Chwalba, Andrzej 82n222
Cohn, Adolf Jakub 53
Cohn, Józef 100, 101n25
Cohn, Mojżesz 88, 90, 91, 99, 100, 100n21, 100n24, 101n24, 102
Corrsin, Stephen D. xxviiin31
Cylkow, Izaak xxviii, 49, 51
Czacki, Tadeusz 197
Dankowicz, Szymon xxix, 51, 53, 53n127
Davidson, Israel 169n31n32
Davis, Edward 112, 119n25, 122n43, 128n62

Davis, Moshe xii, 160, 168n27, 189
Dembitz, Lewis N. 160
Deutsch, Gotthard 180
Drachman, Bernard 160, 168
Dreyfus, Alfred 180
Dropsie, Moses Aaron 160
Dynner, Glenn 63n166
Ehrenberg 85
Einhorn, David xxxiv, 131, 136, 143, 153, 170
Eisenbach, Artur 51, 57n139, 60
Elkana, L. 105
Elsenberg, Jakub 22, 33, 48, 48n98
Epstein, Adam 29, 30, 49, 100, 100n21, 101, 192
Epstein, Jakub 27
Epstein, Mikołaj 53
Errant, S. W. 100
Esman, Janusz 11
Ezra, Abraham ibn 19
Fajans, Maksymilian 53
Feibelmann, Simon Halevi 7
Feilchenfeld, Moses ben Josef 7, 7n289, 13, 16, 18, 18n90, 21, 22, 187
Feinkind 85
Felsanthel, Bernhard 112n12, 136, 183
Fijałkowski, Antoni Melchior 82, 82n220, 85
Flatau, Isaak 26
Flatau, M. 29, 30
Forelle, Józef 51
Frankel, Jacob 38n66, 116, 160n3
Frankel, Zacharias xxiv, xxv, xxvi, 51n118, 52, 90, 175
Franz, Joseph 184
Friedland, Eric xii, 155
Friedländer, David xxi, xxin12
Friedman, Murray 110n1
Friedmann, Bernhard 99
Funk, Isaac Kauffman 180
Furness, Frank 118
Geiger, Abraham xxii, xxiin14, xxiv, 89, 89n4, 99, 100, 112n12, 175, 183
Gelber, Natan M. xi
Ginzberg, Louis 180–181

Glücksberg, Jan 29
Goldman, Bernard 53
Goldman, Jerzy 53
Goldschmidt, Abraham Meyer xxviii, 21–23, 23n9, 28, 28n31, 29, 29n32, 33, 40
Goldschmidt, Julian 23n9
Gorczakow, Mikhail 192
Gottheil, Gustav 124, 184
Gottheil, Richard 180
Graetz, Heinrich xxv, 18, 21, 25, 41n75, 55, 86, 87, 89n4, 90, 102, 106, 107, 175, 183, 184, 187
Gross, Charles 183
Guttmann, Jakob 93, 203
Hensel, Jürgen 25n20
Herzberg 197
Hirsch, Emil G. 121, 177
Hirsch, Samson Raphael xxv, xxvi, 106
Hirsch, Samuel 136, 141, 142, 142n37, 143–146, 148–150, 166
Hochheimer, Henry 121, 160, 161, 173
Hog, Ezechiel 41n76
Holdheim, Samuel xxii, xxiii, xxiiin16, xxxiv, 132, 143, 153
Homer 16
Huebsch, Adolph 121
Hundert, Gershon xvi
Illowizi, Henry 126
Isaac, rabbi from Rogozna 5
Isaacs, Abram S. 183
Isaacs, Samuel Mayer 160, 182
Isserles, Moses 39n69
Jacobs, George 121, 124, 164
Jacobs, Henry S. 168
Jacobson, Israel xx
Jacobson, Jacob 5n15
Jastrauer, Abraham — see Jastrow Abraham.
Jastrow, Abraham 7n28, 11, 11n49, 12, 13n56
Jastrow, Alice Esther 108, 121n37
Jastrow, Annie M. 121n37, 185
Jastrow (Wolfssohn), Bertha 19, 20, 22, 85, 92n17
Jastrow, Carl Eduard (Karl) 108, 121n37

Jastrow, Chaim (Herman) 13, 13n58, 88, 101n27
Jastrow, Isaac 12n50, 13, 13n59, 88, 91n11
Jastrow, Jette 13n56
Jastrow, Johanna Maria (Nelli) 108, 121n37
Jastrow, Joseph 99, 99n13, 104n4, 121n37, 122, 123, 147
Jastrow, Moritz (Morris) 85, 92n17, 104n4, 121n37, 122, 123, 180, 185
Jastrow, Wilhelm 85, 92n17, 104n4, 121n37
Jellinek, Adolf 148, 168
Jerchower, Seth xvi
Joël, Manuel xxv, 15, 18, 25, 86, 100, 175, 187
Justman, Zygmunt 51
Kalisch, Isidor 130, 130n1, 131, 133, 136, 150, 153, 166
Kemlein, Sophia 8
Kiron, Artur xvi, 9n35
Kohen, Bernard 33
Kohler, Kaufmann 124, 180, 184, 186, 186n47
Kohn, Abraham 49
Kohut, Alexander xxxii, 160, 168, 169, 175, 177
Konitz, Samuel 33
Korzeniowski 197
Kościuszko, Tadeusz 75
Krajewski 85
Kramsztyk, Izaak xxviii, 34, 57n139, 83, 85, 86, 101
Kramsztyk, Stanisław 53
Krasiński, Ignacy 75
Kraszewski, Józef Ignacy 103, 103n36, 197
Kraushar, Aleksander 23n9, 53, 53n126, 54, 194
Krauskopf, Joseph 123, 126, 183, 184
Krauss, Samuel 176
Kremer, Elijah ben Shlomo Zalman xxv
Kronenberg, Ludwik 29
Kronenberg, Samuel 27
Kubit, Lidia xvi
Kurczewski, Marceli 68

Ladeburg, Leopold 99
Landau, Wolf 18
Landshutter 27
Lansberger, Franz 184
Laskowski, Feliks 11
Leeser, Isaac xxxii, xxxiv, 107, 108, 130, 143, 160–164, 166, 173, 182, 185
Lehman, Marcus 106
Leifer, Judith xvi
Lelewel, Joachim 66, 75
Lesser, Aleksander xxxn37, 53, 66, 77, 78n211, 80
Levin, Chaim 13n58
Levy, Jacob 175–177
Libelt, Karol 14
Lilienthal, Max 148, 150, 182
Loew, Immanuel 176
Lowenthal, Aleksander 53
Lubliner, Ludwik O. 60
Lubliner, M. 193
Łukasiewicz, Józef 14
Luzzatto, Salomon David 175
Maimonides xviii, 24, 164, 169
Makowski, Krzysztof A. xi, xvi, 8, 10
Malczewski Skarbek, Franciszek xxin12
Malinowski, T. 88
Mannheimer, Isaac Noah xxv, xxx, xxxn37, 40, 40n71, 66n179, 148, 170
Marek, Lucjan 56n134
Marmur, Dov vii
Mayer, Luis 90
Mazurkiewicz, L. 88
Meir, Abraham ben 19
Meir, Izaak 57
Meir, Jonas 92
Meisels, Baer (Ber) viii, 66, 66n172, 77, 82, 82n220, 83, 83n226, 84, 84n227n228, 85, 86, 88, 91, 170, 187
Mendelshon, Moses ben Mendel 7
Mendelssohn, Moses xviii, xviiin2, xix, xxi, xxv, 97, 197
Merzbach, Henryk 30
Merzbach, Ludwik 10n42
Merzbacher, Leo 153
Meyer, Herman 33, 87, 100, 102, 102n33

Meyer, Michael A. xx, xxvi, xxvii, xxviiin31, 40
Mickiewicz, Adam 75
Mielziener, Moses 121
Milowicz, W. 88
Mochnacki 75
Monasch, Ber Loebel 41, 41n75
Monasch, Izydor 41, 41n75, 51n118
Montefiore, Moses 61
Moore, Geo F. 180
Moraczewska, Bibianna 66
Morais, Sabato xxxii, 126, 130, 141, 142, 160, 161, 164, 168–170, 173, 184
Muchanow, Pavel 34, 48n97, 82, 192
Natanson, brothers 53
Natanson, Henryk 33, 58, 100, 101
Natanson, Ludwik 33, 50
Nemirovsky, Igor vii
Neufeld, Daniel 53, 57n139, 97, 98, 98n8, 99n17, 101, 197
Nicholas I, tsar 74
Niemojowski, Jan Nepomucen 87
Nussbaum, Hilary 50
Oppman, Artur 96n2
Orgelbrand, Samuel 33, 197
Orgelbrant, Moses 93
Orzeszkowa, Eliza 46
Paprocki, Aleksander 53
Paprocki, Gustaw 53
Peiper, Maksymilian 10n42
Pereira Mendes, Abraham 168
Pereira Mendes, Henry xxxii, 160, 168
Perles, Joseph 86, 175, 183
Philippson, Ludwik 101n28
Philipson, David 123
Pillati, Henryk 67, 77, 78n211
Plessner, Elias 7
Polano, Hyman 164
Polonsky, Antony vii, xvi, 59
Popliński 14
Posner, Dawid 91
Poznański, Samuel A. xxviii, 170
Proffitt, Kevin xvi
Przemysław II 2, 2n2
Raisin, Jacob S. 60, 60n153n154, 97, 192
Rapaport, Samuel Loeb 175

Raphall, Morris 160
Rashi (Rabbi Shlomo Itzhaki) 102, 102n30, 105
Rice (Reiss), Abraham Joseph xxxi
Romanowski, Mieczysław 96n2
Rosen, Izaak Simon 27, 29
Rosen, Mathias 25, 30, 30n38, 33, 57n139, 58
Rosenfeld, Isidor 104, 104n3
Rosenthal, Ludwik A. 7
Rosin, David xxv, 18, 19, 25, 86, 187
Rothschild, Samson xii, 104, 105, 108n21
Rotwand, Stanisław 53, 85
Ruderman, David B. xvi
Rundbaken 51
Rutkowski, Zdzisław 68
Rymarkiewicz 14
Sachs, Michael xxv, 7, 15, 16, 16n79, 17, 17n80, 18–20, 40n71, 41, 66n179, 155, 170, 175, 187
Salinger, Stanisław 29
Saperstein, Marc vii
Sarna, Jonathan vii, xvi
Schechter, Solomon 170, 177, 178, 185, 186
Schlenker 85
Schneeberger, H. 168
Schorr, Moses xxix, 170n38
Schreiner, Stefan vii, xvi
Schünemann-Pott, Friedrich 141
Sigismund I the Old, the king 2
Simson, Sampson 162
Singer, Isidor 179, 180
Słowacki, Juliusz 75
Sofer, Moses xxv
Sokoloff, Michael 179
Sola Mendes, Frederick de 160, 168
Solis-Cohen, Solomon 160, 169
Sowiński, Józef L. 75
Stern, Simon 183
Sulzberger, Mayer 160, 183, 184
Sulzer, Solomon xxx
Surowiecki, Wawrzyniec 62
Szacki, Jakub xi, 85
Szold, Benjamin xii, xxxii, 114, 120, 121, 124, 146–150, 152–157, 160, 161, 167–170, 173, 184, 185
Szold, Henrietta vii, xii, xiv, 147, 147n54, 183, 184
Szold-Jastrow, Rachel 147
Szołdrski Władysław 3n6
Tabak, Robert 110n2
Taylor-Kucia, Jessica vii
Teller, David 144
Thalgrün, Stanisław 53
Thon, Ozjasz xxix
Tilles, Anna vii
Toeplitz, Henryk L. 33, 53, 194, 195, 197
Toeplitz, Teodor 53n124
Tugendhold, Jakub 57n139, 59, 84, 84n227, 192
Turkułł, Ignacy 61
Unszlicht, Maksymilian 53
Vedol, Sharona vii
W., Paulina 15
Wagenfisz, Leon 53
Waryłkiewicz, Z. 88
Weil, Chaim ben Yakov 7
Wielkopolski, Aleksander 57, 59, 82
Williams, William H. 164
Willstätter, Benjamin 93, 203
Wise, Aaron 160, 168
Wise, Isaac Mayer xxxiii, xxxiv, xxxv, 116, 119, 119n22, 120, 122, 123, 124, 126, 130–134, 136, 138–140, 144, 148, 150, 153, 161–163, 166, 167, 184, 189
Wodziński, Marcin xi, 63n166, 72n196
Wohl, Henryk 53
Wolf, a teacher 13
Wolf, Joseph xx
Wolffssohn, Augusta 104n4
Wolfshon, Moses 50
Wolfsohn, Louis 29
Wolfssohn, Bertha — see Jastrow, Bertha.
Wysocki, J. 88
Zarchin, Michael M. 6
Zilbersztejn, Sara 25n20, 28, 29, 34, 40, 44
Zimmerek 11
Żmichowska, Narcyza 66
Zola, Garry xvi
Zuckermann, Benedict xxv
Zunz, Leopold xxiii, 16, 175, 183

www.ingramcontent.com/pod-product-compliance
Lightning Source LLC
Chambersburg PA
CBHW051112230426
43667CB00014B/2546